The Diary Of Lieutenant Desmond Mulholland MC

Peter Jesson

Peacock Press

The Diary Of Lieutenant Desmond Mulholland MC
© 2014 Peter Jesson

All rights reserved. No part of this publication may be reproduced, stored in a retrieval system, transmitted in any form or by any means electronic, mechanical, including photocopying, recording or otherwise without prior consent of the copyright holders.

ISBN 978-1-908904-45-4

Published by Peacock Press, 2014
Scout Bottom Farm
Mytholmroyd
Hebden Bridge
HX7 5JS (UK)

Design and artwork
D&P Design and Print
Worcestershire

Printed by Lightning Source, UK

Front cover: painting of Desmond *by Arthur C. Michael*

The Diary Of Lieutenant Desmond Mulholland MC

Peter Jesson

Peacock Press

DEDICATION

Second-Lieutenant Desmond Mulholland 107259,
The Duke of Cornwall's Light Infantry.

ACKNOWLEDGEMENTS

My very special thanks go to Irene for starting the typing of the diary and giving me the enthusiasm to get it finished and to Mandy for taking over and doing the lion's share of the work including a huge amount of translation and other research. On a trip to Germany in 2013 she made a rather large detour to visit the site of one of the POW camps that Desmond was in, and photographed it widely. Without their enthusiasm and hard work Desmond's writings would still be in a box in the attic!!

Thank you Paul for your three months of patience!!

A big thank you to David for all his tireless work in the design of the book and his endless patience while I was bombarding him with amendments and queries.

There are a number of people on the island of Guernsey who have been an enormous help to me over the years of research and in the arrangements for the publication and launch of the book:

To Keith who sent me an endless supply of information and, from the very early stages, guided me to those who could help me get the project off the ground:

To Helen who helped with Uncle Mickie's paintings held by the Museums Department and who had to put up with my continual badgering;

To Shaun who offered his help to try and establish the facts of Desmond's arrest by the Germans and his patience in guiding my wife and I round Castle Cornet to see if we could find the place of imprisonment;

To Lina who, by a miraculous piece of good fortune, met my cousin Brian on a coach in Italy and established the contact with the Martel family on Guernsey;

To Marie for all her help with the more intricate details of Desmond's time on Guernsey in 1940 with Philip Martel and their arrest by the Germans;

To the Société Guernesaise for their help with the details of my Great Aunt and Uncle's deportation and for, very rightly, convincing me to become a member.

To Susan for her very detailed research into my family on Guernsey, her time in being a guide through the Royal Courts and the records at the Greffe on Guernsey and for all her time in arranging the book launch.

To Brian for all his support and help with the family records.

To the trusty band of proof readers who, thankfully, were very thorough.

Last but not least to my wife Ann for putting up with the months I spent in my office on the computer and my continual chatter about Desmond.

Without all these people I would have seriously struggled to achieve the right result.

MAP OF THE CHANNEL ISLANDS

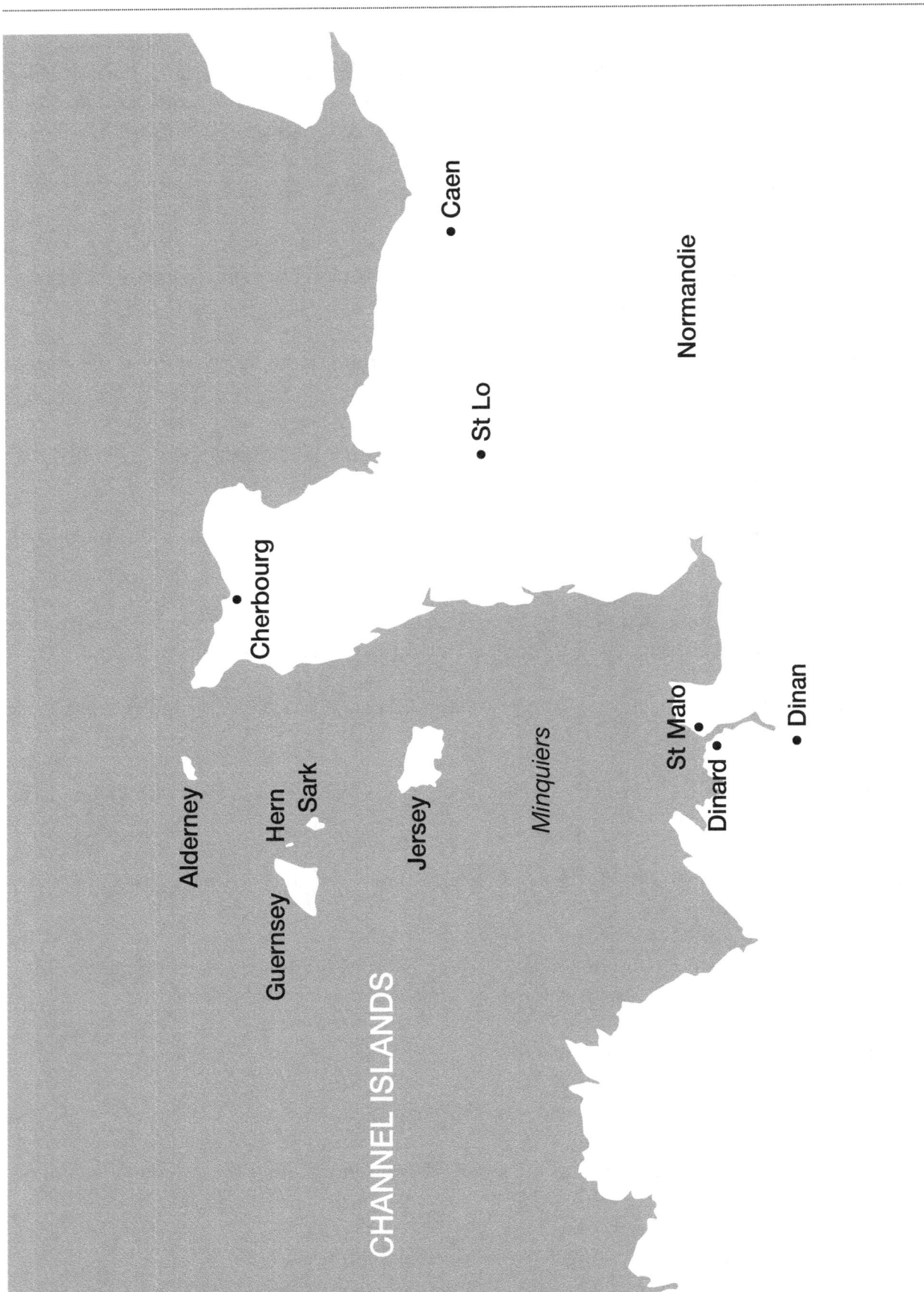

FOREWORD

I am delighted to have been invited to write the Foreword to The Diary of Lieutenant Desmond Mulholland MC and to have had the privilege of reading the book before publication.

I congratulate Peter Jesson on having the foresight to appreciate the important contribution that the Diary makes to our understanding of the Second World War, and in particular, of the Guernsey people who, in so many different ways, played a part in the events that unfolded during those terrible years.

The Introduction Peter has written and the footnotes he has added throughout the Diary help to place the work in its proper context and to enable the reader to understand what Lt Mulholland was writing. They are an invaluable and integral addition to the work.

The Diary provides a fascinating picture of the tedious and mundane routine of life inside Prisoner of War Camps and of one man's attitude to it. People, like me, who have watched "The Great Escape" and similar films or television programmes may have the impression that every captive spent their entire waking hours plotting their escape and return to the UK.

That is far from the case. Mulholland refers to escapees but shows little desire to join their ranks, much as he longed for the freedom he would enjoy at the end of the War.

Instead, his way of coping was to keep himself occupied, to educate himself and to improve his mind so that he could better enjoy a fulfilled life once he was free. What a tragedy it is that he was never able to do so! He wrote "The only thing to do here is to work; in work you can forget yourself and prepare for the time after the war: life here is too personal to contemplate deeply." And later "Prison life makes me see people and things as they really are. How do I see myself? Working to prevent myself thinking; living in a world of imagination which pays little attention to physical troubles".

He greatly benefitted from being with some very able people who were able to lecture and educate their fellow prisoners. He particularly enjoyed the study and appreciation of music and one senses his longing to be free and to be able to attend and enjoy a full orchestral concert.

Above all else, he occupied himself with reading and writing, including writing his diary.

Sadly, we learn little about the failures of the mission that led to his surrender and subsequent enforced captivity; a mission that Winston Churchill described as "a fiasco". The likely reason for his silence is that his diary was read (and censored) by his captors.

We do however learn of his frustration that he did not delay his surrender for another 24 hours when the rescue party that had finally been sent might have been able to meet up and bring him home. However, he does not hide his guilt at having implicated other members of his family especially his beloved mother who assisted him when he was hiding in Guernsey from the Germans. The lack of news of her whereabouts and of what had befallen her is a constant source of worry to him.

We also learn of his feelings of embarrassment and shame at having surrendered and of how he eventually manages to cope with that aided by the understanding and sympathy of others.

Above all else, the lasting impression I am left with is of the futility of war and the tragic waste brought about by it. Here was a brave, intelligent man determined and committed to make the best of his life and to do what he could for his Island and his country. He had so much to give yet so many years were wasted while he languished in enforced captivity.

I am left marvelling at his qualities and values and wondering what might have been if he had been able to pursue his chosen career.

I commend this book to all who are interested in the Second World War or in the achievements of distinguished Guernsey men or simply in the study of human nature.

R J Collas
Bailiff of Guernsey
January 2014

INTRODUCTION

Desmond Mulholland was born in Wandsworth, South London on 17th July 1919 to John Edward Mulholland, who was an Army Intelligence Officer in World War I, and Dorothy Madeline Mulholland, née Moorhouse. Dorothy was a sister to Gladys Jesson née Moorhouse, (my grandmother and Desmond's aunty). Desmond and my father (Russell Jesson) first met in about 1922. They used to spend their school holidays with their grandfather and grandmother, Edward (Grandpa) and Mary (Nanny) Moorhouse.

From r to l: My father (Russell), Nanny Moorhouse, Desmond +
my father's sister Barbara taken at what I believe is Petit Bot Bay in about 1928.

Edward Moorhouse was a journalist and a writer of books about horse racing. He had been involved in the editing of the "Sporting Life" and was also co-founder and first secretary of the Thoroughbred Breeders Association. Edward and Mary moved to Guernsey in 1921 and lived in a house called "Les Douvres", Rue de la Motte in the parish of St. Martin. This house is now a hotel. My father and my father's parents used to spend summer holidays at "Les Douvres".

Les Douvres in 1931

By 1932 Great Aunt Dorothy had divorced from her husband and, with her son Desmond, also went to live at "Les Douvres". Desmond was educated at Elizabeth College, St Peter Port from 1932 until 1936. When they were in their late teens, Desmond and my father used to have "high old times" going to dances and beach parties. My father always said that he and Desmond were much more like brothers than cousins owing to their close relationship. Both Desmond and his mother were very accomplished pianists and were also great connoisseurs of classical music.

In the mid 1930's my great aunt Dorothy remarried to Arthur Cadogan Michael, an artist living locally, known by the family, including Desmond, as "Uncle Mickie". They lived at a house called "Le Paradou", Les Resbouquets, in the Parish of Forest on Guernsey. Uncle Mickie had become a very accomplished portrait painter in oils and water colours. Some of his paintings remain on the island, with a few in the Museum and one that hangs in the Guernsey Royal Court.

Desmond and my father shared digs in London when my father was studying medicine and Desmond was studying law. Desmond eventually passed his exams and qualified as a barrister at Gray's Inn. The family sold "Les Douvres" in 1936 and moved to a house called "Les Préaux", La Route De Sausmerez in the parish of St. Martin on the outskirts of St. Peter Port. On 11th February 1939 my Great Grandfather, Edward Moorhouse, died very suddenly and two months later Les Préaux was sold. Prior to this in 1936 Edward and Mary had purchased La Ruette Farm, La Fosse de Bas also in the parish of St. Martin, so Mary went to live there. During the war she lived in flats that she and her late husband owned at Grange Terrace and Grange Place near Elizabeth College in Grange Road, St Peter Port.

Desmond later enlisted in the Royal Guernsey Light Infantry at Les Beaucamps camp in the Parish of Castel. The photograph below, taken at Les Beaucamps, shows Desmond being carried on the shoulders of his colleagues.

Courtesy of Guernsey Museums & Galleries, States of Guernsey, 2013.

From Left to Right (front row) :
Private Loaring, Private Desmond, Sergeant E.A.Guilbert. Sergeant Guilbert is one of the soldiers holding Lieutenant Desmond Mulholland on his shoulder. Private Stonbridge(?) is standing behind Desmond (second soldier from the left). Standing behind the soldier with the accordion (over his right shoulder) is Drum Major H. Le Page.

Desmond in the uniform of the Royal Guernsey Light Infantry
(Otherwise known as the Guernsey Militia.)

In September 1939, when war was declared, my father was with the family on Guernsey and he decided to join up, left the island and was eventually accepted into the Royal Navy. Desmond, a fluent French speaker, had started studying French law at Caen University, with the idea of becoming a lawyer on Guernsey. He too left Guernsey to join the Army and was attached to the Duke of Cornwall Light Infantry.

After discussion between the UK government of 1940 and the Jersey and Guernsey authorities, it was decided that the islands should be demilitarised and all traces of the island militia were to be hidden, including uniforms and weapons. This, in the main, was to reduce the risk of a full blown battle for the islands and the inherent damage that would cause. That decision was made finally on 19th June 1940 and by then many islanders had left for the mainland of England. On 28th June the islands were bombed by the German air force and a large number of islanders were killed or injured. The occupation of the Channel Islands by German forces began on 30th June 1940 with Guernsey being occupied first, trapping my great grandmother (Mary Moorhouse) my great aunt Dorothy and her husband (Uncle Mickie) on the island. Jersey was occupied the next day, followed by the occupation of the other islands over the next few days. It was not long before the Prime Minister, Winston Churchill, decided to test the German defences on Guernsey. A force of special volunteers was selected. The operation, code-named "Ambassador", had a number of objectives amongst which was the destruction of Guernsey's airfield.

The prequel to Operation Ambassador was "Operation Anger". This was to be the fact finding part of the main operation. First to land on Guernsey, on 6th July 1940, was Lt. Hubert Nicolle of the Royal Hampshire Regiment, his brief being to find out the strength of the German forces. Nicolle had been a resident of the island before the occupation and a member of the Guernsey Militia. Three days later he was joined by Desmond Mulholland and Philip Martel, a Lieutenant in the Hampshire Regiment, and another ex pupil of Elizabeth College. Both were residents of Guernsey before the war and had also been in the Royal Guernsey Militia. Martel worked at the family jewelery business in The Arcade in St. Peter Port. Their orders were to land secretly ahead of the raiding parties one of which was to land at Petit Bot and the other at Le Gouffre on the south coast of Guernsey, and guide them to the selected targets. Desmond and Philip Martel were told they had to be in civilian clothes and could, if caught, be shot as spies.

After arriving at Plymouth on the evening of 9th July 1940, they hung around for an hour or two waiting for authorisation from Churchill to proceed. This instruction never came so they went ahead anyway and joined the submarine. Shortly after midnight on 10th July 1940, they arrived off the coast of Guernsey and were rowed ashore in the submarine's dinghy by a member of the crew landing at Le Jaonnet, a small bay in the south of the island. Hubert Nicolle quickly briefed them as to the situation on the island. He told them that a curfew had been imposed and that the Germans had changed the time by one hour, also that you could move around freely during the daytime as the Germans were not interfering with anyone. When they were half way up the cliff path, they noticed that the canvas dinghy that Hubert was in had overturned and they returned to the beach and helped to drag it ashore, bail it out and refloat it. The help of Philip Martel and Desmond had been vital, as the dinghy was damaged and leaking fast but Nicolle did manage on the second attempt to get back to the submarine.

Le Jaonnet Bay, Guernsey

Nicolle was to return to Guernsey on 4th September 1940. This time he was in the company of Lieutenant James Symes, also a Guernsey man and of the Hampshire Regiment. Unfortunately they suffered the same fate as Desmond Mulholland and Philip Martel, finishing up in various German POW camps.

Bad weather then led to the postponement of Operation Ambassador, but Desmond and Philip Martel having no means of communication and no way of knowing that the plans had been changed, were on their own and in enemy territory. Everything possible went wrong with "Operation Ambassador": bad weather, bad planning, delays, boats not in a fit condition to sail, compasses not working etc. and finally no means of communication with the men on the ground. They waited at Le Jaonnet for two nights, but the submarine did not appear. They then layed low for about three weeks and made two attempts to escape. Desmond and Philip Martel were all the time on the look out for ways to escape. During this time they managed to purloin a couple of bicycles. A good watch was being kept on all the fishing boats by the Germans but they did manage to acquire a boat at Perelle and made out to sea. Neither knew much about boats and nearly went on the rocks, all they managed to do was give themselves a good fright and they returned to land. Added to the continual strain of hiding from the Germans, there was also danger for their families who they had visited from time to time. For several days they slept at La Cour de Longue in St. Saviours, which was owned by Colonel Cantan whose wife was the Dame of Sark's daughter. Escape was uppermost in their minds. They decided to visit the Dame of Sark, hoping she would know of a Sark fisherman to take them back to England. They travelled over on the Sark boat with their stolen bicycles. This must have been so nerve racking as there were Germans on the boat. Unfortunately the Dame of Sark was in Guernsey at the dentist so they missed her but they did manage to find out that the Germans had all the fishing boats in the harbour and the approach tunnel well guarded. The Dame did visit them at La Cour de Longue the next day. They also stayed in a barn next to a house in Vazon, but even here they did not escape attention, as the lady of the house spotted them and recognised them. This could not go on. Apart from the continual strain, they were now understandably jumpy. There was danger to their families as well as to the people who knew where they were. So they decided to give themselves up.

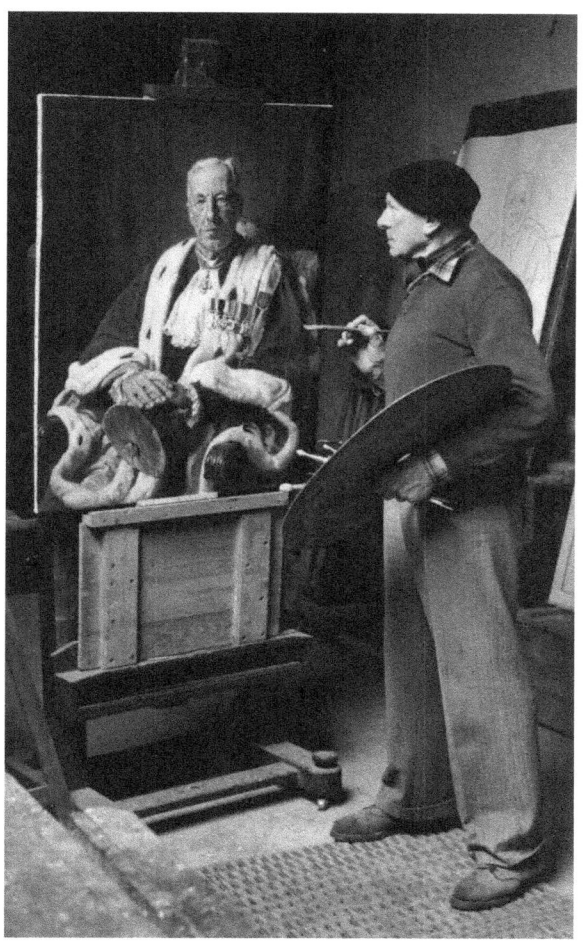

Uncle Mickie painting Sir Ambrose Sherwill

Major Ambrose Sherwill, who was then His Majesty's Procureur and President of the Island's Controlling Committee, was up very early one morning in his home Havelet House. He heard a knock on the back door and, thinking it was the milkman, he opened the door to find Desmond Mulholland and Philip Martel. Major Sherwill knew Desmond as a friend of his daughter. They were invited in and related their story. They told him that they were done in and that their nerves could take no more. Sherwill asked if they were quite determined to give themselves up and they both agreed that they were. As they had landed in civilian clothes they would be shot as spies if caught so the only way to save their lives was to find them uniforms. Sherwill discussed the risks with his wife but she brushed aside his grim warnings and proceeded to give them a breakfast of eggs, which they ate ravenously. Next they were sent to an attic room to sleep.

In the meantime Sherwill took his wife's Fiat car and went in search of a friend who would assist him in obtaining some uniforms. The initial plan was to burgle a house of a Guernsey Militia officer who had gone to England, but the friend knew of uniforms at the Town Arsenal, so they drove there passing a German soldier on the way. In the Arsenal they found a chest full of service dress uniforms and selected uniforms that looked as if they would fit. One of these uniforms had first war medals attached so they were cut off but a mark was left which they tried to hide. Next they spotted the Guernsey Militia buttons. The wife of the caretaker of the Arsenal came to the rescue and she did a heroic job of speedily cutting off the buttons and replacing them with British Army buttons. Finally Sherwill piled the uniforms into the car, dropped off his friend and drove home, terrified that a German might stop him and ask for a lift.

Back at Havelet House, Desmond and Philip Martel were woken, given dinner and dressed. A last minute snag occurred. They were a pair of braces short so Sherwill had to sacrifice his own!! Then Sherwill telephoned the Germans to inform them that two British Officers had surrendered to him. He managed to convince the Germans that they had arrived on the island in uniform but had acquired some civilian clothes to get to Havelet House. The civilian clothes were made into two brown paper parcels and Sherwill, Desmond and Philip Martel set off to the German headquarters, which was then situated at the Channel Islands Hotel. On the way Sherwill impressed upon Desmond and Philip Martel that they must say nothing, only their name, rank and number, a fact that he had to remind them of sharply whilst they were being questioned. The two of them were kept at the hotel overnight.

This whole ordeal had been unnecessary, if only they had known that on the very morning that they gave themselves up, their rescue had already been arranged. Another Guernseyman, Stanley Ferbrache also serving in the Hampshire Regiment, had volunteered to go by motor torpedo boat to Guernsey to find them. He landed at Le Jaonnet and spent the night on the cliffs, only to hear rumours that two British officers had just given themselves up. This was confirmed by Desmond's mother. He was too late, by less than a week.

They were then both flown to France where they were separated and questioned at length. Each night their trousers were taken away from them to prevent them from escaping. Whilst in France Philip Martel became seriously ill and so Desmond was sent on alone to various POW camps in Germany, Poland and Czechoslovakia, including Oflag IX-A/H at Spangenberg in Germany, Stalag XX-A at Thorn in Poland and Oflag VII-B at Eichstätt, also in Germany. They did meet up again, at Oflag VIB at Warburg in October 1941.

From l to r: Philip Martel, Bob Huelin (from Jersey), Michael Mellish, Major Carey and John Laine at Oflag VIIB at Eichstätt.

Meanwhile, my great aunt Dorothy, Desmond's mother, was arrested for harbouring Desmond. She was sent to a prison of sorts at the Hotel de la Gare in Saint-Lô, the capital of the Manche department in Normandy, where she had to report daily to the local German Commander. Her husband, Uncle Mickie, later requested to be allowed to join her and permission was given. In January 1941 she was released and the two of them were sent back to Guernsey but, on 28th September 1942, a large number of men, women and children who were not born on Guernsey were rounded up and shipped off to three POW camps in Germany (Biberach, Laufen and Dorsten). This was in retaliation for Germans being rounded up elsewhere at the request of the British government. We know that Aunt Dorothy and Uncle Mickie were sent to Ilag V-B, a civilian POW camp, at Biberach in Southern Germany, as she sent a card to my grandmother (her sister) on 24th April 1945 to say that their camp had been relieved by the French but she did not know when they would be home. The card was addressed "Internierungslager Biberach". Ironically Desmond was at Oflag VII-B in Eichstätt during the same period that his mother and stepfather were imprisoned at the camp at Biberach, only some 100 miles distant from Eichstätt. Neither of them knew this of course. Desmond became very depressed by the separation from his family and friends and felt very responsible for what had happened to his mother.

He also felt very guilty about the harm he may have done to those remaining on Guernsey and often wondered if he would ever be accepted back into the island society. He also worried that he would be court martialled for giving himself up to the Germans so readily, instead of making a better effort to escape.

Desmond kept a hand-written diary of his time as a prisoner of war which was censored by the Germans on a regular basis as is evidenced by the "Geprüft" ("Approved") stamp on each page, so he had to be circumspect about the facts he recorded. The diary and notebook were taken from him on a number of occasions and only the record of his first year of imprisonment survived. He regularly recorded events and facts in his note book and then, sometimes two or three weeks later, he transferrd these into his diary. Occasionally these facts get a little muddled due to the delay so the reader will perhaps notice that something like a POW camp may have the wrong number attached to it. Desmond regularly uses French words and phrases which is still very common on Guernsey.

Whilst in various POW camps he met a number of people who were to become very well known, such as the late Airey Neave MP, who later became a prisoner at Colditz Castle and the late Michael Goodliffe, actor who, ironically, was at school with my father at St. Edmund's School in Canterbury, Kent. During his time of imprisonment

Desmond read widely and studied German, Russian, Italian and shorthand. He was very ably coached in these by other prisoners. Whilst in Oflag VIIB at Eichstätt, he passed the Royal Society of Arts Exam in Russian in Advanced Grade. He became very keen on the idea of becoming a legal journalist on his return to the UK before going back to the law.

On 12th April 1945 at Eichstätt (Oflag VIIB) they were told they would be moving south in two days time. There had been rumours beforehand that they would be moved as the war in Europe came into its final stages. They were all packed and ready to go. A few thousand officers taking as many clothes and as much food as they could possibly carry as they did not know what lay ahead. Two officers placed a pole between their shoulders with their bags hanging from it. Their departure was not in an orderly fashion, not a military column but men walking in groups of two or three. They were about 15 minutes out of the camp when a plane flew over them. It was recognised as an American reconnaissance plane. Then they heard two fighters dropping bombs across the valley and before they knew what was happening machine gun fire was being aimed at them. Philip Martel went to the left and put his head in a ditch with a German soldier and was safe, but a friend who went to the right side of the road was killed. The planes came around a second time. After they had left, the officers ran back to the camp as quickly as they could. The first back straight away put the letters "POW" on the roof. The camp had been left in disarray, as they were not expecting to return. 14 Officers had been killed and 46 injured by friendly fire that day. The Officers refused to march by day again. Orders were issued that they would leave the next day at dusk. They marched in stages staying in various farms on the way before they reached Moosburg, which was probably Stalag VIIA, the final camp. This camp was situated nearer to Munich. It was a huge camp with many nationalities. Desmond was finally repatriated to the UK in May 1945, just after the Channel Islands had been liberated.

The family all eventually moved back to Guernsey with my grandparents, great aunt Dorothy, Uncle Mickie and great grandmother living in the converted farm buildings in La Fosse opposite the "Bella Luce Hotel". My father got special leave to visit his family in late 1945. My first visit to see them was in July 1947.

Major Ambrose Sherwill became Bailiff of Guernsey in 1946 and remained in that office until 1959. He was knighted in 1949 and died on Alderney in 1968.

I hope that all who read Desmond's account of life in a POW camp will get as much pleasure as I did from his wonderful, descriptive way of recording what must have been the worst kind of drudgery and deprivation imaginable. The mental pain and anguish that shows in the diary remained with him.

Peter Jesson

I am writing this on Dec 5th and I hope my memory allows me to give an accurate report (the writing is bad but I hope it will improve).

Tuesday July 30th (1940)

After a wakeful night I arose about 8 o'clock: the bed had been hard and the guards had been in and out with much noise at regular intervals. It was a glorious morning and the sun, shining from behind the islands, made the clear blue sea look most tempting, but I was locked in my room and the sea was about a 20 foot drop from the sill of my window. My thoughts seemed numbed and I could hardly realise that I was not at liberty to walk out into the wide world. I had not yet begun to think of the inevitable step that I had taken and I was hoping to leave the island and those terrible days behind me. I didn't want to face my friends as one who has surrendered himself, though, as I write this, I am convinced that our action was the only sane one. My breakfast was brought in by one of the troops, Cornish, a boy from Jersey who had got marooned in the island by the speedy departure of the mail boat. A sentry accompanied him and only a casual greeting was allowed. My mind somehow went back to the days when Grandpa used to say, "Don't talk unless you have something to say." Most of what I say could, without loss to my audience, be left unsaid. Some chicken roll, tomatoes and a cup of tea; "Not bad if we always live like this," I thought, but they were airy thoughts as you will see. A razor and some hot water were procured for me and I removed my week's black growth: it was rather Bohemian. Some magazines were brought; awful picture books and I used them as a sort of anaesthetic. But most of this lovely July morning I spent on my window sill looking at the fishing boats and being brought home to reality by the large German sentry who sang to himself and smoked English cigarettes: was there really a war on? Lunch at last came and with it perhaps my last real meat: two lamb chops and a cup of tea. I did not have long to enjoy this for a soldier rushed in and cried, "Flugplatz"[1] and I realised we were off. We were led out to a waiting grey Standard[2] in which I took the front seat. The boys were on the wall and "thumbs up" raised my hopes. We tore up the New Road, along the Fort Road, past the dear old Préaux,[3] along the Forest Road and up to the asphalt tarmac. How often have I walked these sympathetic roads? There were a lot of Messerschmitts[4] on the airport and a large black Junker[5] being loaded with tomatoes by two Dutchmen of my acquaintance. After some moments we were instructed to board the plane. Two seats were placed for us and we sat in this crate like interior surrounded by melons and tomatoes. We were soon skimming over the West boundary fence and heading for Jersey. The Paradou[6] looked so small: did Mummy know I was up there? When would I see her again and, God, I hope she'll be safe. Soon Jersey was below us and I thought of my rugby II trip: not games this time! A shot rang out. Spitfires were my first thought but as we didn't career seawards I realised, thankfully I fear, that it was our light-hearted gunner who, with a mechanic and a young officer were taking us from home. The Minquiers[7] passed below us and soon we were over the French coast and I recognised St Malo[8] and Dinard.[9] The flight became a little bumpy now and in a few minutes we turned round and down and landed on a huge flying field. When we came to rest we were ordered out and caused a great sensation among the German guards and French workers. The airmen digging and working on planes were clad in shorts and the poor French looked very hot and tired. We

1 German: airfield.
2 Vehicle manufactured by Standard Motor Co. Probably a light utility vehicle.
3 Desmond's Grandparents' house in Guernsey (see Introduction).
4 German fighter aircraft.
5 German military aircraft.
6 "Uncle Mickie's" house in Guernsey (see Introduction).
7 A group of islands and rocks 15km south of Jersey.
8 A walled port city in Brittany in north western France.
9 A commune in the Ille et Vilaine department in Brittany in north western France.

learnt that we were at Dinan[10] and then came an embarrassing experience so we were very glad to getback into the now unloaded plane. We realised that we had not been expected. I guessed that our next stop would be Rennes[11] and at 3.30, an hour after our departure, we came to rest on Rennes airport. A car was waiting for us but we were put in the charge of a tall, khaki coated soldier and with two guards we were marched to the terminal buildings. There were many French at work digging and I was unable to detect their feelings. Telephoning was done and after some time we were marched to a waiting car and, in the company of a bouncing young air officer, we left the airport at great speed in an Opel Kapitän[12]: we passed some wrecked French planes and numerous road barriers. We suddenly turned into a camp full of French prisoners; roughly dressed and unshaven who were queuing up for some meal. We were led straight to an office where we waited for more telephoning to be done: we were not expected. When we left the camp we felt many eyes burning into us but my eyes were on the ground: the sight of all this captive humanity had shaken me. On the road again and soon we came to the heart of Rennes, full of Germans and, what surprised me, a great many French uniforms. We got out in a huge square and were taken into the Hotel de Ville,[13] where, after having been led into various large rooms, we came to rest in what appeared to be a guardroom and an office. We had to wait for some time but the time did not hang for a military band was organising itself outside with much movement and noise. Two or three officers came to us and with them two interpreters. The man, in English, asked us who we were and where we had come from and, after some conference, we were handed over to a soldier who marched us out, past the band who were now loudly playing to no one. We went along a crowded street beside a canal but we were not marked out and I could not gauge the public feeling. Were we among friends or enemies? Along a shady walk where we passed a girl reading a Penguin: she smiled, which pleased me: we still had a friend. We were being followed by two little boys who whistled Tipperary and La Marseillaise[14]. Our escort was not at all sure of where to take us and after many questions we arrived at the Rue de l'Orient where we turned into a gate and beheld a camp of British huts surrounded by barbed wire and full of assortedly clad men: many in English uniforms, but certainly not British. A German officer appeared and, after some conversation, we were sent off to the French CO[15], a pleasant old Captain who sent us on to a British troop. We had begun to feel a bit lost and this meeting put our dusty, hot hopes into the air. The long hut was hot but about 20 soldiers, led by a very superior sergeant of REs[16] gave us a great welcome and made us quite at home. An English speaking Red Cross lady was there and was very charming and told us where her hopes lay. The men got to work to make us two beds and we sat down with them to slop potato soup and some bread and cheese sent them by French friends who had been most kind to them. We were glad to get a wash and then went to see the few French officers who looked after the troops. During our conversation the German NCO[17] came in and told us to follow him which we did and we were led to a tin shed next to the shower baths: here two beds, tarpaulin springs and a straw palliasse[18] and a French coloured counterpane. The NCO, who spoke a little English, commiserated with us and hoped for a speedy conclusion to this war. Then, as it became dark, I flung myself on to this bed and could have wept. Hot, dirty, tired, dispirited, having no idea what the future would bring, I fell into a merciful sleep with only the heavy pace of our sentry entering my dreamless hours.

10 A walled Breton town and a commune in the Côtes d'Armor department of north western France.
11 Capital of the region of Brittany in north western France.
12 A luxury German car.
13 French: Town Hall
14 National anthem of France.
15 Military abbreviation: Commanding Officer.
16 Military abbreviation: Royal Engineers.
17 Military abbreviation: Non-commissioned Officer.
18 A straw filled mattress.

Wednesday July 31st

I was awake pretty early and outside it was a glorious morning, the sun streaming through the lattice grill. One of the Dolmetschers (Interpreters) came in with a razor, some soap, chocolate and bread that had been sent by the soldiers. We shaved and no sooner had we finished than the NCO arrived and told us to get ready, which was not a long task: we then went out and at the gate of the camp we were met by some men with GFP on their shoulders which we later found to be "Gestapo Feldpolizei".[19] We were shown to different cars and we were soon flashing out of Rennes in the St Malo direction. The NCO with me spoke very good French and he had only just been called up. In build and appearance he was not unlike Daddy. Before long I began to recognise the route as I had been along it at Whitsun 1939. We crossed the Rance[20] at Dinan, getting a glorious view and I remembered how I had posed for a photo on this very bridge. Through Dinan and the Château d'Anne[21] and on to the Dinard Road. We passed a great many convoys and troops erecting telegraph poles: also a number of returning refugees being recognisable by the bedding on the roof. What sights these poor people must have had to bear. We soon got into Dinard itself and pulled up at the Hotel Bellevue. I was shown into the hall and given a seat: of Martel[22] there was no sign. I was feeling distinctly nervous and my nervousness was not alleviated by the arrival of a number of officers covered with medals. It was not long before I was taken out on to the veranda where I was told to sit down at a table already occupied by an officer and a young airman. The officer was a bigly built man with glasses and wearing a very smart uniform. He took my particulars and, in excellent English, he questioned me for about an hour and that hour was not one of my most pleasant memories. It came to an end at last and when the interrogating officer and a distinguished elderly officer had taken their leave, I was taken downstairs by an interpreter and given some stew, though my appetite was not at its best. M was at another table with an interpreter and a number of other soldiers were scattered over the room. After the meal I was led back to the veranda and so passed a long afternoon, listening to the interpreter, a Münster[23] professor, reading bad novels and looking out at the bright blue bay where the well-loaded vedettes[24] plied (their trade)[25] between Dinard and St Malo. The tide went down so slowly and the time dragged itself on to 7 o'clock. I did everything I could to put thought out of my head but it was difficult. The long afternoon came to an end and I was taken back to the dining room. Brown army bread with a harsh, bitter but not unattractive taste, various French and English tinned stuffs and black coffee. I ate a great deal and argued politics: the conclusion reached, "You are English: I am German." Still it was all very interesting. The time passed quickly in this way and at 11 we were taken up to the top of the house and put in separate rooms with a guard on the landing: our clothes were removed and there was nothing left for me but to climb into the little bed. Our fate was still in the balance and we had no idea what would happen or what had happened: still we were still alive and though very much harassed mentally, were physically intact. I hope I will never have to wait alone again with such a terrible anxiety on my head. Still, sleep comes to all who wait.

---

19   German: Secret Field Police – secret Military police of the German Wehrmacht in WW2.
20   River Rance.
21   Tower of the Duchesse Anne built in the 14th century.
22   Philip Martel MC, Hampshire Regiment - Desmond's colleague who accompanied him on Operation Anger, the scouting mission to Guernsey (see Introduction).
23   A university city in Westphalia, Germany.
24   French: a small steamer or motor boat.
25   Desmond doesn't actually say 'their trade' but I think it is what he means.

The Diary Of Lieutenant Desmond Mulholland MC

Thursday August 1st

I was awakened about 7 o'clock by Krabb, who was Martel's interpreter. I opened my window and looked from 5 stories on to a deserted street: no holiday makers this year. It was a lovely morning and I almost felt like a bathe. Krabb, a Münster schoolmaster, speaking very correct English, full of very trite remarks, brought me a piece of soap and I used my sheet as a towel. Breakfast consisted of brown rye bread and a tin of cheap salmon. This hotel had been used by the English and was full of stores. We went up to the veranda and watched the sun rise over St Malo and the vedettes preparing for their daily task. I buried myself in a book of short stories, interrupted by a game of Russian billiards. It was not easy to be natural for we had no idea what our fate was to be. About midday the English speaking Captain returned and my heart dropped. After about 10 minutes he seemed satisfied as to our connection with Jerbourg[26] and for the next few minutes we talked of this and that. He had done a great deal of travelling in the Empire and I drew my own conclusions. When he had departed, M and I were allowed to come together and from that moment the attitude of our guards changed. We were taken to a lunch of army stew and when we had finished M and I took on the Interpreters at Billiards and so passed quite a pleasant afternoon though we were still in the dark as to our future. It was a glorious afternoon and I envied the happy young swimmers their liberty. The bay, bright blue in the sun, was full of red sailed craft skimming here and there like a farmyard of ducks with an occasional ferry boat acting the intruding goose. After supper of bread and salmon (3d at Woolworths) we had a match of billiards between "Tommy and Jerry" as Krabb put it. He sent out for some wine and it was hard to think of us being at war. These men, however, were all civilians till May and had not acquired that "Soldaten" veneer[27]. At 11 it was time to go to bed and though we were no nearer a decision I felt more easy and was soon asleep.

Friday August 2nd

Krabb was in early and again gave me some soap. He produced some marmalade which was a welcome change and the morning ran on similar lines as the day before and the large bay turned from misty grey to bright blue and at about 11 o'clock when a number of settees were brought out, our hopes went from rosy red to deep blue. They were not made easier by the arrival of the Captain, a young, gay, good-looking Bavarian, who came to talk to Krabb, my interpreter having taken his farewell of us. I heard G[28] mentioned and glanced at M. Now we would hear. The captain soon left and Krabb, with a smiling face, told us that we were to leave for a prison camp that afternoon. The GHQ[29] had decided our case and the Captain had spoken very heartily in our favour. I think they were all genuinely pleased. After lunch of pea stew we took our leave of K and the Captain: we had been well treated and were grateful. Both in the same car, we headed for Rennes with an officer for escort. He spoke no English so I had time to think over the future: we were lead to believe that we should soon be taken to Germany. In about an hour's time we were turning into the old camp "Camp des Pionniers".[30] The officer shook hands on taking his leave of us and we were amiably received by the NCO. We were allotted to a Nissen hut (a type of corrugated iron tunnel hut) in the compound reserved for the Malgache, i.e. Madagascans. The soldiers were very pleased to see us safely back and quickly got our beds rigged up. One of them was in a bad way with dysentery and I hoped I should

---

26   The Jerbourg Peninsula is the south eastern point of Guernsey where a small, unsuccessful commando raid landed on 14th July 1940.

27   German: soldier's (veneer).

28   Germany, presumably.

29   German or Gestapo headquarters, presumably.

30   French: Pioneers' Camp (known to the Germans as Frontstalag 133.

be preserved from that complaint. They were well supplied with food from the kind Rennais[31] and they made us a cup of tea on the hut stove. Titch, red faced, bulbous nosed and head clipped, was the fireman and he carried out his duties with much swearing, not because he didn't like the job but because it was his wont to swear. I never learnt his name and all I knew was that he was an "old sweat" put into the AMPC[32] who played the cornet, drank beer and was most amiable. The French Capitaine Frémont invited us to dinner which we took in a little kitchen attached to his office. It was hot and flies swarmed but we did justice to what was quite a good meal, cheese soup, raie beurrée[33], peas and a mobile[34] Camembert and life in that hot, dirty, ugly camp became quite bearable. At 9 o'clock we wished our troops goodnight and made our way to our hut. The N-----s were war dancing and it made a great impression on me. How much happier they must have been in their barbaric jungle than in this "civilised" world. We had had an exciting day and sleep soon came upon me. The shed was huge and we felt like pygmies in this dirty, dark and barren dwelling. I don't think I'll mind the embankment after this war.

Saturday August 3rd

I was woken by one of the troops who brought us some tea which was fortunately sweet, for I think French cook house tea would bear very little resemblance to its English namesake. I had slept quite well and felt much easier in my mind. There was no issue of breakfast so after a wash we went over to the hut and there found some bread and chocolate and also some hot water for a shave. I left my moustache and hope to have it when I return to England. I spent the morning in getting acquainted. We were not expected to dine with the French officers, why I have no idea, but the oberleutnant[35] said so. There were Poles and Belgians in the camp, the latter sharing a hut with our boys, as well as French. I met two very charming Poilus[36], two students, one from Rennes the other Paris, who spent most of their time with our boys and trying to learn English. Raymond Martin was very bitter against his officers and I began to realise why France had so soon collapsed. The Belgians had very little time for the French and vice versa. Lunch was some rice and fat and I was very grateful to the Rennes gifts. There was nothing to do in the afternoon but sleep with a book: Peking Picnic by Ann Bridge which took me out of this fly infested tin camp. At about 5.30 the men made some tea but the heat in their hut was absolutely stifling and flies just clouded. We ate bread and jam and gave our potato soup to the Belgians. Our lads were very cheerful and 'Bing' Harris crooned his way to happiness and Yorkshire accents mingled with the Welsh singsong. After tea we played tip and run in the dusty yard watched by a crowd of open mouthed French men. When we had finished the N-----s did some war dancing to the accompaniment of tin tom toms: was this to show that they also knew some mad games? Appell[37] was at 9 and so we went to our hut. It was very hot and the sight of the mooching prisoners was not inspiring. The camp was surrounded by barbed wire with 4 elevated MG posts[38]. A Belgian sergeant, with a tiny mouche, i.e. a little lower lip beard, who answered to Ma, Ma came and ran down the French and the Belgian officers, of how they had left their men and departed in fine cars accompanied by their wives. We had no form of lighting so all we

---

31 French: the people of Rennes.
32 Military abbreviation: Automatic Message Processing Centre.
33 French: skate cooked in butter.
34 I am not sure if this word is transcribed correctly. Desmond could be referring to a runny Camembert(?).
35 German: Senior Lieutenant.
36 French: French soldiers (slang).
37 German: Roll call of prisoners.
38 Military abbreviation: Machine Gun post.

could do was retire to bed, a sack full of straw and a French counterpane. I had luckily obtained a British great coat and a towel: my scrounging days had begun.

Sunday August 4th

I was up pretty early and went and took a shower with one of the troops: this was further proof that the camp was British built. It was cool and refreshing and I was glad to find that kind friends had sent in bread, butter and meat paste so we made a reasonable meal all crowded round the little table. I read and talked all the morning and lunch was some potatoes with what I am convinced was horse: still I was only too glad to eat anything. I had a long chat with Sgt. Victor Maclean from Ballywater[39] who worked for the Mulholland family, he was a grand, good hearted fellow. There was a football match in the afternoon and the N-----s enjoyed themselves immensely. I made the acquaintance of some of the doctors and one or two were from Caen[40]. They invited us to take a cup of tea which was very welcome and later a French Pastor came to see us. He preached an excellent sermon in English and we sung a few hymns: it was somehow rather inspiring to hear these rough, good hearted lads singing so sweetly in this corrugated shack. He took our names to send them to some English lady in Dinard. When he left it was time to attend the concert organised by a lively, bright "Adjutant"[41] from St Malo, Monsieur Benedict: he was the type who shook hands over and over again and called you "mon ami"[42] when he first met: he knew all St Malo and organised it from Church festivals to café réunions[43]. A stage had been put up in the yard and an orchestra dressed in white shirts and flowing red neck ties droned out windy tunes. Titch was blowing a trombone and Victor was masterly on the drums! We had a Ukrainian choir which was delightful: a sad peasant lullaby and these boys seemed to take you away to their little village homes and see their sad and lonely families. Then the N-----s war danced and sang unmelodiously, to my ear, patriotic songs. Two or three comedians and we English sang "My Bonnie", "In the Stores"[44], "Tipperary" and "Pack up Your Troubles". We were very well received especially my final thumbs up, so popular among the French. It was a fine effort in this grilling sun and put new life into everyone. The day was over now and one that I shall not forget: you can forget even in the most dismal surroundings. I soon went to sleep. We saw the Ouest Éclair[45] every day but there was little real news and the RAF were continually over to bomb airports. They asked the public to wait till August 15th: no one knew for what: still one was able to build up hopes.

Monday August 5th to Saturday August 10th

These days were so similar that I feel you would be bored by my memory searchings so I will group them together. I was usually woken by one of the boys who brought a petrol can of tea over after they had finished and I went and had a shower. A piece of bread and jam or cheese (stronger the better! Try it yourself it is very good!) and then the day wandered on. Discussing the news and "Bobards" (rumours) with the doctors, talking of old times and future times with Raymond, talking about the army with the troops, reading Peking Picnic and a number of very

---

39	A village in County Down, Northern Ireland.
40	A commune in north western France.
41	An officer in each regiment who assists the Commanding Officer in matters of business, duty and discipline.
42	French: my friend.
43	French: get togethers/meetings.
44	Presumably 'The Quartermaster's Stores'.
45	A daily regional French newspaper published in Rennes 1899-1944.

bad novels, sleeping in the afternoon and playing tip and run in the evening and then going to bed. Martel got a bad attack of dysentery and I was trying, without much success, to get him rice and proper food: he was pretty bad and passing blood and all night long he was out of bed: the flies worried him terribly and he had no energy to shake them off. I felt most awfully sorry for him. I procured a battle dress from Victor and taught the Frenchmen darts. The ration food was usually potatoes and we thanked God for our kind friends in Rennes who were always sending us good things to eat. I wrote to Geneviève and hoped for an answer but I had no energy and got most awfully depressed. Eating in the hot and stuffy hut and having nothing to do was getting me down. The men went out working now and again but they were mostly not fit enough. I still had a horror of having to reface the GFPs. One bright spot was Victor: always bright and smiling and his action in forcing me to accept 20 marks will be repaid if I can get in touch with him. Cpl Veryard was also most helpful in looking after M. Sergt Tether, who hopes, after the war, to become a priest was always a very fine companion. The camp was dreary but those fellows and their kindness will be one of the good things of 'Le Camp des Pionniers'. I also learnt that clothes washing is no child's play. Saturday 12 o'clock I was informed that all officers were to leave at 2pm for La Caserne Colombier[46] in Rennes so I had to collect my kit. M told me that he did not feel up to travelling so I saw the German NCO who said he would find him an ambulance and have him transported. I took my leave of him and have never seen him from that day to this. At about 3 pm, the usual hour's hanging about having been observed, we were piled into a lorry, 32 of us and, after being seen off by a vast number of German officers, we left in the direction of Rennes. We drove for about ¼ of an hour, but the lorry was closed and, when we were ordered to get out, we found ourselves in front of a large gateway: we were hustled through this and came upon a large courtyard, a machine gun menacing some wire, at one end. We had to give our particulars and were then allotted rooms. I with Capt Frémont and some other officers were allotted to a huge barrack room on the third floor of Batiment[47] R. I kept a bed, two wooden trestles with boards between, for Martel, but our room was not overcrowded for all the doctors moved off and I was left alone with the Captain. I found a straw palliasse and got some coarse canvas sheets and two blankets from a very superior lieutenant, de Roubaix by name, who was chef d'étage.[48] He was very pale, limped and carried his head on one side: combined with this, he spoke slow and pedantic French and referred to me as "Mon Petit"[49] from our first meeting. He seemed to act the old aristocrat inviting you to his spacious château. He came sufficiently to earth to warn us of fleas, though personally I never suffered from them, or rather caught them. I was worried about having no pay but was told that the mess would not require me to pay for my meals, the usual rate being 15 francs a day. It was now about 6.30, the time for the first service of dinner, there being about 800 officers which necessitated this procedure. We had some soupe aux legumes,[50] gigot[51] and haricot beans and some cheese. It was pleasant to sit down to a real table and drink some rather bitter cider: as everyone used his own penknife, I felt a little lost but was able to borrow one. After the meal I was besieged by a host of enquiries and had many questions to answer. Apart from the main entrance court, there was a cloister surrounding an inner court where a volley ball and basket ball were installed. I spent most of my evening walking with a bearded sailor and a very charming Chasseur,[52] Captain Bachelerie, who spoke perfect English with a decided Oxford accent: his wife was a Welsh girl and as an English professor he spent his spare time writing a book on the Gaelic tongues. He was "reformé", ie. released on medical grounds after a short time. Most of the prisoners walked the cloisters, the place had been a monastery in the 16th Century, or they played a game of quoits, throwing metal disks on to a board. We had to be in our rooms by 9.30

46   French: Colombier Barracks.
47   French: Building
48   French: Leader for that particular floor of the building.
49   French: My little one.
50   French: vegetable soup.
51   French: leg of lamb.
52   French: a light armed French soldier.

and lights out by 10. I was quite tired and, though my bed was very hard, I soon fell asleep. I had by now acquired a very attractive nightshirt, white with a pink neck design: very sweet!

***[53]

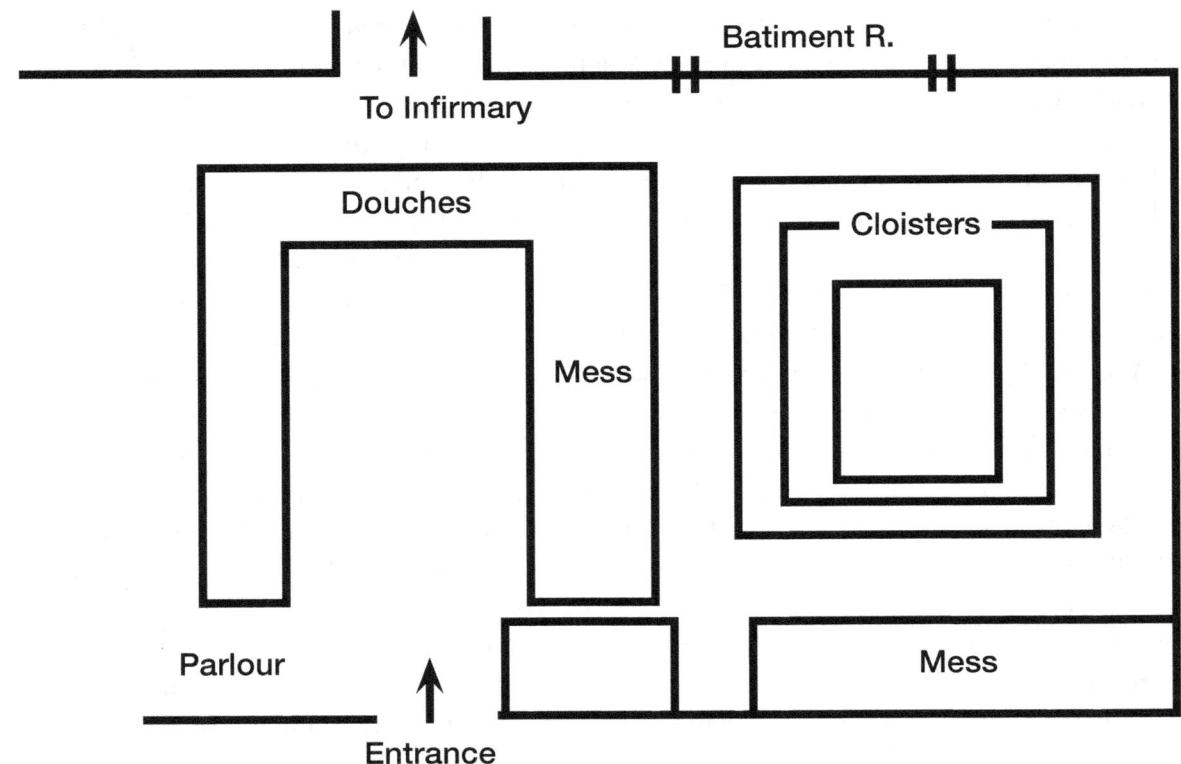

Sunday August 11th

I woke up about 7.30 with the sun pouring into the room and had a wash, there were a lot of taps on the second floor. There was one stand up WC for three floors, pretty inadequate in my opinion. The building was a barracks and was composed of a great number of large and small rooms. Ours was one of the largest rooms with two windows and two skylights: it was rather dark and noisy as it was used as a ping pong room as well as being a connecting room. Breakfast was of sweet tea and French troop bread which always tastes and usually is, half mouldy. I bought a copy of L'Ouest Éclair, which I used to peruse at the Association in Caen, though it was no longer the same paper? The air raids were beginning on England and we were losing British Somaliland.[54] After the meal I was taken by Bachelerie to a Protestant service where I met the same Pasteur,[55] Monsieur xxxxx[56], as we had met last week. We sang some hymns and the service was not dissimilar to that of the C of E. He was carrying letters for friends and promised to get in touch with Geneviève. When it was over I went to visit the infirmary, expecting to find Martel. He was not there but I was able to meet a Pte[57] Thomas England, Hamps, who had been

53   Here Desmond has drawn a sketch showing the layout of the barracks.
54   This is now North West Somalia.
55   French: Pastor
56   The name of the Pastor has been crossed out.
57   Military abbreviation: Private.

wounded in the Rennes air raid as the other English boys. Two troop trains, one English, a refugee train and an ammunition train all in the station at once and blown up by 3 bombers. About 600 British killed and the station master found shot!? While chatting with him, a lady from the Red Cross arrived and gave us some money which had been subscribed by Rennes ladies for English prisoners. I left England with 200fr and took 100fr. When I returned to room 45, I discovered some cards to fill in for the French Red Cross and I sent a French military card to Mummy. I sent two of these in all but both were returned "inadmis"[58] about 3 weeks later. I was taken along to lunch by a dentist and went to the other mess, called the Rosary. I was with two air force officers and except that the meat was tough and we had a good runny Camembert, I forget the meal. After it I paid a call on a Lieutenant Delbarre, Raymond's platoon officer and the only officer for whom he had a good word! I found a powerfully built young man supporting a "fantaisiste"[59] beard; sideboards then a shaved portion followed by a goatee beard. With him was a little Zouave[60] officer. I always knew him as Zouave. I also met two very charming Cavaliers[61], Charles de Brosses, a wealthy young aristocrat who loved bridge and described everything as "Mon cher, c'est impayable"[62] and his more serious friend Marcel Boyer, a Paris business man: I always remember him with his pipe. Both wore beautifully polished boots and spurs and their little room was very neatly laid out. Two beds, a table and cloth and plenty of photographs. They at once invited me to tea at 4.30: "Nous connaissons des anglais"[63] and de Brosses had met many in Dinard, among them Lady Curtis. His favourite pose was making tea and smoking innumerable cigarettes in a long holder. I spent the afternoon on my bed, sleeping and reading "I am Jonathan Scrivener"[64] a really enthralling novel which I advise all to read. At 4.30 I presented myself and found an excellent cup of tea waiting for me: it was made on a little alcohol stove: it was served with sweet biscuits, "petits toasts", and troop biscuits and honey. A very enjoyable afternoon which was the forerunner of many which I spent with these two in their pleasant little room. It was the nearest approach to home that I had met and have met since I have been a prisoner. I did not go down to supper as I had an attack of mild dysentery which is not much fun. I went to bed early, feeling miserable and homesick: perhaps it was that feeling that made me burst into verse. It was a lovely evening and the lovely blue, silver sky formed much too beautiful a background to the AA post[65] on the modern, white block of flats just outside the walls. Still sleep is a comfort and I had the hope of the arrival of my cards. "Ignorance is Bliss."

---

58   French: Presumably an abbreviation of inadmissible.
59   French: whimsical, weird, fanciful.
60   French: The title given to certain light infantry regiments serving in the French army in French North Africa.
61   French: A Private in a cavalry regiment.
62   French: My dear chap, it's priceless (i.e. extremely funny).
63   French: We know some English people.
64   "I am Jonathon Scrivener", a novel by Claude Houghton, published in 1930.
65   Military abbreviation: Anti aircraft post.

Monotony

In the evening light the houses form a silhouette against the sky,
Roof tops, chimneys, then a church or two and then some trees.
These are all that I can see beyond my prison walls. Below me soldiers try
To throw some metal rings on to a board, while officers in twos and threes
Walk round and round.

I am imprisoned here and yet my mind is seldom in these walls,
Usually it lives the lives of those I read about in books
And spends its evenings in a London club in which a trumpet drawls
And people dance and love and drink. But men with homelost looks
Walk round and round.

Often my mind walks out on to the cliffs not always quite alone
For with it goes a pretty face, a girl who holds my arm and smiles
And by her silence comforts me. I tell her then my hopes and from my tone
She knows how much they mean. But here the prisoners, talking, slouching, covering miles
Walk round and round.

Desmond Mulholland

Monday August 12th

I woke up in time to get a cup of tea but I purposely ate nothing as I still did not feel too well and had passed rather an uncomfortable night. I visited the library which had a number of volumes but everything I wanted to read was in use. The librarian was a bearded, affected poilu:[66] he was limpid and seemed to hang in mid air. He was a priest by profession and his appearance, if nothing else, was really most Christ-like. With much bowing and hand rubbing he addressed me in English and asked me what my opinion of his rather inferior accent was. He then placed P Bourget's "L'Ecuyère"[67] into my hand. It was an early 20th Century romantic tale which all ended well. I then visited the infirmary and the French MO[68] looked me over and gave me some Epsom salts and told me to return tomorrow. I ate no lunch and spent the afternoon asleep. About 4 o'clock I went into the bar which the French had been able to obtain and drank a jus de raisin: this is made from grape juice and is most refreshing. I visited the Canteen and bought some note books and a tin of Greengage jam and a small pot of honey. I made the acquaintance of Jean Valéry, which was indeed lucky for me as I was to spend many enjoyable and useful hours in his company. He must be about 40 years of age, has very refined tastes: rather feminine in manner and appearance and walks with that movement that gives the impression of putting his hands and feet forward at the same time.

66   This is an informal term for a French WW1 infantryman
67   "L'Equyère" (The Equerry), a novel by Paul Bourget, published in 1921.
68   Military abbreviation: Medical Officer.

He spoke quite good English having been with the BEF[69] and he suggested that we should exchange languages. I did not feel inclined to do so but soon changed my mind and my work with him has helped me unquestionably both in French and in constructive writing. I purchased a bottle of Vichy[70] and was given a tin of Gloria milk.[71] I made the acquaintance of a Caennais[72] who knew many of my friends and was later instrumental in conveying a letter to Zabette. His name was Fevrier. I went to bed pretty early and soon fell asleep. I thank God that I don't suffer from insomnia.

Tuesday August 13th

I felt much better and made short work of some bread. I visited the infirmary and took a few cigarettes and books to England. I had by now recovered so at 11.30 I went to lunch. The food was not bad and I was able to get some boiled rice when I wanted it. The mess sergeant was a very decent fellow and he always had the latest news and was always ready to help officers. I wish I had asked him for help earlier on. I read all the afternoon: it was very hot in the room. A great number of Medicos left as also did Capt Frémont so I was all alone. A pharmacien[73] from Lamballe[74] forced me to take 100fr: I have his name. He told me to go into the small room he had vacated: it was occupied by a Jewish doctor who had been retained and this had made him very depressed. He was a Rumanian born Jew and had studied with the aid of the money he earned leading an orchestra on transatlantic cruises. Since his retainment he had neither eaten nor gone to bed. I did not feel like keeping his company: just as well I did not go into that room for when no answer could be obtained from his room the next morning, his door was broken down and he was found dead in his bed: an overdose of laudanum.[75] If I had kept him company, it is possible that he would not have taken this terrible step. Still, though I am not frightened, the thought of a man dying next to me does not fill me with pleasure. Anyway, after supper I was invited to transport my effects to room 38, on the same floor but in a room in the gable end with three large windows. The occupants were all Engineers and mostly Captains. They made me quite at home and I spent many happy hours with them. Capt Sanglier, short, fat, cynical and good hearted. Capt "l'Admiral" Pirot? So called for his magnificent Bohemian beard and his love of the sea and his yacht. A perfectly charming Nantois,[76] Capt Vallée, quiet but as generous and good hearted as anyone I know. Lt Picot, who was soon released, just as well for he snored most terribly and Cmdt Barbottin who spent all his time with le Général, rather to our advantage. I told them my story and so started the happy souvenir of Chambre[77] 38 which I shall always keep. We talked for some time and I amused them a lot by my interpretation of French jokes. I was called Poupée[78] on my demand, though this later became Roger: that story will one day be told. Ask me about it!

69 Military abbreviation: British Expeditionary Force.
70 A brand of bottled water.
71 A brand of evaporated milk.
72 French: a person from Caen.
73 French: Pharmacist.
74 A commune in the Côtes d'Armor department of Brittany in north western France.
75 Laudanum is an opium preparation used as a pain killer.
76 French: A person from Nantes.
77 French: (bed) room.
78 French: doll, puppet.

Wednesday August 14th

From now on I can give you this day as a typical one of my life.

I used to get up about 8.15 and rush down to the mess where I drank a lot of tea and ate bread and jam: sometimes we had butter or milk and English army biscuits. A red haired servant friend of mine used to slip me a few packets. Then I would buy a paper and read about the air raids, for they had just begun. I would now play basket or volley ball and then do some dumb bell exercises. I had then raised a sweat so a good wash and a shave helped the morning along till 10.30 when I took my composition to Valéry and we would compose notes, then I would read and practise up my pronunciation which helped me very much: he kept me from using too much slang, a bad habit. I was so thankful that I spoke the language. 11.30 and lunch soon came, usually a tin of something and some meat and potatoes and fruit to follow if we were lucky. I then paid England a visit and we swapped yarns: he was recovering slowly from his shrapnel wounds. I read lying on my bed: among the books I read were Flaubert's "Salammbô",[79] a very difficult novel but most instructive, Pierre Benoît's "Monsieur de la Ferté"[80] and "L'Oublié"[81], two good novels. One or two Anatole France[82] and a few odd light novels: I'm afraid I wasted the afternoons. At 3 I would often play some basket but this was very hot and dirty. If I did not go to tea with de Brosses or Bonnefaut at his "Colombier Club", I had a beer with Valéry. Bonnefaut was an aviator who had flown in Finland and Norway and been made prisoner for some civil offence. He spoke English perfectly having been educated at Eastbourne College and Christ Church where he did no work but collected a double blue, rowing and rugby. He styled himself Le Marquis de Bonnefaut but many believed him to be an illegitimate son of a famous demimondaine.[83] He was full of good stories and when wearing his monocle he played the gentleman to perfection. He lived in a room which was divided into partitions by a great many volumes full of military records, and, in the space between the shelves, he and his roommates had installed themselves, as in cubicles. They were a very cheery crowd: La Rivière, who was a ranch proprietor in South America, spoke very perfect English and in his mondaine existence he had come across Hobson, St Sauveur and others. He was always scrupulously polite and would have looked at his best in a double breasted dinner coat leaning nonchalantly against the chimney piece, and gently flicking his cigarette ash into the fire and smiling charmingly at his very attractive lady friend. She would have to be attractive and must inevitably call him Darling, drawing the word out to make it more romantic. Then a young musician called Coudere who, with his friend Kampman, an American born Frenchman with a great love for Shakespeare and the violin, spent most of their time in the music room, where through their kind permission I was able to pass many happy hours struggling with a piece of Liszt.[84] A jovial Captain from Caen, a friend of and bearing a distinct resemblance to my old friend Monsieur Spriet. These bright spirits had formed themselves into the Colombier's Club where they served tea every afternoon and organised themselves a sitting room with Divans and vulgar drawings produced by one of their midst. I used to often visit them in the evenings when they were usually discussing food with the bright, Parisian little Vaguemestre[85], i.e. the post NCO. He, it was, who obtained my beret for me and he was always ready to give me tins of food, though I've no idea where he got them from. I wish I had taken these friends into my confidence instead of relying entirely on Barbu, Bernard, etc who seemed to think that they had a lifetime before them. Still, perhaps it is fate that leads us. I used to attend the first service of supper, usually a soup and then some meat and usually some fruit that came from the Canteen. I used to enjoy their Petit Rennais biscuits of which

---

79 "Salaambô", a historical novel by Gustave Flaubert, published in 1862.
80 "Monsieur de la Ferté", a novel by Pierre Benoît, published in 1934.
81 "L'Oublié" (The Forgotten Man), a novel by Pierre Benoît, published in 1922.
82 Anatole France (1844-1924), a French poet, journalist and novelist.
83 A woman living an extravagant and hedonistic lifestyle.
84 Franz Liszt (1811-1886), a Hungarian composer, pianist, conductor and teacher.
85 French: Post orderly

I ate a vast quantity. A short walk round the cloister and then I would adjourn to the room and play Belote[86] with Sanglier and Pinel till about 9 o'clock. It got dark about now so I prepared myself for bed, though before doing this I used to dash off my French composition for Valéry and the number of mistakes was in proportion to the speed at which I composed it. It was not often that I was asleep before eleven o'clock as we had lots to talk about though we might have saved our breath. At last peace and quiet fell on the room. Once it was broken. Sunday August 18th in the early morning, the sky of Rennes was ablaze with fire and it was a glorious sight though I was very thankful that not a plane was hit. The raid had apparently been directed against the airports, both of Rennes and Dinan! There was usually quite an amount of German air activity and encouraging rumours came in from the town. So my usual day was passed, uselessly as I look at it now, but it was difficult to realise that prison life would go on and on and not suddenly come to an end in the proximate future. One or two things do stand out however. One day I received 100 francs from a Monsieur Kate, an American who gave his address as La Croix Rouge,[87] Rennes, and with this gift was a request for me to ask for anything that I might desire. I was able to obtain some socks but we left the town before I could get anything effective. Whether I shall ever hear from him again remains to be seen. The news that Geneviève had left for the zone non occupée[88] was rather a shock to me, however I was very grateful to Monsieur C--- for sending my letters. Towards the end of my stay, August 24th, three English soldiers arrived. A Sgt Keppel of the Gloucesters, dark skinned and wearing a huge moustache, an old Corporal of the Lancs Fusiliers and young Driver Edgar, RASC.[89] These men had been captured well on in May and since then they had been employed in a German convoy and were having quite a pleasant time. They used to come up and chat with me in the evenings: it was pleasant to meet some English men as I had almost lost myself among the French. Those who stand out in my memory are Eric Schiller, a young cavalier,[90] very smart and dapper, [91] speaking perfect English: he was always a mine of information: the red haired mess waiter and the little Vaguemestre. So the days rolled by, the last Sunday being particularly noteworthy. We had a lecture and demonstration on Fencing by a very athletic Colonel: he was always in the forefront of the PT enthusiasts. To end his talk he gave a display of fencing: épée and sabre fighting with an adversary who had been a member of the French Olympic Games fencing team. It was a very fine spectacle and amusing or perhaps instructive in that the Colonel's adversary was released the following day on the grounds of an infirmity in both legs! He was one of many who were liberated: somebody knew his job!

Thursday August 29th

At about 9.30 the order was received that all officers were to leave the camp. The bombshell had come and yours truly was not prepared: he wished to help himself but was advised to wait: one man did not wait. Still fate again. Anyway at 11 o'clock, a sackful of belongings under my arm and two blankets round my neck, I was standing in the courtyard, waiting for the order to move off. It was not long before we were marched out of the gate where, on the Champ de Mars, a great many battered Parisian buses were waiting for us. Once inside we had to wait for some considerable time and were able to admire the galaxy of female talent that gazed upon us. I know myself and I am surprised that I was not more moved by the sight. I could not attribute this phenomenon to being blasé. I don't think that I have ever been so long without seeing a female form. Can it be that the less one sees, the less one wants: God forbid that I should stay here too long! Soon the convoy moved off, and we passed through the main Place de Rennes with its flowery gardens and huge municipal buildings. We soon came on to the Canal along

86	A French card game.
87	French: The Red Cross.
88	French: The free zone (i.e. not occupied by the Germans).
89	Military abbreviation: Royal Army Service Corps.
90	French: A Private in a cavalry regiment.
91	

which I had been marched: my destiny was no more certain now than it had been then. Along the canal the buses went until we crossed the dirty stream and pulled up outside a large barracks. There were a great many guards and we were all, 800 of us, rushed through the iron gates which were locked behind us. The sight that met our eyes was not a pleasant one, we who had grown soft in the comparative comfort of a cloistered monastery: right in front of our eyes was a vast patch of dusty, marching gravel with two forlorn netball stands trying to cheer up the complete misery of the yard. On the right there was the usual five storied French barrack building and on the left a more modern, but lower replica. Straight in front was a more sympathetic building, the clock house which might, with a great stretch of the imagination, be likened to a little château, lost in it some rather windswept and tattered trees. Barbed wire and sentries were everywhere. We were counted and pushed into buildings on the left. A great many large rooms, stone floored, or at least I think they were stone for dirt and the capacity number of wooden trestles that served as beds did not leave much of the floor visible. We from room 38 kept together and piled ourselves into a ground floor room. I felt so depressed that I could have wept, though I have learnt by now that this was comparative luxury. "No lunch" was the cry but after about 2 hours of panic, very prevalent among the French army, or what remained of them, some meat and bread was brought. "Oh we have no plates," I heard. That didn't stop me. "What's wrong with your fingers and a table," and, quick off the mark, I gorged myself on gristle and fat. Some of our friends had been getting busy and I was told to take my things over to the clock house. Here I found a little room on the first floor with just enough room to take 10 beds. I had by now obtained a palliasse, scrounging does not take long to learn, and I made up my bed, a very lopsided one I fear, and one which broke numerous times, between Vallée and Triplet, a young "train" officer who became a very good friend to me. We were all together with a few additions. Amath, i.e. a large, good natured Norman, two rather dreary Captains, Le Cirod and de Buisson (I think the de was the best part of this fellow: he always looked sad and when he did speak it was usually with his mouth full) and Soulignac, a short, active, almost square figure of a man, so often seen in professional centre forwards. The first thing we did was to prepare some disinfectant and sweep up the floor. The place was alive with mosquitoes that seemed to have formed a university in the palliasses. Old Le Gros swamped his whole bed with flea powder: it was apparently his fetish and it was lucky he had this streak for it was his only claim to originality. This "déménagement"[92] took us quickly through the afternoon and at about 7 o'clock some soup was brought up. We sat in our room and it was here that we took all our meals: it was very crowded but at least it was in peace. Some tables had been brought up as had plates and spoons and the poor Colonel of Intendance[93] was flashing his gold teeth and squeaking his head off to try and organise some form of system into things which is very difficult when you have about 800 men shouting at once and never waiting to receive an answer: instead of a Colonel, he was treated rather like a Hyde Park speaker addressing a working class audience on the advantages of having a rich and landed gentry. Most meals went to those who were quickest off the mark. We had a nominative Appell and then we were all counted. Renaud had some fun whereas de Moidrey had some bad luck. The courtyard, though I never saw anything resembling a court, had to be vacated by 9 o'clock. We had to cross to the other building to get a wash and when I saw the serried rows of beds I felt grateful to the initiative of some of my friends. I fear that I am a person who sits down and says "Oh well, it might be worse and I must make the best of it." I see that if bodily[94] counts for anything in one's social make up the motto must be "It might be better and I won't make the worst of it." To Him who knocks shall it be answered and all inside must be treated as deaf. After such an eventful day it was not long before my hard, lopsided palliasse rocked me to sleep. Take no heed of the morrow: how true for a prisoner.

---

92   French: moving (house).

93   French: The Commissariat Colonel (charged with supplying provisions and stores).

94   I think there must be a word missing here as the sentence does not make sense.

Friday August 30th

When I woke up about 7.30 I found a cup of tea by my bed: what service! Le Gros, who always got up and washed at crack of dawn – he needed to do this because he spent such a long time rubbing himself with eau de Cologne that had he risen at a normal hour, his toilet would not be finished before his bedtime – had been over to the men's side of the camp and had got a dixie[95] full of tea. This was the regular breakfast and he, fortunately, was the tea fetcher though we others always intended to do it but of course never did: it is so easy to intend to do these things and one can feel genuinely sorry that one has not done one's duty as long as someone else has done it. Appell was at 8 and I found it quite chilly on the square which later in the day became a furnace. I spent the morning with Valéry and we did some work, watching the "boules" players: they played with iron bowls and hurled them along a dirt covered alley. Here we were always under the eagle eye of a sentry and even to look out of top windows was an offence. Everyone wanted to know our fate, it was to be liberated, we heard from one side and I was preparing to disguise myself en soldat français[96] and so be released with them: this was the vainest of my hopes. The other party held the view that we should be taken to Germany and I must say that I could not help taking this pessimistic view. The food question, after much argument, had been settled and some soup turned up at lunchtime: we were also able to buy some rather inferior cider and the canteen officers were attempting to reorganise themselves. The weather was of brilliant sunshine so with a book, a bad one called "Le Poste sur la Dune",[97] I went and sat out in the sun. The locality chosen for this sunbathing later became known as Le Lido and it was situated between the large barracks and the vast exterior wall. Here, every afternoon semi nude officers reclining in Riviera like postures were to be seen and in the short time of our stay our backs went through all those sunburn tints, white, pale pink, agonising red and then various hues of brown. In this way the first afternoon soon passed and at about 6.30 some meat and potatoes came. A walk round and round the yard and then Appell at 8 o'clock A game of Piquet or Belote[98] and the day was over. The news service was still being carriered and the figures were practically identical except with the great difference that the sides were reversed. Triplet and I talked long into the night until the snores of our roommates drowned our whispers.

Saturday August 31st

This day was as its preceding one and I spent the morning wandering about collecting les derniers bobards[99] and talking to V. Conversations with him were always entertaining and we travelled into the lands of literature and art. It was today that he spoke of teaching me Italian: he speaks like a native having relations in Italy and always having an Italian servant. We read some of Stendhal's "Tour d'Italie"[100] together and V painted such pictures of this land of sun and indolence that I became and still am burned with an enthusiasm to visit it when this unhappy war is over. I was able to procure "Bel Ami", by Guy de Maupassant[101] from a library that had been opened: it is the life of a journalist and this, with all V's descriptions of this great profession, made me long to enter the brotherhood: I miss Grandpa now, even though I cannot communicate with him. I played a game of basket ball in the afternoon: it was

---

95   A large metal pot used for cooking and making tea.
96   French: as a French soldier.
97   "La Poste sur la Dune" (The Post (mil) in the Dunes), a novel by Marie le Franc published in 1928.
98   Popular French card games.
99   French: the latest rumours.
100   Stendhal was the pen name of writer Marie-Henri Beyle (1783-1842). He wrote extensively about Italy although I have not been able to identify a work entitled "Tour of Italy".
101   "Bel Ami" (published in English in 1903 as "Bel Ami or, the History of a Scoundrel: A Novel"), Guy de Maupassant's second novel published in 1885.

hot and dirty and a shower was most welcome to wash off the coats of dust. The showers here were really excellent: luckily something was. I was surprised and pleased to get a letter from Zabette. Caen was as it had been and though sorry to hear of my misfortune, she was glad to be able to write to me and she told me that she had posted a parcel containing a pullover, a pipe and some tobacco for me: it has never reached me. It was a comfort to hear that I was not completely cut off from the outside world. The day soon passed as did the Sunday, most of which was spent in waiting for the Pasteur who never came, and the Monday, when I played volley ball and sunbathed. The Canteen was working again and we were able to help out the poor rations with tinned stuffs. One day we had hard boiled eggs in tomato sauce: I wonder how long before I eat another.

Tuesday September 3rd

This augured to be as monotonous as any of the others until after supper when my attention was called to a large body of prisoners coming towards us along the canal bank. We were informed that they were 400 officers from St Lô.[102] We had no idea where they would sleep. We all stood by to watch them in. Imagine my astonishment when I saw Douglas McLeod, in civilian clothes with a number of others in civvies all of whom I took to be Channel Islanders. One tall young officer in battle dress and a beret, was the only uniformed Englishman. I think Mac must have been surprised to see me. I must have looked very odd for I was wearing a beret, some light blue sailor trousers and a French Canvas jacket. Their first question was as to the whereabouts of M. Then, a fat, red faced, cheery, Pickwickian[103] figure gabbled something into my ear about two G[104] ladies being in St Lô at the Hotel de la Gare[105]. This made me feel miserable and has caused me and still does cause me many sleepless hours. You can guess the terrible thoughts that came to my mind. My informant was Capt Connors, later to be known as "Hash". He was

---

102	A commune in north western France and capital of the Manche department in Normandy.
103	A reference to "Pickwick Papers" by Charles Dickens.
104	Here Desmond is referring to Guernsey rather than German(y) which he usually references with a G. He is obviously worried that the 2 ladies are his mother and Martel's half sister.
105	French: The Station Hotel.

BEKANNTMACHUNG

DIE beiden im Juli ds. Jrs. auf der Insel Guernsey zu Erkundungszwecken an Land gesetzten englischen Offiziere haben sich zeitweise bei ihren Angehoerigen aufgehalten, ohne dass die deutsche Militaerbehoerde hievon Kenntnis erhalten hat. Diese Angehoerigen sind:

Frau Adale Masurier, Geb. Martel,
'Westcroft,' Queen's Rd., St. Peter Port.

Frau Dorothy Madeleine Michael, GEB. MOORHOUSE.
"Le Paradou," Forest.

Um eine Unterstuetzung von weiteren englischen Ausspaehversuchen auf den besetzten britischen Kanalinseln von seiten der Zivilbevoelkerung zu unterbinden, wurde vom zustaendigen Armee Ober-Kommando angeordnet, dass die beiden Frauen nach einem auf dem Festland gelegenen Platz, der mindestens 15 km von der Kueste entfernt ist, gebracht werden und sich dort taeglich bei der Feldkommandantur zu melden haben.

FELDKOMMANDANTUR 515.

Der Feldkommandant:
gez. SCHUMACHER,

NOTICE

BOTH British Officers who, in July last, had been put ashore on the Island of Guernsey for the purpose of reconnoitring, stayed for a time with their relatives, without the German Military Authorities having been notified.

These relatives are:

Mrs. Adale Masurier, née Martel,
'Westcroft,' Queen's Rd., St. Peter Port.

Mrs. Dorothy Madeleine Michael, NÉE MOORHOUSE.
"Le Paradou," Forest.

In order to stop any support by the civilian population of further English reconnaissance attempts on the occupied British Channel Islands, orders were issued by the competent Army Chief-Command that both women must be transferred to a place situated on the mainland at least 15 km away from the coast, and that there they must report daily at the Feldkommandantur.

FELDKOMMANDANTUR 515.

Der Feldkommandant:
(signed) SCHUMACHER,

Announcement of the arrest of Desmond's mother and Philip Martel's half sister by the German authorities.

wearing a battered grey pork pie, a linen coat and a bow tie and his hands were full of boots and pots and pans: he looked and talked like one complete model. There were three officers from Jersey, one of them an RAF officer who had had an interesting but hard luck experience. The fellow in uniform was Colin Watson, Gordon Highlanders, who had been ambushed near Cherbourg: in this action Spence, Helen Arnould's newly wedded husband, had been killed: poor Helen. I later came to appreciate this quiet unenthusiastic Scot and it was great good fortune for me to fall in with him. With the party was a very distinguished looking gentleman, tall, upright and soldierly. He was Col Gibbs, who, though on the retired list, had been interned under the German alien decrees: his wife is a French lady and he has his house in Normandy. He was sent to a military camp on account of his long military connections, having served for many years in the army veterinary corps. I remember my friend Michel Meyer speaking of an English man living near St Lô and M knew his daughter: it was rather strange that I never came across them during my stay at Caen. The first work was to get bedding for these new arrivals and there was a great deal of pushing and fighting and general unpleasantness. The French seem to have lost even the semblance of discipline: at last the English party found a quiet corner in a corridor and with palliasses and blankets they were able to make themselves reasonably comfortable: not a complaint from any of them whereas people were cursing and complaining around them. The camp was all confusion: another chance lost. It was well after ten when I climbed into bed: shall I ever be able to go anywhere without meeting old acquaintances? I am so glad that we were joined together. I had been getting very depressed of late and attributing my present position entirely to my own lack of tenacity and to my overestimating the dangers of remaining, I foresaw Cms[106] and general disgrace, "letting the regiment down": young man flees to the colonies driven there by a wave of embittered public opinion. No one to talk to who could appreciate and understand my difficult position. Now all this was changed. We threshed the problem out and at last I had real sympathisers: you cannot realise what a moral pleasure this was for me. From now on my fear was for what Connors had told me and as I write this (18.12.40), I am no nearer the solution.

Wednesday September 4th

Appell was a lengthy proceeding and much counting was necessary. The Commandant was now a "Marin à cinq galons"[107] who, with many other sailors, had come from St Lô. They had been on AA[108] and coast defence work and so had fallen into the hands of the enemy. I had more to do with some of these gentlemen at a later period. My day was now much brighter for Connors had brought a store of milk and tea and other foodstuffs with him when he left Guernsey: the prisoners left the island on Thursday August 1st. Our appearance may have had a connection with the departure but I do not think that it was entirely on our account because the Jersey prisoners had been in Cherbourg for some ten days. Connors, a grocer by trade and thereby a gastronomic expert, as his size and conversation confirmed, was always ready to boil up some water in a borrowed electric kettle, and make us a cup of "steaming" "Lipton"[109] or just plain tea which was always acceptable. I spent most of my time with them and soon made the acquaintance and, I hope, the friendship of Col Gibbs and his little party. Weysom, RMA[110] was the other Sarnian[111] and turned out to be a very sound chap. At home he is the proprietor of Bella Luce[112] and an ale house under the market and I soon placed him as one of Herbert Stephenson's[113] opponents for election to the States. When not playing bridge, he was to be seen perusing, with enormous concentration, a page of an out of date stamp catalogue. I thought that he must be a very great collector and I don't think I'm wrong in my assumption but, from his general conversation, he appeared to be interested only in the sea and the next cup of tea! I later came to appreciate this latter trait as you, who are used to your third and fourth cup will do, when you are cut off completely from "God's own drink". Weysom had a great scheme for a trawler fleet operating from Guernsey after the war. I wonder if we shall see his sensible idea put into action. Plenty of conversation on old times with Mac, if he could be drawn from bridge or detective novels, and so many pleasant hours were spent. Everyone wanted to know the reason for this collecting of prisoners especially when all the "Congé professionelle"[114] prisoners returned. We were allowed no contact with the men and in all ways life was much more severe. The weather was as brilliant as ever and the overcrowded rooms were most uncomfortable: everything pointed to a short stay, the end of which would be the beginning of the long trek. The liberation optimists were not so prominent. Still food was fairly plentiful and the Canteen was working again.

---

106   Courts martial.
107   French: a sailor with five stripes.
108   Military abbreviation: Anti aircraft.
109   A brand of tea.
110   Military abbreviation: Royal Marines Artillery.
111   A person from Guernsey.
112   A hotel on Guernsey.
113   Herbert Stephenson was a Guernsey resident standing for election to the Island Parliament (The States).
114   French: Professional discharge prisoners.

Thursday September 5th

This morning Mac created a great impression by appearing in a kilt (a Cameron soldier gave it to him) and I had given him my battle dress. The rest of the contingent had been given French uniforms. I stupidly missed an opportunity of getting a pair of boots. I contacted a St Lô interpreter who promised to make enquiries as to the identity of the ladies. Whatever efforts he made were unfortunately unavailing and I am still desirous of the information. I played a strenuous game of basket ball, took a shower and the morning slipped by. The afternoon on the Lido! A cup of tea and supper was upon us and soon this uneventful day drew to a close. Appell was very lengthy for we had to march round the yard in single file to be counted. Multiples of five are rather hard!

Friday September 6th

Just such another day: grilling hot, the heat not even affected by the strong wind of the camp rumours. After an afternoon in the sun I was invited to join in a game of deck quoits with a very expert and sunburnt sailor, a Capt de Gaguerand, a painter by profession, cultured, intelligent and speaking perfect English. Colin Watson and I made up the four. We had just begun the game when we saw several German officers arrive and shortly after the order for an assemblé général[115] was ordered. (The lido was situated behind the barracks. Several of us used to congregate every afternoon and, with a stretch of the imagination, one could be on Petit Port[116]: the occasional flushing of the WC gave a surf like impression and a whiff of chlorine completed the effect). We stood about for an hour and at last the camp CO told us that we must collect our things and be ready to move off the next day. We were all annoyed at being kept standing about in the hot sun and we English hated having to wait for our tea. Supper soon came and with it a great treat: salmon, cheese, grapes and jam, all that was left over and my last real meal. All conversation turned on our destination: some said Neuilly[117] "pour le tirage",[118] others Germany, and this was the belief of the lorry driver who brought up the rations. Personally I did not worry for many reasons! After supper I walked with Col Gibbs, the precursor of many walks: the heat was grilling. We got no news so nothing remained but to go to bed.

---

115 French: a General Meeting.
116 A rocky and exposed cove on Guernsey.
117 Neuilly Sur Seine, a commune in the western suburbs of Paris.
118 French: pulling/hauling of carts, barges, etc or quarrying for stone. There were quarries around Neuilly at this time.

Saturday September 7th

I was up at 6 and managed to get a good wash before tea came. After some parading we moved off at 8.15. Our procession wound its way through the depressed city: women, their eyes filled with tears and sadness, watched the departure of their loved ones. Many Anti English posters adorned the house walls but I don't think that they were taken very seriously: I thought of the Union Jacks in July 1938. Our miserable tour soon ended and at the station we found a third class German train waiting to receive us. Strange to say, a German officer picked me out as English even though I was dressed as a Frenchman and was amongst the French. After about an hour the order to embark was given and we climbed into our respective coaches, 40 to a coach. Rations were issued: a loaf of bread, two tins of cheap English salmon and two tins of French bully bully, commonly known as "singe".[119] We set off at midday and our speed was about 15mph. At every frequent halt the guards leapt out and lined the route: two always travelled on the running boards of each coach. We followed the Paris route till we got to Sillé Le Guillaume[120] then we took the Rouen[121] direction. We reached Alençon[122] at 9 pm where some nurses gave us water and lovely fresh bread. The soldiers, when not watched by an NCO, were very kind in fetching us water and shut their eyes to the buying of wine. They all looked very tired of their present existence and one or two incidents lead me to think that their appearance did not belie their feelings. When it became dark we had to shut the windows and the heat was stifling. I put a rug on the floor and, with my sack for a pillow, I soon fell asleep. The carriage seats were wood and not very easy on one's person: the floor was hard but at least I could stretch out. During the night we turned off at Rouen and took the Amiens[123] route.

Sunday September 8th

I was up at 7 after a tolerable night and found it to be a heavenly morning with our train pulling through thick woods from which the morning mists were slowly rising. We ate some bread and then I settled into a book (Axelle by P Benoît).[124] At Forges les Eaux[125] we once again took the Paris route: where were we going? At Gisors[126] the station was full of good friends who gave us bread, water and wine: it seemed as if the whole town was there. The country was flat but everywhere I got the impression of travelling through a deserted land full of discontented people. We had to lunch off singe, more stringy and liquid than our bully beef: soon after this bite we were through Pontoise[127] where some damage had been done and a bridge or two were down. From now on the countryside was very ugly: little houses, dirty and cramped, overpowered by an occasional, deserted factory. At Creil[128] I was very lucky. A very pretty brunette dressed in white got into a train next to ours and she had soon sent us, via a guard, her L'Illustration[129] and a tin of sweets. I was soon told that she was an American so I called to her in English. She was surprised and pleased to be thus addressed and she soon told me that she was a journalist working in the Paris office of Time and Life and a one time writer on The Daily Mirror. I got her address and promised to write to

119 French: monkey.
120 A commune in the Sarthe department in north western France.
121 Capital of Upper Normandy in northern France.
122 A commune in Normandy, capital of the Orne department.
123 A city and commune in northern France.
124 "Axelle" a novel by Pierre Benoît, published in 1928.
125 A commune in the Seine-Maritime department of Upper Normandy.
126 A commune in the metropolitan area of Paris.
127 A commune in the north western suburbs of Paris.
128 A commune in the Oise department of northern France.
129 A French weekly newspaper published in Paris from 1843 to 1944.

her: the lady reporter was the only name I knew. She said her US correspondence was cut off and just before we moved I found out she was engaged: smart work, Mullholland, and as our conversation ended she terminated our short acquaintance by blowing me a kiss! I immediately wrote to her hoping that if she received it she might be able to communicate via USA with England. Perhaps it was quick work but a POW hasn't got all day. We turned on to the Compiègne[130] route and at Pont-Ste-Maxence[131] I gave my letter to a charming little Red Cross girl and I hope it reached its destination of 52, Avenue des Champs Elysées. We reached Compiègne at 5.30 and turned off for Laon.[132] Apples were thrown to us as we passed through villages, which seemed more dead than alive. At 10 we reached Laon and spent the whole night in a siding. Once again onto the floor where, strange to say, I dreamt of Jean Watson. My impressions for the day had been: a green, civilised desert: no life, no hope, no spirit.

Monday September 9th

I arose, longing for a wash, about 7 o'clock. It was pouring with rain and was decidedly colder and the sight of our siding was very dreary. Some bread and chocolate was our apology for eggs and bacon and at 7.15 we left Laon for St Quentin.[133] At Tergnier[134] we got some bread and from here it was pretty certain that Germany was our destination. We passed through St Quentin and Le Cateau[135] and I thought of the 1914 BEF,[136] suffering and fighting.[137] At one station we saw a sight that tore our hearts. A train of French troops, 35 to a cattle truck: they were allowed down to do their toilet and my thoughts turned to galley slaves, as they hung over the edge of the trucks in search of air. We sent over some bread and when they pulled out they raised a cheer. France may be "pourri"[138] but the spirit is there as it always will be. At 12.45 we stopped at a place called Aulnoye:[139] here the platform was covered with German officials: the men and women hardly dared speak to us and I could feel that the occupier was driving his foot into the soil and driving French freedom with it: like seed it will lose itself for a time and then spring up a thousand fold. It was very ugly here and the light rain made it no more cheerful. At 12 o'clock I entered Belgium for the first time in my life. We stopped at Quévy[140] and were allowed out. There was a lot of handshaking and a stampede for a tap to get a vague wash. Rumour has it that three lads have slipped. Our officer, a last war prisoner is quite pleasant: fairly considerate and turning a blind eye to the showers of letters that fell from the train as we pulled out of almost any station. We stopped at Mons[141] where there was quite a deal of destruction. The scenery was ugly: huge black slag heaps and rows of dirty little tenements. The huge factories had not been damaged: intentionally, I suppose. Soon the country became open and appeared very fertile, many large herds against a background of woods. Here and there small shell holes brought us back to reality and often we passed tank blocks and defensive positions. There were not many villages that had come through unscathed.

130 A commune in the Oise department of northern France.
131 A commune in the Oise department of northern France.
132 The capital city in the Aisne department of Picardy in northern France.
133 A commune in the Aisne department of Picardy in northern France.
134 A commune in the Aisne department of Picardy in northern France.
135 Le Cateau-Cambrésis is a commune in the Nord department of Northern France.
136 Abbreviation: British Expeditionary Force.
137 Probably a reference to the battle of Cateau on 26 August 1914 in which 7,812 allied soldiers were killed, wounded or taken prisoner.
138 French: rotten.
139 Aulnoye-Aymeries is a commune in the Nord department of northern France.
140 A Walloon municipality in the Belgian province of Hainaut.
141 A Walloon city and municipality in the Belgian province of Hainaut.

The people were very subdued but I did not get that desert impression that I had received in France. Louvain[142] was slightly damaged and then a station absolutely ruined. From here the country became flatter and I saw the first great windmill. The rain had cleared and the sky gave us a lovely red sunset, amidst angry clouds. Not much further I hope: this type of travelling is not much fun though I could never complain when I think of the poor men.

Tuesday September 10th

I did not sleep very well owing to the cold and when I got up I found that we were at a station in Holland, Roermond.[143] At 8.15 we crossed into Germany having passed through a flat, swampy moorland of heather and pines, bathed in thick mist. We stopped for two hours at Dalheim[144] where the station was full of troops and equipment trains. After Dalheim the scenery was wooded and very fertile. The first large town was Rreyndt[145] where the factories were hard at work: very few young men were to be seen but children swarmed everywhere: the cheers were no longer for us now. I may be mistaken but the older folk were not enthusiastic. The towns are very clean and bear a strong resemblance to our towns except for the almost total lack of street life. At 11.30 we crossed the Rhine and were soon at Düsseldorf:[146] there were a few bomb marks. We waited here for some time and after a short journey were in the industrial Westphalia. Here were hills covered with pines and right in the midst of this severe beauty were smoking chimneys and huge factories at full pressure. One of these towns, Wuppertal[147], stands on a shallow gushing torrent which winds its way through the town. Communication in the town is by way of an elevated, suspended tramway. At Haspe[148] were steel works and a petrol refinery. We stopped at a large station called Hagen and I was amazed to see no form of sarcasm or even of enthusiasm: everyone was supremely indifferent. When we left Westphalia we came on to flat well cultivated land. We often passed groups of prisoners who in one place were working on an autostrade,[149] a most impressive piece of work. At Soest[150] we stopped for two hours and were able to get a real wash: I even shaved, leaving myself a chin beard! At 7 we started again through rather uninteresting scenery, very similar to parts of England with its well cultivated fields and its compact little houses, just like the suburbs of any English town. As dusk fell, much earlier as we moved eastwards, we began to pass through the imposing Hartz mountains, their slopes thickly covered with pine trees: the forestation here is very well cared for. My general impressions of the day: I saw much that surprised me: the country looked very well cared for and every inch was used. I will one day be able to say more?

---

142   Capital of the province of Flemish Brabant.
143   A city, municipality and diocese in the south eastern part of the Netherlands.
144   Dalheim is actually a commune and town in Luxembourg.
145   I have not been able to identify this town. It may be incorrectly transcribed.
146   Capital city of the German State of North Rhine-Westphalia.
147   A city in North Rhine-Westphalia.
148   Hagen-Haspe is a borough in the city of Hagen in North Rhine-Westphalia.
149   Italian: highway. I think Desmond is confusing Italian and German (autobahn).
150   A town in North Rhine-Westphalia.

Wednesday September 11th

I woke up about 6.30: it was raining hard and we were passing through flat cultivated country: we came on to towns, Nordhausen, Berga[151] and stopped at Sangerhausen[152] where we chatted with a Poilu[153] who was being taken to Hospital. From now the scenery became rougher though still well cultivated and enormous tracts of potatoes. I remember seeing a little cart drawn by a huge brown dog. The thing that struck me was the fact that though the country was so well cared for, it was very rare to see anyone working in the fields. We were now in Saxony and often went through large towns, Eisleben,[154] Angersdorf,[155] Halle,[156] Drieskan[157] where there was a pylon depot: the electric system seems to be well gridded. We passed a few damaged Ms[158] which cheered me up. Rain was still streaming down and it was bitterly cold. At Speisenhaus, a suburb of Leipzig[159], was a large aero factory with rows of chassis waiting to be assembled. At 12.30 we went through Riesa[160] and then crossed the Elbe.[161] We had now been in the train for four days and our rations were giving out and we had no bread at all. There was always a mythical hot meal in store which, like so many things, always remained mythical. The railway system is very vast and seems in good condition: they are even laying new iron sleepers! What did I hear before? It would appear that our journey was not prepared for we were always stopping in the most out of the way places and the officer went off and telephoned for instructions. The allotment gardens are very well looked after and I have seen no slums: perhaps our long journey is for propaganda purposes. Several passenger trains have passed but they are mostly empty: but the population must be fairly large for new houses are going up everywhere. Cars are not plentiful but the railway has many cistern trucks. At 3.45 we came to a suburb of Dresden[162] where we were given some brown, square loaves and a hot drink called tea: it was red and tasted like nothing on earth. We were served by young men in splendid grey uniforms: ARD[163] I think. Everyone here wears a uniform: the railwaymen in blue with a variety of coloured caps: customs men in green, the police in navy blue with superb top boots. There was no one in the stations and pretty girls were not to be seen! Are there any? The town of Dresden is very large, though the streets are empty. One voice was heard to say, "Bon Courage"[164]: was it a voice crying in the Wilderness or the beginning of a gale? As dusk came on us we were passing through thick woods of spruce and Scotch pine: the country was becoming very mountainous and beautiful: the sight of three baby stags playing in a clearing did not detract from the beauty, I can assure you.

151   Both Nordhausen and Berga are in the German State of Thuringia.
152   A town in Saxony-Anhalt.
153   French: a French soldier (slang).
154   A town in Saxony-Anhalt, Germany
155   A village and former municipality in the Saalekreis district, Saxony-Anhalt.
156   Halle (Saale), a city in the southern part of Saxony Anhalt.
157   I have not been able to identify this town. It may be incorrectly transcribed.
158   Presumably Messerschmitts (fighter aircraft)?
159   City in the State of Saxony.
160   A town in the district of Meissen in Saxony.
161   River Elbe.
162   Capital city of Saxony.
163   Military abbreviation: Aircraft Repair or Receiving Depot.
164   French: Bear up/be brave.

Thursday September 12th

When I woke up we were at Nossen:[165] the rain was coming down as hard as ever but our guards leapt out just as numerously. The country was flat again and seemed prosperous. We passed through Mannsdorf[166], a little village with spruce white houses and a lot of derisive cheering from its young inhabitants. We were still in Silesia. At Mannsdorf we were kept waiting for about an hour, when we were ordered to get out. I joined the English party and we were soon en route, passing through a type of heath land, heather and scrubby trees. This was a training area for we passed barracks and squads undergoing training: they did not look A1 troops. After about 5kms we entered a huge camp surrounded by double lines of barbed wire and bristling with machine guns. We passed through the men's camp, full of English and Poles and went into a separated compound: there we were lined up and counted three or four times and an apology was extended: we were not expected and would not stay long!! We went, 26 at a time into barrack rooms, the floor piled high with wood wool. Our dinner was a sort of mongol soup[167] and bad, unpeeled potatoes. Then came the usual tumult. Everyone outside with kit to go to the showers: then inside again; this was repeated several times and at last we were left in peace. Connors now came to the fore and in a miraculous way was able to produce a pot of tea: manna from heaven. We had a chat with some of the troops, most RAMC[168] who were running the infirmary. The complement of the camp was 1000 but a great many were out on working parties. Our supper was a pig swill of bad potatoes and bread. As evening drew on, it became very chilly and I had a sharp walk, finishing the evening with a chat with a RAMC.[169] RSM:[170] his life was not too bad as he did well by running the infirmary. The majority of the lads were from the 51st[171] and were taken at St Valery.[172] They had had to march here, about 400 miles and it was not all fun and we heard one or two hair raising tales! It was dark at 8 o'clock so I threw myself down on the floor and it was but a few minutes before I fell asleep lulled by Connors' succulent snores.

Friday September 13th

The German NCO got us up about 6 though I had been awake for an hour. An urn full of coffee was outside: the coffee was Ersatz[173] (grilled barley, I believe) but it was pleasantly sweet. After a wait of two hours, we were marched off to the showers. Once inside, our clothes were taken from us and numbers attached to them: the same number was given to us to hang round our necks and we moved into a steam room: my hair was capably cut and I did not risk being clipped all over. From thence we went into a lovely hot douche. A little Scotchman serving with the Foreign Legion, who acted as interpreter to the French, asked me if I wanted a shave. When I told him that I was growing a beard he gave me such a look that, in my shame, I hastened to the barber and was once again made respectable: my strong Bohemian faith did not hold for long! Our clothes, smelling strongly of gas, were returned to us and we were all moved off to another part of the camp: before we left the showers, the soldiers forced some cigarettes onto us: they were a happy crowd and their only complaint was the absence of almost all food. We were kept waiting for another hour and then our luggage was gone through for maps etc. Waiting for a train will be a

---

165 A town in the district of Meissen in Saxony.
166 A town in Saxony-Anhalt.
167 A split pea and tomato soup.
168 Military abbreviation: Royal Army Medical Corps.
169 Military abbreviation: Royal Army Medical Corps.
170 Military abbreviation: Regimental Sergeant Major.
171 The 51st is a reference to a Territorial Highland Division.
172 St-Valery-Sur-Somme, a commune in the Somme department in northern France.
173 i.e. substitute coffee

pleasure to me! Tommies[174] then came and carried our luggage into a hut where lunch soon came up, bad potatoes and salt fish soup, a little goes a long way. These poor boys live like this all the time and they had never heard a word from home. In the afternoon I learnt to play Auction bridge: I soon picked it up and the afternoon soon passed. Supper was of bread, sausage (Wurst), and some English margarine (loot, I suppose). We went out about 6 and, to our joy, the English lads were singing: it was lovely to hear and we were all intensely moved when they sang La Marseillaise followed by "The King". I could feel the thrill in the air and I had nothing to say but words of admiration for their courage and cheerfulness in the face of such adversity. Their discipline was excellent and their bearing soldierly: comparing this to the French prisoners, I felt a thrill of pride. A great deal can be done with a nation that can stand adversity in this way. An example of doggedness was of a little miner who, on an escape, had got within 35kms of the Russian border before he had been apprehended: "I'll try again in the Spring": though he knew what it would mean to fail again. Appell was the usual muddle and we were quite glad to be ordered off to collect rations. The German officer told us that we were leaving for a fine château and our journey would be short: "Bon voyage"[175] he said!! It was dark by now and, weary but elated by what I had seen, I climbed into my top bunk. The last happy words I heard "Ils ont du culot, vos gars!"[176]

Saturday September 14th

I woke up about 3 o'clock and found everyone putting their luggage outside. After some hanging about I went back to bed until five when some hot drink arrived. At 6 we were en route having bade farewell to the English lads and I felt a pang when I thought of the awful winter they would have to go through. We were halted for an hour just before the station and it was cold, wet and miserable. At 9.30 we boarded our luxurious train carriages for the colonels and cattle trucks, 38 to each, for us. We had some bread and tinned blood "wurst"[177] and settled down to play bridge. As there was only one small window, I saw very little of the scenery. Most of the time we seemed to be going backwards, but I suppose we progressed a little. The train rattled down steep valleys, bordered with pines and little white chalets standing out against the surrounding green: little rushing streams broke up the dense hillsides. At 7 we got to a little village where we were able to get some water and stretch our legs: a village nestling in the hills skirted by a crystal clear brook. Once we were on the move we tried to settle down for the night but sleep was out of the question: fortunately we had some fine singers amongst us and it was thrilling to hear their voices ringing through the crowded truck to the accompaniment of the rattling rails. Toto Manon, a tiny, Parisian "aspirant"[178] then livened the proceedings by imitations of "Maurice"[179] and the telling of many rude and funny stories. The grumbling of some of our neighbours was shocking: they imagined that they alone were uncomfortable. France has reached a state of indiscipline and egoism that brokers no good for the future. My philosophy is "Well, it might be worse" and that possibility is always there.

---

174   Military slang: British troops.
175   French: Have a good journey.
176   French: They've got some nerve/balls, your lads.
177   German: sausage.
178   French: an Officer Designate in the French Army
179   Maurice Chevalier, a French actor, singer and entertainer (1888-1972).

Sunday September 15th

We staggered out about 6 o'clock after one of my most uncomfortable nights. Neustadt[180] was the name of the town which we had soon left behind on our march across a flat, uninteresting pasture land. The villages were very neat with little tidy white houses and the little children, in Tyrolean suits and long white socks stared at us with curious eyes. After 2 hours (8kms) we came to Langendorf,[181] a large village full of soldiers and brown shirts, even the little girls wore swastika armlets. We turned off the main road and a large white house well skirted with barbed wire met our eyes: once inside we were lined up and issued with some hot coffee. A German officer then read out the camp orders and we were, after the usual turmoil, formed into 7 companies: Colin, Mac and I in the 2ième,[182] the others in the 7ième.[183] We had to stand about for 2 hours and then we went inside to a bowl of cabbage soup: the cooking arrangements looked clean and hygienic, large aluminium inn boilers filled with soup. Our bedroom was No 6 on the ground floor: 30 occupants in double decker bunks with wood wool mattresses. I got a bottom bunk right away from the window and getting to it meant squeezing sideways through two rows of beds. Cupboards were in the corridor and we three got one between us. We did not unpack our sacks because we were waiting for the "fouille"[184] searching. Bridge was our only consolation and this we played till 5 when we drew our bread ration, one loaf for 5 days, some butter which was very good, and some coffee. More bridge and then bed at 8 as lights out soon after 9. Washing accommodation was very poor: each man had a basin and there were about 3 taps on each floor: we were much too numerous for this place and I got the impression of a foyer of a theatre during the interval when everyone dives for a drink and talks of the play as fast and as loudly as they can.

Monday September 16th

I slept very well and was up about 7, got a wash and ate some bread and butter: the bread was scrupulously divided. Appell was at 9 o'clock and then we each received a card which I sent home. After roll call we examined the famous park: it was a quarter the size of Les Préaux[185] and was surrounded by double apron and dannert[186] barbed wire with a machine gun post at each corner. It made me feel more a prisoner than ever: it was too tantalising. The country within my reach but impossible to attain whereas the other camps were just camps, pure and simple, and the other world was almost forgotten. Lunch, the precursor of all our lunches here, was of soup. We queued up outside the kitchen, were each handed a bowl and a spoon, filed past the boilers where our bowls were filled up, passed through into another room where we fought for a stand by the table, drank our soup, put down our bowls and walked out: the ideal soup kitchen. We managed to get to a table and play some bridge though we had just enough room to sit on the little wooden stools which were in insufficient quantity for our large numbers. Hash managed to bribe some hot water and we had a tea session. The others have a pleasant room on the top floor with a view on the park and seem comparatively comfortable. Soup and butter at 7 and then bed. A day passed: a useless day. I feel that my life is not my own and the desire to be alone has never been so strong. I can never take a walk without someone

---

180 I think Desmond may be confused here. There is a Neustadt in Germany but it is not in the area close to Mannsdorf. There is, however, a Neudorf very close to Mannsdorf.
181 A town in Saxony-Anhalt.
182 French: the 2nd (company).
183 French: the 7th (company).
184 French: searching (of a suspect).
185 Desmond's Grandparents' house in Guernsey (see Introduction).
186 A concertina type barbed wire which could be carried in a compact coil and then stretched to form a barrier without any vertical supports.

coming up to interrupt me. It rained hard all day: Lord knows what the winter will be like and God help us if an epidemic breaks out.

Tuesday September 17th

We were outside at 7.30 for a searching when everything must be declared. The 7th company began and as they went through at 40 to the hour, I realised that we should be some time. It was very cold and to crown it all, it began to rain. At 12 we were told to stack our luggage in a cellar and we should be sent for later. We got some soup for a change and then settled down to bridge, as we had not been allowed any books. We got some sausage in the evening and oh, I was so hungry. An incident will show how bestial we have become! At lunch, in the refectory room, we saw some crusts left over: without a moment's hesitation, we precipitated ourselves upon them and scoffed them. I hesitate to think of our behaviour at a tea party. Appell at 8 was outside in the yard and we had to hang about for a very long time. Then bed: is it possible that I used to go to bed in the early hours of the morning?

Wednesday September 18th

We were ordered out of our rooms by 7.30 because our corridor was to be used for searching. I had a walk with a very charming painter, Capt de Gaguerand. He feels as I do and it has been weighing on me very much lately: that we have all been thinking of our rights and never doing our duty, "Nous avons demandé nos droits sans faire nos devoirs."[187] The aftermath of the war will be hard but we must keep a set of values before us, taking the good from the old, culture, the idea of religion, science, and adapt these to the new surroundings. Take the old wine and put it into new bottles, but these bottles will know what is going in and will know what to do to avoid being damaged. Some French with Valéry, who feels very depressed with this new life of bustle and supervision. Soup again of bean flour and microscopic bits of meat. I was searched during the afternoon, losing my penknife and my note books. There was no regularity in the search! A bumper supper night! Two helpings of potato soup and then, at the instigation of the pleasant, French speaking kitchen officer, we had some "rabiot" (army slang for remains) from lunch. I did not sleep very well as I was suffering from terrible toothache: a filled tooth which had always given me trouble and had at last given up the ghost on a piece of hard bread during our voyage.

As the days were so monotonous at this Oflag[188] VIII H, I will give a daily programme and then each week insert any points of interest over and above the daily round. My usual hour of rising was 7.30. I then did some exercises and did my ablutions in the corridor: this was not easy for I had to take a pretty comprehensive wash, there being no form of bathing arrangements. Then we ate our bread, always three slices and butter or margarine and drank some coffee: this breakfast was taken in the corridor where we had to fight to get near a table and we usually ate standing up. From now till Appell I wrote up my diary and took a walk round the garden. Appell at 9 was in the courtyard and lasted about a quarter of an hour: there was always a lot of noise and complaining and a great deal of sshing. After Appell I walked with either Colonel Gibbs or Valéry until about 10. The garden was always very crowded and in time became very near to a muddy bog. At 10 I went up to Valéry's corridor, which was lighter and warmer than ours, and did some French until Sept 20th when I started Italian and continued with this as well as doing a French composition. This took us to 11.30 when we took a stroll in the garden. Lunch was by companies and we lined up anytime between 11.30 and 12.30. We had soup every day and the selection was small: cabbage

187   French: We have demanded our rights without doing our duty.
188   German: A Prisoner of War Camp for Officers only.

soup, potato soup, bean flour, barley or carrots. At 1 o'clock I made my way to a room on the first floor and there took an English conversation class: my method seemed quite successful and my pupils made great strides. I commenced with a dictation from a Dickens' book, I then explained the words and got each member of the class to use the word in a sentence: we then had general conversation, usually taking a special subject e.g. motoring, wireless, sport etc. I had a very pleasant audience, most young regular officers from the Artillerie Coloniale[189] and we had some amusing hours together as they were all fairly fluent. I was not a grammarian and never attempted to give grammatical explanations and I think this helped to keep the issue clear. From 2 onwards I did an Italian exercise and usually a French composition: it was not easy to work well because our corridor was noisy, dark, draughty and damp: not conducive to great mental effort but I did my best. About 4 o'clock V and I used to take a walk which was an English lesson for him; he was fluent but his pronunciation was very foreign and he had many mannerisms. He was a good pupil for he liked to be corrected and always made a note of his mistakes. The evening was a complete turmoil from now on. The coffee arrived about 4.45 and, if the supper was cold, it accompanied the coffee: these dishes were also very stereotyped either white cheese (curds) or jam, or three boiled potatoes in their skins. When we had a hot supper, about twice a week, we had to line up between 5.30 and 6.30: these dishes suffered from the usual monotony either noodle soup or semolina soup, beetroot salad or a vegetable soup. After every meal pandemonium was let loose: everyone queued up on the chance of getting a second helping: I was lucky three or four times. The general impression to be drawn was of feeding time at the zoo, pushing, shoving, shouting, groaning: all the mannerisms that distinguish animals from men. Some attempts were made to organise these "rabiot"[190] queues but without much success. After supper, till Appell Mac, Weysom, Colin and I played bridge, stopping for an interval about 7 o'clock when we consumed some bread and beer: this latter was perhaps the greatest luxury: it was of two kinds, light or dark and both were excellent, the dark very much resembling our own brown ale. Appell was at 8.15, usually in the courtyard where we had to hang about for a considerable time: we were counted in the ranks and recounted as we filed into the building. I usually read till about 9.30 and then went to bed. The room was always stuffy as the occupants were very averse to "courant d'air"[191] and expostulated violently when a window even looked as though it might be open. I usually slept very well, the atmosphere in the room acting as an anaesthetic. The sanitary arrangements were very primitive: a lean to shed in the courtyard with a long board, no form of drainage whatsoever: the indoor WCs, 4 in number were opened at 9pm but the general cleanliness and decency of the inhabitants was such that the flushes were invariably blocked up with stale food, old socks and the like. Discomfort and noise were the key notes of our existence.

Week beginning Thursday September 19th

This week was jaundiced by the agony of toothache, a pain that colours with dreariness the entire outlook. I was able to get some aspirins from the German doctor but it was not till Monday that I got relief. On Monday afternoon at about 1.30 I left the camp with an energetic hearty naval officer, Cmdt Casankuve, who we called "hands across the sea", for he was speechless when his hands were in his pockets! We took a bus to Sternberg[192], a journey of about 9kms across the flat, cultivated plain, skirting along the foot of the pine hills. At Sternberg, quite a large market town with cobbled streets and overhanging houses, we were conducted by our fat, jolly Rhineland sentry to the dentists' houses. We had to wait for some time in the waiting room, a long dark chamber with the usual pile of periodicals and the familiar uncomfortable chairs and advertisements calendars. After an hour we went into the surgery, rather old fashioned and not over clean, and, what I had never seen before, two operating chairs:

189   French: Colonial Artillery
190   French: second helpings, extras
191   French: draughts
192   A town in the Parchim district of the State of Mecklenburg-Vorpommern.

in one of these, a lady dentist was operating on a little girl. I had the unpleasant experience of having to watch the dentist, a bull necked, heavy man with a long angry duelling scar across one cheek, operating on my comrade and adopting a manner which was anything but bedside. My turn came to sit in the chair, took one look at my tooth and said "Aus."[193] He jabbed his syringe into me, left me for a few minutes and then returned with a pair of evil looking pincers, gripped me by the shoulders, took hold of the tooth and with a violent tug, removed it. His injection had not taken and you can imagine what I felt. The dentist grinned, grunted "Gut"[194] and disappeared. There was nothing for it but to grin and bear it as Mr Godfrey's little cat advises. We walked back to the bus, but as it was late and our sentry wanted to smoke we went up a side street and waited. From here we got a fine view of the church, a very ornate, oriental building: as it was an Austrian Catholic church, the cross was set up at an angle and not perpendicular. On our way home the guard had great fun with two young girls: life does not change much. I was again struck by the emptiness of the town though the shops seemed fairly well stocked. During this week I made the acquaintance of a very attractive naval lieutenant, who spoke very perfect English having done a lot of yachting at Cowes and having business connections in England: his name was des Raux. He was a great friend of the Falry's and Vivi Cocheri, who is now married and he had met Hobson and De Boislambert on shooting expeditions near Varaville.[195] My reading was from a book "L'abbaye d'Evolagne":[196] it was a study of the character and changes in that character, of a woman whose husband decides to become a monk. It was heavy and tragic but the author had put a great deal into her work and the general effect was of sincerity and the rule of fate. Sunday evening thoughts: - Life is going to be hard and we must forget many of our old pleasures: compare this Sunday with others, a stroll in the park with Jean, lunch at the Troc[197] and then to Eton for tea, back to town for a glass of brown, nutty sherry and then on to dinner at Gray's Inn[198] followed by a stroll in the dusk lighted gardens with the scent of the flowers drenching the London air!

Week beginning Thursday September 26th

This week was made rather worrying by the news that has been brought in by the German NCO interpreter, a tall, dark, insinuating fellow. The rumour was that the British had gone to Dakar,[199] demanded that the town should join de Gaulle[200] and, on receiving a refusal, the warships had opened fire on the town and bombed it with their aircraft: a British cruiser and a French submarine were the casualties. The general feeling here is that the Germans must have been using the port and our action is endorsed by the majority but the truth is very obscure. The anti English element is from the sailors led by La Perouse, but they are in a very definite majority and their supporters are recruited from the senior officers entirely. A general discussion of La P's paper led to my realising the preponderance of sympathy that is for us. The others are looked upon as traitors, unfit to be called officers. Still my eyes have been opened to what Democracy can stoop to. A rumour that King George had abdicated was being circulated: also that peace terms by Germany had been put forward to France, 35 milliard d'or,[201] north

---

193	German: out
194	German: good.
195	A commune in the Calvados department of lower Normandy, France.
196	French: "The Monastery of Evolagne." I have not been able to identify this work.
197	Presumably the London Trocadero.
198	The Honourable Society of Gray's Inn, commonly known as Gray's Inn, is one of the four Inns of Court in London to which the barristers of England and Wales belong.
199	Capital of Senegal.
200	Charles de Gaulle(1890-1970), leader of the Free French Forces in WW2.
201	French: a billion in gold

of the Somme and Alsace[202] and Lorraine.[203] Italy requires Savoy,[204] Corsica,[205] Tunis,[206] Djibouti.[207] These are considered too harsh and Ribbentrop[208] has gone to Rome to mediate. All this is rumour: it is terrible to have no real true news: believe nothing is the best policy. Sunday was a big day when we had a slice of roast meat and some gravy! One lovely evening of student songs in which I took a prominent part and brought back old memories. We put forward an application to be transferred to an English camp; I personally find life interesting but it is not too easy for those of us who do not speak French. Another rumour was that Japan had declared war: this would not assist our fleet distribution and would certainly bring America in. This week's reading was André Gide "Les Faux Monnayeurs":[209] a distinct resemblance to A Huxley:[210] that same cynical, rather vicious narrative and that counter point style of leaping from one period to another in successive chapters. Strong impressions: High mass in the garden and some lovely singing: suddenly the youth movement marching down the road burst into commanded song. Fine voices but what different thoughts: one was for love and peace, the other for war and hatred: is this to be our new creed?

Week beginning Thursday October 3rd

I attended a protestant service held in the ornate little catholic chapel adjoining the main building: our prison had once been a monastery. The service, similar to our own C of E, was conducted by a German Pasteur who gave us a sermon in French written by a French Pasteur: an invocation to keep ourselves from falling into the deep, black well of uninspiring prison life. The sound of organ music was a great joy. I thought so hard of Mummy: I wonder if she knew. We were issued with an advance of pay of 10 marks: we English only receiving half pay as a reprisal? We are paid in Lagergeld.[211] Also we are only allowed one letter a month instead of the Frenchman's seven! Also a reprisal, some thinking: pleasure must be kept but must be an accessory to work and not the aim of work. Perouse is a large aggressive man who rolls his way along with his cap on the side of his head: he is usually to be seen in a tête à tête[212] with some young man and takes on a very plotting air. I am much appreciating the descriptive style of Dickens. I read a passage each day to my class: nothing escapes his eye and his similes are remarkably apt. On Sundays we have a protestant service in the refectory when a captain reads the service to us: I appreciate the quietness and the simplicity, so like a meeting of Friends. A great stroke of luck when I scrounged some hot water and Hash made us some tea: he was able to put some milk into it which he had saved: it tasted like nectar. I had been doing some laundry: not an easy matter with cold water and a limited supply of soap. I will not throw my laundry on the floor without thinking of the difficulties of this pastime. What strength those old French washerwomen must have as they scrub at the river's edge. My Italian was progressing well and I did some conversation with V: a few months in a family would soon put me right. V has talked of introducing me to Wickham Steed[213] after the war and I am thinking very seriously of a journalistic career: I mean to start from the

202   On France's eastern border, adjacent to Germany.
203   French region bordering Germany, Belgium and Luxembourg.
204   French region bordering Italy and Switzerland.
205   A French Island in the Mediterranean west of Italy.
206   i.e. Tunisia, the smallest country in North Africa and under French rule in 1940.
207   A country in the Horn of Africa.
208   Ulrich Friedrich Wilhelm Joachim von Ribbentrop (1893-1946) was Foreign Minister of Nazi Germany from 1938-1945.
209   "Les Faux Monnayeurs" ("The Counterfeiters"), a novel by André Gide published in 1925.
210   Aldous Leonard Huxley (1894-1963), an English writer.
211   An internal currency used to pay prisoners in German Prisoner of War Camps and also Concentration Camps.
212   French: in deep conversation.
213   Henry Wickham Steed (1871-1956) was a British journalist and historian and was editor of The Times from 1919 to 1922.

bottom and work really hard. I was still on the same book: I find the characters too young and precocious and, if they represent modern democratic youth, then reforms are most necessary. Reading is not easy: everywhere is penetrated by distracting conversation and real concentration, which this book requires, is almost impossible. The corridor had at last been made more habitable by the building of a partition between us and the main door: we were no longer driven crazy by the shouts of "La porte, la porte!"[214] Japan has taken steps in Indo China and now controls a very important railway. Our little Anglophile friend, Hervier, is most indignant. He is a journalist on the foreign side of Le Matin:[215] he speaks English, German, Spanish and Russian: he stresses the latter very strongly. A series of lectures were now in progress. German, Spanish, Literature and the like. I had no particular desire to attend them and I was really quite busy.

Thursday October 10th

Today came rumours and later confirmation of our impending departure by orders of the Germans and in no way connected with our application: rather extraordinary that they should both fall together.

Friday October 11th

After a great deal of hanging about we received some pay: 24 marks and we were definitely informed that we should be leaving on the following morning. A general came to inspect the camp and we had some croquette potatoes as a big treat. I spent most of the day collecting addresses and taking farewell of my many friends. V was very sorry to say goodbye but we shall most definitely meet when all this is finished and he has invited me to stay at his home in Montpellier.[216] After Appell I went up to see Boyer and De Brosses and partook of a final cup of tea which they surreptitiously made on their alcohol stove, the last in their possession.

Saturday October 12th

We were up bright and early and by 8.30 had shaken hands with everyone: many were those who came up and told us what faith and friendship they had for England: they asked us to take away a bon souvenir[217] and to remember that the dissension in the camp came from the old, the senior and the minority. We lined up opposite the others for Appell and, as soon as that ceremony was over, the Captain adjutant of the camp told us to move along. Before we could take a step, the French burst into song and we quickly recognised "The King". Everyone stood to attention, our guards shuffling uncomfortably from one foot to another. Then came "Tipperary" and, as we moved off, I felt a pang of sorrow and admiration: we were leaving friends behind us, and I, especially, was leaving a friend who had influenced and helped me more than any other man I have met. In his quiet, unassuming, gently distinguished way he had put new faith into me, given me something to work for: a life of work for truth and information, for travel and help: I think he brought out Grandpa's spirit in me, ambition tempered with a sense of what is right: it sounds very self righteous but it is what I feel.

214   French: The door, the door.
215   A French daily newspaper created in 1883 and discontinued in 1944.
216   A city in southern France, capital of the Languedoc-Roussillon region and the Hérault department.
217   French: a happy memory.

Our lorry was speeding on the road to Sternberg which we soon passed through, then up a mountain road skirted by chestnut trees: once on the summit of these hills, we passed through flat, dusty, plain land, occasionally flashing through little villages, deserted except for the geese meandering about the market squares. Our NCO guard was full of life and ruderies, having been a prisoner in the last war: he was a good soul and was good enough to give us each a croissant, really delicious white bread. After about 1 ½ hours of dusty travelling (we were now almost unrecognisable for the coating of dust on our faces) we entered mountainous country and climbed in and out of thickly wooded mountain tracks, one minute gazing into the depths of a valley, another minute peering up at towering hills. At 12.30 we emerged into a valley and after passing a few wooden huts we saw the familiar letters OFLAG but this time VIII G. Our immediate arrival was not a great success for our driver mistook the turning and, after being ordered by an officer to clear out, he backed into a quagmire and for the next 20 minutes we were all pushing and shoving to extricate the diesel smelling lorry. The usual barbed wire soon came into view and made us feel at home once again. A number of officers were standing in front of what was obviously a commandeered hotel and, after we had descended, we were inspected by a distinguished looking, red faced old gentleman who I rightly took to be the Commandant. He issued orders through a bespectacled, pimply, youth who grinned at us with a row of bad teeth, and ordered us, in fluent English, to go inside. When inside, we were led into a large, parquet floored room and our baggage was searched: I was relieved of the new cut throat razor that I had bought at the Langendorf Canteen the day before. An orderly brought us in some potato soup and I ate as much as possible. Then we were marched by the Interpreter out of the camp to the Kommandantur[218] buildings. Here we found some magnificent showers and it was a relief to wash all over. I discovered that this place, Bad Johannesbrunn,[219] was a thermal spa which accounted for the well appointed shower baths and the position of this large hotel in such a deserted countryside. When back in the camp, we made the acquaintance of the other prisoners, about 12 in number. They were the engine room of the merchant cruiser HMS Vandyck[220] which had been bombed and sunk off Norway. They were not officially commissioned and it had only been by representation to the American ambassador that they had left the Stalag[221] of Lamsdorf:[222] they were a mixed bag but at least they were English. It struck me as odd that such a huge camp (built for 800) should have such few prisoners. The answer, Mr Racky said, was that the camp would not be completed till after the Spring offensive on England?! We were allowed to remain in the garden, that is a gravelled space in front of the house till 5 o'clock then we were all marched upstairs, 6 of us occupied a small room equipped with 5 double decker beds: the 3 others had a room. There was a stove in the room and also a wash basin and the floor was parquet. The usual wood wool mattresses, blue mattress covers and pillows and a blanket each. The supper was all ready for us and we were not worried by a strange diet: white cheese, brown bread (5 to a loaf) butter and Ersatz coffee, unsweetened. We had this meal in a little common room and the six orderlies, who had also been at Lamsdorf waited on us. After supper I played some bridge and, at 9, Appell was in the rooms: two guards were all the time on the landing and when lights were put out at 10 our door was locked and, if a midnight sortie was necessary, everyone was awakened by the rattling of the janitor's keys. There was a very fine tiled wash house just along the corridor. The system of only being allowed out when escorted and being locked in at night was aggravating and nerve racking. Bad Johannesbrunn is in the Sudeten Mountains at an altitude of 400ms. This hotel, which is our prison, is above the river, which runs shallow and swiftly through rich green fields bordered by high hills covered with tall pines, interspersed with silver birch and chestnut. The stream cannot be seen from here but we look straight across at the thickly coated hills. The air is very bracing but warm only for a short time, as the sun rises very little above the encircling trees.

218 German: Oflag Headquarters.
219 A town in the Sudeten Mountains.
220 HMS Vandyck was bombed and sunk by Luftwaffe aircraft in Norwegian waters on 10th of June 1940.
221 German: Prisoner of War Camp.
222 Lamsdorf (German spelling). A town in Silesia, Poland. Stalag VIII B was based here.

Sunday October 13th

We were awakened at 6.30 and our trousers and shoes which had been removed the night before were returned to us: breakfast was what we had saved from the night before. 9 o'clock was Appell and the Colonel Commandant inspected us and asked us a few questions. The rest of the morning was spent walking up and down and sitting in the sun which was very warm when it had properly risen. The air was very bracing and fresh and it felt very healthy. Lunch was one of the usual soups with the difference that we were able to get a second helping. The cooking arrangements were those of the German garrison and we used to get what they left. I had to spend the afternoon asleep as there was nothing else to do: the seamen were not a very interesting crowd and their Liverpool accents were almost incomprehensible. Supper was at 5.30 and we were issued with a tasty cheddar type of cheese. Then came the usual bridge and so a useless day drew to a close. The only bright spark of the day was when Colin and I had our heads clipped and we looked very like two convicts: I can't quite think why I had it done: mostly to see what I would look like and I was not afraid of female criticism!?

Monday October 14th

There was a sharp frost on the ground but it soon warmed up with the rising of the sun. We were searched after Appell and I was pleased to get my Italian notes back and also to have one or two Dickens. I lost my diaries though. After lunch we went for a walk in the company of four sentries: along the route we came about 6kms through high pines. We had a fine view of the rushing stream and the small villages on the mountainside. The colouring was a basic green, glittering with autumn tints, framed in the bright blue of the skies. I felt quite tired after this slight exertion and we sat down to potato soup and jam, having made some toast on the fire which was a very welcome change. The sentries had been removed from the landing and we could leave our rooms in freedom: this had a great moral effect: I did not feel quite such a prisoner. I was soon asleep though the cold nights necessitated my sleeping inside blankets, and, not using my sheet.

Tuesday October 15th

Life was equally dull here so I will not weary you. Our day began at 6.30. I was up early and did some exercises before the open wash house window: then breakfast, usually toast from the night before and a few cold potatoes if possible. We had this in a little room adjoining the large dining room: here we had a fire and, as it was the old billiard zimmer,[223] the green decoration was quite restful: here were garden chairs and little tables and it was very cosy. Appell was at 9 and did not last long. The Camp Officer, a school master by profession, was a very considerate soul and was always pleasant and polite and we once had a very amusing evening with him! I walked hard for about half an hour as it was decidedly "nippy". Then I sat down, either inside or out, and wrote up my Italian, attended Racky's one and only useless German class, or read "Martin Chuzzlewit"[224] which I was very much enjoying: I read it before when I hurt my leg in Oct 1932! and I must say that it was as though I had never read it. Lunch of one of the usual soups was at 1 o'clock: once we had a meatless rissole which made a change. The afternoon was taken up either by reading or going out for a walk. Supper at 6 with the usual dishes except that here we were always sure of some boiled potatoes. From tea till Appell in the rooms we played bridge. Lights out at ten and we usually talked till about 11: sleep soon came to me though I usually spent a restless night.

223   German: room.
224   "The Life and Adventures of Martin Chuzzlewit" by Charles Dickens, published in 1844.

Week beginning Tuesday October 15th

I ordered an English German Grammar and a French Italian Grammar from J Gross. Heidelberg[225] (They turned up at Oflag IXA about the beginning of December). Wednesday afternoon passed quickly with a douche and then a walk on the other side of the river which was full of enormous trout. We rested in a large field bounded by the river and gloriously coloured woods. I wrote my first letter to Aunty 15.10.40. The mornings were very frosty and my hands suffered terribly. On Friday we had a TAB[226] injection: here it is done down in the right breast and it was very efficiently done. Connors got down to dishing up tea after lunch and we made it a daily habit, sometimes taking cocoa instead of tea. About 80 French doctors arrived who had been made prisoner in the Maginot line:[227] they had had no news from home and had not been very well looked after. They had passed through Lamsdorf in their wanderings and had been very impressed by our lads. Saturday was spent in chatting to the Frenchmen and in peeling potatoes, a job for which we volunteered: it was a cold job but the knack came at last. I sent a letter to Zabette. Sunday morning was very frosty and it gave a Christmas card effect. I got the nucleus of an English class together: some of the doctors speak quite good English and they are all very Anglophile. Col Gibbs has been doctoring the Commandant's horse and, as a reward, he has been given a fire in his room: this is very nice for him, for though he keeps better here he finds it very cold at night. I ordered a number of Tauchnitz[228] books. Lunch changed slightly when we had some very salty cod. My class, organised as before, started off before lunch for one hour. Received my identity plaque: a real convict now! Hash has been busy with Tangye, his son's spirit. Poor H takes everything very literally. Tangye, a courtier of Farouk,[229] speaks excellent English and H tells us of schools which operate in the other world.

Week beginning Tuesday October 22nd

Washing clothes was made much easier with soda. The French officers gave me some real coffee: the taste was quite forgotten to me and it was a treat to get it again. Beer had arrived but was not up to the last camp's standard. We got a fire in our room: the stoves are high of glazed tiles and give out a great heat. Walking is not easy now for 100 walkers on the 80 yard strip does not leave much room. I did most of my walking now, before Appell. I finished "Martin Chuzzlewit": the murder of Tigg by Jonas was a masterly piece of writing and Tom and Ruth Pinch scenes had such a warming charm.

On Thursday we had a second TAB, this time in the left breast. I started a book on Penguins by Cherry Kearton,[230] translated into French. I wrote to Mummy after tea, 24.10.40. Old Moore prophesies the end of the war for Oct 25th: well here we are! I read Zadig, one of Voltaire's "Contes",[231] "He was loved not because he was intelligent, not because he was good but because he was chief magistrate." A table rapping session was held under H's supervision.

---

225   Publisher based in New York.
226   An inoculation to give protection against typhoid.
227   Named after the French Minister of War, André Maginot, a line of concrete fortifications, tank obstacles, artillery casemates, machine gun posts and other defences which France constructed along its borders with Germany and Italy in the run up to WW2.
228   A family of German Printers and Publishers.
229   Desmond spells this Pharook in the original text but I think he may be referring to King Farouk 1 of Egypt (1920-1965).
230   Cherry Kearton (1871-1940), one of the world's earliest wildlife photographers and writers.
231   "Zadig" by Voltaire, a French Enlightenment writer, published in 1747.

He prayed and sung a hymn and then we waited but nothing happened: Choppin, the orderly took it all very seriously and made us laugh! "Il n'y a point de mal dont il ne naisse un bien".[232] "La bile rend colère et malade: mais sans la bile l'homme ne saurait vivre".[233] "Tout est dangereux et tout est necessaire".[234] "Quand on est aimé d'une belle femme on se tire toujours d'affaire dans ce monde".[235] Snow came on Oct 26th and the countryside took on a guise of fairy land. A terrific thrill when two Red Cross parcels came for Thorp, the old steward of the Vandyck. The tins of food thrilled us and it was almost unbelievable to think of. This parcel had been despatched on August 2nd. Walking was now impossible so I trotted round under the veranda. We had a little service in the Hotel chapel, Beatty read the prayers and Thorp the sermon, a product of the American bible society. We finished with "The King". Old Choppin was at the organ and acquitted himself quite well.

Monday October 28th

The latest rumour is that the war is over?! The snow was by now 6" deep. We were told to be ready to leave by 4 o'clock as we were leaving: our camp was to be taken over by Generals, two English amongst them, and the rooms were being better furnished with tasty furniture: still, I suppose a General must have a spring bed. At 4 we climbed into two lorries and were soon speeding along snow covered lanes bordered by trees borne down with snow: the sight of two deer playing in the snow pleased me very much. At 5.30 we reached Troppau,[236] a fairly large town with large shops and cafés and full of troops. We hustled through the station into a waiting carriage and were soon on the move. There were good lights of acetylene and I was able to read a rather dull detective book: at 10.30 we ate some blutwurst[237] and bread and then I made myself comfortable on the wooden seat and dozed fitfully. We had passed Ratibor[238] and Oppeln[239] and stopped at various other stations. About midnight we were woken up and told to get out. Our guards were of one NCO and three sentries.

Tuesday October 29th

We were now at Breslau[240] which was a huge station. We were marched, via a subway to the waiting room and received the news that our next train was at 6 o'clock. I was very amazed at the great number of travellers and the place was swarming with uniforms. I very soon got down on to the floor and, covered with blankets, I was soon asleep. I woke up at 3 and there were still just as many travellers: they must have to wait a long time for connections. I woke up again at 5 and some nurses, one of whom spoke English, gave us some soup. We then moved to another platform and after half an hour's wait we boarded a local train. There was a great deal of activity in the station and I saw two great streamlined trains, one the Berlin-Bratislava express. There were as many troops as ever and I saw one or two tender farewells: here the most tender farewell always ends up with the inevitable salute. Dawn

---

232 French: There exists no evil from which good may not be born.
233 French: Worry makes one angry and ill. But man cannot live without worry.
234 French: Everything is dangerous and everything is necessary.
235 French: When one is loved by a beautiful woman, one can always cope in this world.
236 The Principality of Troppau (German spelling) is situated around the Upper Silesian city of Opava in the modern day Czech Republic.
237 German: blood sausage (similar to black pudding).
238 Ratibor (German spelling), a town in southern Poland.
239 Oppeln (German spelling), a city in southern Poland on the Oder River. Capital of Upper Silesia.
240 Breslau (German spelling), the largest city in western Poland.

soon broke and a vestige of snow still lay on the ground: we passed through "Neumarkt"[241] (but did not stop for the sales!). We got out at Liegnitz[242] and had half an hour of very cold waiting. The next train, which was pretty well heated, took us through Arnsdorf,[243] Haynau[244] and Gôrlitz:[245] from the carriage map we knew that we were en route for Dresden and the country through which we were passing was flat, well cultivated and quite fertile. We passed groups of English, Belgian and French prisoners who were working sometimes on the lines, sometimes in woodcutting gangs. Bautzen[246] was an attractive 12th century town. The morning passed on with bridge and reading, often interrupted by people trying to climb into our carriage! At about 2.15 we passed into some very wooded country and I recognised it as the outskirts of Dresden. At Dresden Neustadt[247] where we got out, we received some hot tea from the Red Cross, much better than the tea we had received during our outward journey. We crossed over the station and after half an hour's wait we got into a fresh train moving in the opposite direction: our new coach was quieter and better sprung than the others. It was snowing heavily and, after we had passed through the well kept industrial suburbs, we passed Neiderau.[248] We were now en route for Leipsig,[249] the route we had followed before only this time a blizzard was gradually whitening the countryside, flat and uninteresting. We crossed the Elbe and stopped at Reisa[250], and with my reading a modern French novel "L'Oiseau Blessé",[251] picked up at Colombier,[252] the journey to Leipsig soon passed. At 6 o'clock we had to jump and were conducted to the "Wartesaal" (waiting room) full of dismal looking tourists. Leipsig is a vast station with a distinct resemblance to Waterloo. The Red Cross brought tea to the Guards! At 8 o'clock we went onto a platform and stood about in the freezing cold till ten o'clock. During that time, three trains pulled out: a hitch somewhere and just a glance at our NCO made me wonder how we had got so far. The blackout was intense and it was easier to lose oneself than to keep in the party: where could an escapee go with no clothes and no food! When we at last got into a coach we had a bit of bread and then I dozed till I was ordered out at Halle.[253] Here we waited in the subway as there was an air raid in progress: in about half an hour, the all clear was sounded and at about 12.30 after a cold, uncomfortable wait during which the Red Cross supplied our guards! with food, we boarded yet another train. I was suffering from a terrible attack of colic, due probably to our change of diet, helped on by the cold.

241   Neumarkt (German spelling), a town in the Krakow district of Poland.
242   Liegnitz (German spelling), a town in south western Poland.
243   Arnsdorf (German spelling), a town in the district of Heilenberg, East Prussia (?).
244   Heynau (German spelling), a small town in the Legnica county in Lower Silesia, south western Poland.
245   Gôrlitz (German spelling), a town in Lower Sileasia, south western Poland or Gôrlitz in Saxony, Germany?
246   Hilltop town in Lower Saxony, Germany.
247   A Railway station in Dresden.
248   In the district of Meissen, Saxony.
249   A city in Saxony.
250   A town in the district of Meissen in Saxony.
251   "L'Oiseau Blessé" (" The Wounded Bird"), a novel by Henri Duvernois, published in 1934.
252   i.e. the Colombier Barracks.
253   A city in the southern part of Saxony-Anhalt.

Wednesday October 30th

I dozed till we got to Sangerhausen[254] and then, half asleep, changed into another train and when I awoke again we were being pushed out at Nordhausen;[255] then we were pushed in again, then out, and I thought the whole world had gone mad. At last we went to the waiting room and there we got some unsweetened coffee to drink: it was at least hot and made me feel much better. After about 3 hours of reading and dozing we went out along the line and stood about in the snow till a carriage was produced for us and we were hitched up to still one more train. We had a bit of bread and prayers for a speedy end to this dreary journey. The NCO seems rather hazy as to the workings of the Deutsche Reichsbahn[256] and we shall probably travel forever. The snow was by now quite deep and we were passing across a vast white plain: we were attached to a goods train and so did not stop at Sollstedt[257] or Leinefelde.[258] The country gradually became more hilly and wooded with little snow clad villages nestling in the valleys. We stopped at Uder[259] and Eichberg[260] after which we went through a long tunnel. The snow was still coming down but did not seem to be settling. At Eschwege,[261] we were shunted about and at last attached to a passenger train and we left the Kassel[262] line for a one track local line. I finished my book by Duvernois[263] which had quite an interesting plot but, like a great many French novels, it suffered from an overflow of sex flowing in the direction contrary to the usual one, that is to say, it was of the gradual development of the love of a father for his adopted daughter, bringing about the rupture of his own marriage. The character of his wife Odette was very well drawn: "Elle tient à rester bonne joueuse avec tout le monde",[264] but she knows all the time that her husband sees through her pose. How often this comes about? At Waldkappel[265] we had quite a long wait, and then off through more interesting country, hilly and pine wooded. A long tunnel and then Spangenberg.[266] An officer was on the station to meet us and we were marched through a little village into a barbed wire compound surrounded by villa like houses with red painted beams. We were taken inside and it was soon my turn to be searched. My particulars were taken and I was relieved of my diaries. We then wrote a card to Geneva with our new address OFLAG IX A.

254   Capital of the district of Mansfeld-Südharz in Saxony-Anhalt.
255   A town on the southern edge of the Harz mountains in the State of Thuringia.
256   The German Railway.
257   A municipality in the district of Nordhausen, Thuringia.
258   A town in the district of Eichsfeld in north western Thuringia.
259   A town in Thuringia.
260   Desmond spells this Eischbergen in the original text but I think he means Eichberg, a town in Thuringia.
261   A town in north eastern Hesse, Germany.
262   A town in northern Hesse.
263   Henri Duvernois (1875-1937).
264   French: She does her utmost to be a good sport with everyone.
265   A small town in the Werra-Meissner-Kreis in northern Hesse.
266   A small town in north eastern Hesse, the location of Oflag IX A/H. There were 2 POW camps, the Upper Camp, housed in the castle itself (Schloss) and the Lower Camp at Elbersdorf.

Oflag IXA at Spangenberg December 1940

Spangenberg 2013

Then a miracle happened: an orderly brought in a tray with a jug of real tea, bread, margarine and some pilchards. A douche followed and our clothes were fumigated and very thoroughly searched. The Naval men, with Wysom and Jones, left us for the top camp: a castle standing on the pinnacle of a tree clad hill: it looked very romantic and very cold! We were now shown to our rooms, the usual beds and trimmings and about 30 officers led by a Capt Forester Fielding who sported a magnificent red beard and a vast moustache. He was in the 2nd Btn[267] of the Sherwood Foresters so we had many mutual acquaintances. We then partook of a heavenly brown stew, tea, bread and cheese which we learnt came from Red Cross parcels which arrived now and again. During supper a DCLI[268] subaltern came and chatted with me but, as it was getting late, Colin and I adjourned to Stube[269] 17. After lights out all the windows were opened and the room was delightfully fresh and airy. There are a crowd of charming fellows and all most helpful. A great factor is that letters and parcels get through fairly quickly so perhaps I shall get some news by Christmas. A news bulletin was given by an officer who spoke German and gets a newspaper.

267   Military abbreviation: Battalion
268   Military abbreviation: Duke of Cornwall's Light Infantry.
269   German: room

Thursday October 31st

I got up about 7.30, made my bed and then went down for a wash; the wash house is fairly well laid out with two enamel troughs and about 30 taps. When the gong sounded we went to the Dining Hall (Speisesaal) and there we found three slices of bread each, tea and of all marvels, fried potatoes, which turns up about once a week. We were at a table with Hash and 3 other officers who let us have some saccharin and a tin of margarine. After breakfast at 9 was Appell, taken by a Major Clout who, as he spoke German, was confidence officer for the camp: the CO is a Lt Col Ford of the Sherwood Foresters. We were very lucky to come when we did for we came in time to be issued with a Red Cross parcel: I suppose that this is some of the subscribed 5 million pounds: the Red Cross quota is one a week but they are nothing like as frequent: still they are most welcome when they do come. A lot of stuff was put in a kitchen pool, another lot in a table pool and we got the rest, some chocolate, sugar, cheese, marmite, coffee, jam, a Lingfold[270] powdered milk. I had a long chat with Major Roberts who I knew when the SFs[271] were in Guernsey: he was made prisoner in Norway. Lunch soon came along, 12.15, and we had minced bully (a looted German issue) and a few potatoes. After lunch I had a lot of conversations: many think of a change! At 3.30 a cup of tea was served and 5.30 Appell soon came along. At supper we had fishcakes (made from the terrible salt cod) and potatoes. At 7 o'clock I visited the library: most Penguin detective tripe but a few good books lost in the pile and dug out by searching and I was able to pick up "Along the Road" by A Huxley.[272] I took a grand wash before bed with a piece of real soap from my parcel. My bed, which I had filled up with wood wool, was much more comfortable. The news was that the Italians were advancing swiftly in Greece.

From now on the days were always framed on the same pattern, so I shall describe a normal day and then divide the diary up into weeks.

I woke up about 7.30, called by the room orderly who put on the lights and shut the windows: black out rules are very stringent indeed. Then I would lie in for a few minutes, getting up about 7.50. A good wash all over and a shave about every third day. There are a lot of beards here but I shall not grow one till my hair looks more civilised! By the 8.15 breakfast gong I had washed and made my bed. Everyone marches over to any meal with a hose under their arm containing numerous tins with saved up fat, salt, sugar, jam, etc: for the most part, mine are empty. The Speisesaal[273] holds the 150 officers very comfortably and they are divided into messes of 7 and each mess has a table: the seating is either on stools or forms and a few "privilégiés"[274] have chairs. Windows are on three sides and the fourth side is taken up with a kitchen hatch and a Canteen room and counter. Three orderlies look after the room and, after each meal, the wooden tables are washed down and the floor swept: every Monday night the place is given a good spring clean. The kitchen is well appointed with two or three boilers, a range and a sink: next to the kitchen is another wash house. The Speisesaal is used as the recreation and is kept well heated with pipes, it is always cleared half an hour before meals except for one representative from each mess who attends to the laying and setting of his own table. There is also a food store where each mess has a locker and only one member is allowed to enter this store. We have a Mess Committee with a Kitchen Officer and also a Canteen Committee. The breakfast menu is usually 4 days of just 3 slices of brown bread and tea: the three specialities come in rotation, fried potatoes, usually on Sundays, porridge, a German issue and very palatable, and semolina usually flavoured with some Ersatz coffee. If we are well up in Red Cross stores, Sunday breakfast is supplemented with either tinned sausage or

---

270   Presumably a brand of powdered milk.
271   Military abbreviation: Sherwood Foresters.
272   "Along the road: notes and essays of a tourist" by Aldous Huxley, published in 1925.
273   German: dining room.
274   French: privileged ones.

bacon. At 9 is Appell: we fall in in five ranks and are inspected by Oberleut[275] Roth, the Camp Officer. A quarter of an hour after Appell, there is compulsory PT and the camp is divided into 4 groups each with a competent instructor, the exercises are not too strenuous but they have the good effect of keeping us flexible in this confined place. From 10 onwards the morning soon passes: there are lectures to attend and the Speisesaal is open for use as a common room. The Canteen opens at 11: most of the articles to be bought have to be ordered and one can expect to wait for at least a month for the arrival of such articles. Beer is issued about three times a week, rather an insipid brown liquid and "pop" is always on sale. Hot water is provided at 11 o'clock for those lucky people who have cocoa, marmite, etc. Lunch is at 12.15 and the menus are pretty well known: always three potatoes cooked in their skins and one slice of bread, then either vegetable stew, fishcakes, Brattling pullvers[276] (a rissole of pigmeal), minced fish, and very occasionally a piece of roast meat. Arrangements are made for the preparing of coffee (usually ersatz unless the Red Cross have been kind). After lunch there are usually lectures. These lectures are held in the two classrooms. Schreibstube[277] 1 and 2, which find themselves in the block where the infirmary is and they are next door to the library: in this block there are also a few senior officers' rooms, with only two or three in each room. The Speisesaal is open in the morning and tea is served at 3.15. We fall in for Appell at 5 o'clock. As supper is not till six, I usually walk during this intervening time. Supper never varies very much: always 3 potatoes, 3 slices of bread, a ration of ersatz dripping and 2 ½ teaspoons full of sugar: the other dishes are either soup, sausage, white or red cheese, fishcakes (made from salt fish). Once a week the kitchen provides a Brot pudding[278], made from bread remains. Tables can also make their own puddings and certain hours are allotted for cooking. After supper the Speisesaal is open again till 9: hot water can be obtained between 7.45 – 8.15. On Wednesday nights at 7.30, the Lecture and Debating Society hold a meeting, and Saturday night is always reserved for the Entertainments Committee. The various circles, French, German, Spanish, Economics hold meetings in the schreibstubes on their allotted evenings. These rooms are used by those desirous of peace and quiet. I retire to one of these rooms as the piano, bought by the mess, is usually being played either by the musician Grayson or by some thumper. At 9 the Speisesaal is cleared and at 10 o'clock the guards come round and count us in our beds: this is the Lights Out time. Discipline in the camp in ensured by the CO, his adjutant, Major Ponsonby, R Corps Signals, and an orderly officer who takers a week's turn of office. The cleanliness of the room at Lights Out is ensured by a room orderly, and in our room this duty falls about once a month. Sunday's programme varies in that breakfast is at 8.45 and at 10 o'clock a service is held in the Speisesaal: Padre MacLean, a regular padre on the Royal Scots always officiates: he is officially of the Church of Scotland. He is dark, young, good looking: his sermons are always most reasonable and helpful and he has one of those soft, sincere voices which command respect and attention. He has a great insight into the significance of every day facts that are related and if not so explained, would pass quite unnoticed. The rest of the day is as always except that at 8.45 the Padre has a small prayer meeting. I always go to this, not really because I pray but the silence is so helpful and I can give all my thoughts to those at home. The evening meeting has all the fervour and austere simplicity of a Quaker meeting. So passes the usual day: I shall take each day but only give those notes and observations and particular events that have struck me as noteworthy.

---

275   German: abbreviation of Oberleutnant, Senior Lieutenant.
276   German: pulver is powder so presumably some sort of dried meat that can be reconstituted into rissoles.
277   German: writing room/office
278   German: bread (pudding).

Week beginning Friday November 1st

There was a walk this afternoon: before allowed on these walks, we have to sign the parole book which binds us just for the duration of the walk. As well as our parole, we have six guards with loaded rifles to protect us from the violent village population! About 50 of us went on the walk and we went across the railway and up a steep hill, past a cotton spinning mill: we halted by the side of a brook and we were not allowed to enter the woods. From our elevated position we got a wonderful view of the Schloss[279] standing on an isolated hill at the strategic junction of four valleys. News: Italy seems to be meeting with some resistance and claims that the Greeks had 300 planes and 60 aerodromes built by Britain. A Huxley, "A critic must not ask himself, does the artist conform with my theory of imitation or distortion, or moral purity or significance <u>but</u> is he competent, has he something to say, is he genuine?"

Saturday November 2nd

"Whether work is good or bad depends entirely on the quality of the character which expresses itself in the work". I went to Lovel Garrett's[280] history lecture: this young man is a master at Cranleigh[281] and had an English trial: he is a cynic, a poseur with knowledge: his pose is that of nonchalant indifference to the so-called everyday civilised manners, especially of dress: he will appear on Appell clad in a woollen cap, unlaced boots, unbuttoned coat and no buttoned trousers, yet he will stand as rigidly and with as imposing a look, as if he were being inspected by the King: slightly bald and with a fringe of black hair he gives himself a Napoleonic stance and appearance. He has great and good ideas of social reform. I shall quote notes from his lectures and his general reasonable trend of ideas will show itself. He has reached the 19th century. He told us of Peel,[282] for whom he has a great admiration and the repeal of the Corn Laws.[283] The lecture soon developed into a general discussion illustrating the relationship between history and our modern position. The conclusion reached was that Economic troubles bring social troubles (a useful debating subject). This argumentative history was as it should be taught: 40 minutes here was more useful to us than hours at school. On this and subsequent Saturdays, the Entertainments Committee produced a show. Tables are thrown together to form a stage about 16' by 8'. A curtain is hung between two of the six wooden pillars and the dressing rooms are blanketed off. We have a foot spotlight and two sides with coloured slides made from toffee papers. The scenery is painted on to paper mounted on Red Cross boxes. The costumes are made from sheets, blankets and assortments of coloured papers, cotton wool for wigs. It is amazing how effective some of the costumes are. This evening's performance was a gala night, "Motley Mockery", written and produced by Eric Langham, a young solicitor, whose spiritual home was the Everyman's Theatre. The revue took its key note from Coward's "Stately Homes of England"[284] and the whole spirit was of intentional or perhaps unintentional snobbery. Funny sketches, lewd and witty dialogues, sketches on stocks solicitors, Queen Elizabeth and the pièce de resistance was the homecoming of the POWs and their forgetfulness of everyday behaviour: the humour reached a really Shavian[285] quality. From an essay of Huxley, I am very much afraid that France's population shortage may bring in black labour, reduce the standard of living and give us a second Portugal.

279 German: Castle i.e. Spangenberg Castle, built in 1253 and the town's landmark.
280 This name was spelled incorrectly in the original text but other sources confirm the correct spelling.
281 An Independent English boarding school, in Cranleigh, Surrey founded in 1865.
282 Sir Robert Peel (1788-1850) became Conservative Prime Minister in 1841.
283 Trade Laws designed to protect cereal producers in the United Kingdom of Great Britain and Ireland against less expensive foreign imports.
284 A reference to Noel Coward's parody of "The Homes of England" poem by Felicia Hemans.
285 i.e. characteristic of George Bernard Shaw or his works.

Sunday November 3rd

I have now got "Heroes and Hero Worship" by Thomas Carlyle.[286] I read the Hero as a divinity. C dealing with pagan religions, saying that wonder at natural quackery can never be a basis and will always stand discovered. Worship is for the man, his body and his mind: hero worship is natural and is good: with it, man loses his desire to work for an ideal: the hero is the ideal in whatever sphere he is admired. I get rather tired of his commiserating with the poor pagans, he says they did their best but had not our divine inspiration: if our present world has been brought about by our increase of inspiration, then let us bow down before Thor: no increased civilisation has brought with it so many comforts and man has become lazy and his beliefs have gone towards a lazy existence: it has been easier to have no ideals, easier to believe in nothing: but youth must realise its duties. I wrote to Uncle Alfred asking for some books on Quakers.

Monday November 4th

Today I started on the German grammar and struggled through the difficulties of the declining article. We rehearsed "Two Gentlemen of Soho" by A P Herbert,[287] written in Shakespearian metre: a study in overstatement and anticlimax. I have the part of a cockney waiter. I am playing an Irish corporal in Sheridan's "Scheming Lieutenant",[288] a nice play that ended happily. Interesting men are Charles Edie, a fair haired Aberdonian Divinity student: he is a sincere, thinking Christian. Littlejohn Cook, from Trinity Hall,[289] has strong social ideas and his knowledge of Russia gives him a chance to voice ideas on modern reconstruction.

Tuesday November 5th

American Election Day. Garrett gave us the Crimean War:[290] the origin was the fear of the Russian bogey (NB London treaty 1915 when Russia received her Crimean demands). The summer, original expedition was made to fight in winter conditions due to a lengthy detour made at the instigation of the French (Do military alliances work on the battle field: are they a diplomatic success?). The war gained nothing for us and the status quo was reinstated. Very important results on army organisation. Laing, a Worksop[291] master, gave his first paper on "Les trois Républiques"[292] at the French circle. Hesitant but instructive, if a little stereotyped. The Hero as a prophet: Islam and Christianity have the same basis: the chaff in any man or thought school will be buried and the whole straw, if it is there, must come to the surface. News most encouraging and we are well settled in Greece.

---

286   "On Heroes, Hero-Worship and the Heroic in History" by Thomas Carlyle, a Scottish philosopher and writer, published in 1841.
287   "Two Gentlemen of Soho", a play by A P Herbert, published in 1927.
288   "St Patrick's Day or The Scheming Lieutenant", a farce in one act, by Richard Brinsley Sheridan, published in 1775.
289   Trinity Hall, Cambridge University.
290   Crimean War (1853-1856), a conflict between the Russian Empire and an alliance of the French Empire, the British Empire, the Ottoman Empire and the Kingdom of Sardinia.
291   Worksop College, an Independent School founded in 1890.
292   French: The Three Republics.

Wednesday November 6th

I wrote to Pat, Daddy and Zabette. Prophet as a poet taking Dante.[293] The prophet tells us what we are to do, vates,[294] poet, what we are to love. Music is the basis of poetry: Dante's poem is a "mystical unfathomable song". At 7.30 a lecture was given in the Speisesaal by Capt (Dr) Cooper on the trend of population of which he has made a study. We will shortly have 25% over 65 and we are reproducing only 600 in the 1000: each family must have three children to reproduce the race. Germany in 1934 had an artificial increase due to pecuniary inducements but this has not been maintained. Why does Japan continue to increase: is it their low standard of life or have they ideals? Social stigma and economic position and, in a lesser degree, the fear of war affect the reproduction. A national religion, a contented and firm home life with a safe future are the essentials. News: Churchill[295] ready to attack in 1943. Very little air activity. Air raid casualties: 14,000 dead and 200,000 wounded.

Thursday November 7th

The tendons of my left foot had swollen up as they did in 1935: due this time to wearing German clogs. I wrote to Mummy: if only I could get a reply that all was well, I should feel so much happier. The Hero as a poet, Shakespeare: a country does not live until it has a voice: do we keep Shakespeare or India? Today we had a jelly served with Weetabix, a very great delicacy. I fear that food plays a very great part in our days, often the only factor that separates them. Rations are not great but I am getting accustomed to them and I'm sure I eat too much when I'm at home. Roosevelt[296] is well in and the Anglo American markets very steady. The Italians are not progressing much.

Friday November 8th

Today I read the Hero as a Priest, Luther and Knox.[297] I get rather tired of Carlyle's smug, civilised 19th century complacency. He will forgive even violence if the ideal be the true motive. Cc this with Ends and Means when good cannot come from an evil tree: also with Macaulay's "Bertrand Barrère":[298] the ideal fanaticism of the few assists the violent tendencies of the unscrupulous who take advantage of the disorganised state of affairs. Violence must be used only by the few and must be well controlled and it must only be used when its threat has been given: it is as harmful to make a threat and not execute it as it is to use unreined influence. A sign of weakness in the face of fanatical strength is an irremediable evil. Some delicious sweets called Ovo sports[299] came from the Geneva Red Cross: this mention may seem as the sublime to the ridiculous but believe me when I say that the deliciousness of the food was most sensible. I attended a meeting of the Shakespeare Society when Major Gee, a Clifton[300] Housemaster, analysed and explained Othello.[301] It was all rather above me but a knowledge of Shakespeare is essential to any writer, if only for his vocabulary. 20,000 words as against 100 of the labourer and 1 of the regular

---

293   Dante Alighieri (1265-1321), a major Italian poet of the Middle Ages (1265-1321).

294   English-Latin noun is a term for a prophet.

295   Sir Winston Leonard Spencer Churchill (1874-1965), Prime Minister from 1940-1945 and again from 1951-1955.

296   Franklin D Roosevelt (1882-1945), 32nd President of the United States.

297   From Thomas Carlyle's "On Heroes, Hero-Worship and the Heroic in History" previously referenced.

298   "On Memoires of Bertrand Barère" by Thomas Babington Macaulay (1800-1859), a British poet, historian and Whig politician who wrote extensively as an essayist and reviewer, published in 1844.

299   A type of glucose/energy sweet.

300   Probably Clifton College, Bristol, an Independent School founded in 1862.

301   "The Tragedy of Othello, the Moor of Venice", by William Shakespeare written in approximately 1603.

soldier. I fear that I have been rather defeated by Carlyle: lack of food, exercise and the terrible sameness of life call for occasional light entertainment and tend to make me less receptive.

Saturday November 9th

Garrett dealt with Gladstone's[302] enlightened premiership 1868-74, in which he abolished the purchase of commission, he disestablished the Irish church. He was unfortunate in alienating all sections of the community and even the Queen was very tired of him: perhaps their characters were too similar. Disraeli,[303] however, was a wonderful flatterer and he sickens one with his treacly compliments: it was the right technique with this rather foolish old woman. The two plays went off very successfully; a great deal of the success was due to the costumes and lighting. F Fielding's fine red beard came off for he was acting a lady: what heart pangs he must have had. News: the Italians seem to have come to a standstill. I wonder if our shipping losses are as heavy as reported.

Sunday November 10th

At 11 Beckwith held a party for his actors: though the beer was watery the general impression was of the usual Sunday morning drinks party: snobbish but agreeable. Perhaps the beer disagreed with me but I slept hard all the afternoon. I played some bridge in the evening but I felt very lazy and I'm afraid I felt rather bored with bridge, much to the detriment of my play. Some men play at least 6 hours of bridge a day. My feeling is that life is going to be hard and I intend to make myself as fit for the struggle as hard work can make me: cards are fun but not essential: it is our duty to learn. Also cards rather bore me: is it that I am not astute enough in counting the cards? I sit down with an inferiority complex and playing is like work, except that I learn nothing except how to count quick tricks! I went to the Padre's meeting and, though I can't get the faith required for praying, I put all my thoughts on to Mummy and I can really sit at the small, polished table which reflects so vividly the scene of Mums in her green chair, glasses before her eyes and knitting in her hands, listening to Uncle Mickie, who is reading from a detective novel with suitable emphasis and much laughter. Hitler made a speech of no compromise: when will it all end?

Monday November 11th

Armistice Day. I worked hard at a German exercise: the time flies by in an oblivious effort. An issue of Red Cross cheese and chocolate, which I fear was soon despatched: I cannot control myself at all, however many resolutions I make. I attended a lecture by Capt (Dr) Nicholls, a brain surgeon wearing a mammoth's unruly red beard: he is a man with a superhuman memory. Though medicine is his profession, he is well qualified to speak in detail upon any subject of which he has read. He spoke of the battles of Korsakov against Masséna:[304] his descriptions were so detailed that it was very difficult not to think of him as an eyewitness. Garrett's class developed into a discussion of general politics and he envisages a union between the right wing labour and left wing conservatives ie Churchill

---

302 William Ewart Gladstone (1809-1898), a British Liberal Statesman who served as Prime Minister 4 times.
303 Benjamin Disraeli (1804-1881), a British Prime Minister, Conservative Statesman, Parliamentarian and literary figure.
304 André Masséna (1758-1817), a French military commander during the Revolutionary and Napoleonic wars. He triumphed over the Russians under Alexander Korsakov at the Second Battle of Zurich in September 1799.

and Morrisson.[305] Two lots of pay were issued, 24 RMS.[306] I had by now started George Eliot's "Silas Marner":[307] an excellent though rather long drawn out style depicting very really the artisan class. Chamberlain's[308] death is reported. What a lot of misery he must carry on his shoulders.

Tuesday November 12th

The weather was and had been rainy and dreary, Garrett was on the Irish problem. George III, by his refusal to let the Catholics set up for election, caused an almost irretrievable grief and the accidental murder of Lord Cavendish[309] completely alienated sympathetic English opinion. Our policy forced the Land of Ireland. Never let anyone think that he has gained a diplomatic victory by a show of force. Silas Marner was a little heavy: early Victorian blissful conclusion. Perhaps life was not so difficult and characters were not so complex. Marner's change in character was taken from the parables of the little children: children can cause such a change. Laing gave his III ième République.[310] When Doumergue[311] could not call the Assemblé Nationale[312] together he resigned and, from thence forward, political life became one of self and party interest and the cause of nationalism, or even ideals of any kind were drowned in the wave of party, political power.

Wednesday November 13th

I attended Pope's German class: this man is married to a German and he could not speak a foreign language better. His views on modern life are most interesting and he is one of the leading Anti Juif.[313] Barrie Grayson gave us a lecture on Psychology in education: he has worked with the LCC[314] and is an expert in his way. Education is fitness for living – Child has born instincts: inquisitiveness and assertiveness and learns by experience. Brute intelligence lasts till 16, then brain acquires real knowledge. Intelligent Quotients obtained from questionnaires but at least 100,000 must be taken. Brain and hand must be made to work in coordination and no copying should be allowed to give rein to imagination e.g. wood with peg holes: child must use intelligence, patience and strength, children are graded. 8-11 is made to act, learn rhythm, to mime, 90% of MDs[315] cured by change of environment. Environment and parent influence is great factor. The system that allows slums and unemployment undermines the health and intelligence of its children. Now de Gaulle partisans have been interned. Italian planes are raiding England.

---

305 Herbert Stanley Morrison (1888-1965) was a British Labour Politician. He held a variety of senior positions in the Cabinet including Home Secretary, Foreign Secretary and Deputy Prime Minister.
306 German Reichsbanknote currency.
307 "Silas Marner, the Weaver of Raviloe", by Mary Anne Evans better known by her pen name, George Eliot, published in 1861.
308 Arthur Neville Chamberlain (1869-1940) British Conservative Politician who served as Prime Minister May 1937 – May 1940. He died of bowel cancer on 9 November 1940.
309 Lord Frederick Charles Cavendish (1836-1882), English Liberal Politician and Chief Secretary for Ireland.
310 French: Third Republic.
311 Pierre Paul Henri Gaston Doumergue (1863-1937) was a French Politician of the Third Republic.
312 French: National Assembly (=House of Commons).
313 French: anti-Semite.
314 London County Council, which was the principal local government for London from 1889 to 1965.
315 Medical diseases maybe?

Thursday November 14th

LG was on the causes of the South African war. Rhodes[316] was a great idealist but also a great holder in the S/A Coy.[317] He provoked Jameson's Raid[318] and lost the support of young Smuts.[319] Gladstone made peace before the utter defeat of the Boers in the first SA War: this was taken as weakness and the defeat of the Imperial forces. After Jameson's raid (financiers' coup to take govt of Jo'burg), the Boers put no more faith in England or J Chamberlain,[320] being convinced he was party to it. The early ill feeling was made by the slavery question and the false missionary reports. I was now reading "A Democrat Dies" by P Frankan:[321] it bears a resemblance to "Acorned Hog"[322] and is of a new political party, tired of self interested politicians and muddling diplomacy taking power. Molotov[323] is in Berlin and de Gaulle has captured Gabon.

Friday November 15th

A long walk along the deserted main road through undulating wooded country. At the Shakespeare Society, Langham gave a paper on the theatre in Shakespeare's day, dealing with the rivalry between the Lord Chamberlain's (Shakespeare's) players and the Lord Admiral's (Jonson's)[324] players. One good remark "Modern theatre has to compete with the cinema: 16th century drama had to compete with the plague". Italians counter attacking in Greece.

Saturday November 16th

Lovely moonlight nights, the Schloss[325] rigidly stereotyped against the sky. LG: the SA war was not a success until Kitchener[326] went out and we lost a great deal of prestige on the continent who, thinking that we were decadent, prepared to strike and did so in 1914: Kaiser[327] supported the Boers.

---

316 Cecil John Rhodes (1853-1902) was an English born South African business man, mining magnate and politician. An ardent believer in British Colonialism, he founded the South African territory of Rhodesia.
317 Military abbreviation: Company.
318 A botched raid by Leander Starr Jameson and his Rhodesian and Bechuanaland policemen which took place between 29 December 1985 and 2 January 1986 against Paul Kruger's Transvaal Republic. It was an inciting factor in the Second Boer War.
319 Jan Christiaan Smuts (1870-1950), a prominent South African and British Commonwealth Statesman, military leader and philosopher who served as Prime Minister in the Union of South Africa from 1919 to 1924 and again from 1939 to 1948.
320 Joseph Chamberlain(1836-1914), a British politician and statesman.
321 I have not been able to identify this book or author.
322 '"Acorned Hog" by James Ian Arbuthnot Frazer (1912-1966), published in 1933.
323 Vyacheslav Mikhailovich Molotov (1890-1986), a Soviet politician and diplomat and leading figure in the Soviet government from the 1920s.
324 i.e. Ben Jonson (1572-1637).
325 German: castle.
326 Field Marshal Horatio Herbert Kitchener (1850-1916).
327 Germany's Kaiser Wilhelm II (1859-1941).

Sunday November 17th

I read German with a French accent which I must cure: the rs particularly. The Smoking Concert was important for the first appearance of the Unterlager[328] Singers: their best song was the lovely melody "Over the sea to Skye".[329] Mansel, an architect who sports an exceedingly military moustache (mine incidentally is coming along very nicely and curling well!), gave a very amusing dumb sketch: the facial expression is superb. Grayson gave us a delightful Schubert[330] impromptu, a 16th Century highly technical, the favourite Turkish March of Mozart[331] and an attractive, melodious, nocturne by a young modern, Arthur Ralph.[332] I am enjoying my novel: what ideals do we want "True freedom, true peace, true justice, individual liberty and safety, culture and thought. For God and beauty and happiness". The Germans report a huge raid on Coventry.

Monday November 18th

MacLean, as usual, preached a good sermon: a story of Gadarene[333] swine. Did they detect a change in the spiritual atmosphere as animals often do? The attitude of the swineherds was more important: they saw the change in the maniac but they were afraid. Like many of us who realise the change, they feared what the change entailed and they preferred to remain as swine.

Our table, consisted of Jacobson, a Jewish South African doctor who had a very disagreeable voice, Bibbings, an amiable Yorkshire railway official, Holland, a long thin Oxford bookseller, with a charming manner and full of witty phrases, Shortman, a territorial QM[334] who loathed the whole world, (Bibbings, in particular, would draw blood from a stone and then say he had been cheated), Hash, Colin and myself. The usual conversation was the running down of fellow prisoners, of Shortman when he had left, of Red Cross parcels, their infrequency and their distribution and of when the next pudding was to be made: conversation that had limited constructive possibilities. The Germans report heavy raids on Hamburg and the Italians claim the torpedoing of a Ramillies class.[335]

The weather was now fine and cold. Our room has a very unsatisfactory heating accommodation and it is quite impossible to work there. The Speisesaal is warm but very noisy with someone crashing at the poor old piano. Still, I prefer warmth and noise, and I am teaching myself to shut my ears. I was able to swop some issue French cigarettes for jam: quite the Shylock.[336] I am very relieved that I am a non smoker. My comrades moan and search the floor for a cigarette stub and, if they are lucky enough to pick one up, they have to set out in search of a light, which may entail a room to room search. I started "The Story of an African Farm" by Olive Schreiner,[337] a story of Boer life in the 19th Century. The Germans announce the bombing of Waterloo Bridge, Paddington and other parts. We retaliated on Hamburg, Kiel and Bremen.

328	German: Lower Camp.
329	"The Skye Boat song", a Scottish folk song recalling the escape of Bonnie Prince Charlie from Uist to the Isle of Skye after his defeat at the Battle of Culloden in 1746.
330	Franz Peter Shubert (1797-1828), an Austrian composer.
331	More correctly known as the Turkish Rondo, the third movement from Piano Sonato No. 11 by Wolfgang Amadeus Mozart .
332	I have not been able to identify this composer.
333	A biblical story.
334	Military abbreviation: Quartermaster.
335	Possibly a reference to HMS Ramillies, a Revenge class Battleship of the Royal Navy.
336	A reference to Shylock, the Jewish usurer in Shakespeare's "The Merchant of Venice".
337	"The Story of an African Farm" by Olive Schreiner , a South African author and anti-war campaigner, published in 1883.

Tuesday November 19th

The walk was across the railway and up the hill: not a very original walk. The autumn tints are still in the trees and they flash effectively in the bright sun. A US Vice Consul came to look round but we had no chance of addressing him. I spend most of my spare time working at German and seem to be making some progress though it is a hard, unattractive language in sound and sight. I addressed the French circle speaking in French with the aid of a few brief notes. A resumé of my talk. France: May 1940 -. Ld Birkenhead anecdote. Introduction. Versailles a) civil effects b) military effects. 1. Sept 1939 – May 2. L'Armistice[338] 1. Effects on territory and people (a) Occupied Zone (b) Free Zone 2. Effect on Navy 3. Effects on army 3. Personal conclusion. La France, pays de la liberté où trop de liberté a comporté l'esclavage.[339] Italians say we had damaged 3 battleships: war in Greece may last 12 months. Mussolini's[340] remark "The great French army melted like snow in the sun when Italy put her army into the field".

Wednesday November 20th

Learnt the Pitman shorthand consonants from Bibbings: sounds not letters count. Nicholls, the doctor with the camera mind, gave us a very interesting lecture on the U.S. Constitution, in which country he was educated. Notes: certain powers reserved to Federal Govt (c.f. Australia, certain powers left to states) e.g. Post, War, Peace, communication, Federal Ct of Industry, House of Representatives: elected for 2 years and sits all the time (NB Wilson's 2nd term with opposition majority). Election on population basis: impeach Federal officers. 35 years of age. Senate: for 6 years, 1/3 change every 2 years. State representation as per state: power to ratify treaties! Standing committees are very strong (c.f. Civil service which does not change with Govt). <u>Executive</u>: President voted for by electoral colleges. Has veto but may be overruled by majority of House and Senate C in C of army, may appoint officers, declare state of war. He may not enter House and introduce party policy. <u>Judicial</u>: US Supreme Ct (Chief Justice + 8 judges for life. Power to decide a motion of constitutionality, guardian of constitution. Administrative. <u>Cabinet</u>: appointed by president but not members of congress: personal secretaries of President. <u>STATES.</u> Law except Federal, taxes except Federal supertax. State executive is governor elected by people and he appoints the state justice: much graft. Call out militia and Nat. Guard. <u>Democrats</u>: low tariffs, states rights (South form Democrat bloc since Civil War). War policy and Anti big business. They followed 3 big depressions. <u>Republicans</u>: Imperialism and Big business. Both parties are conservative but after 1931 a liberal movement e.g. unemployed, blacks, organised labour (i.e. J Lewis and unions of entire trade and not efficient few) moved towards Democrats who went over after Roosevelt had tried to suppress the old men (US Sup Ct judges) and Independents are getting socialist. General impression of politics for their own sake and the means justify the end. Olive Schreiner gives us Bonaparte Blenkins,[341] one of Dickens most displeasing characters could not equal him. Boris, a Hungarian minister in Berlin.[342] What will Turkey do?

---

338   French: The Armistice.
339   French: France, home of freedom or freedom has brought slavery (I think Desmond means enslavement rather than slavery, but it is difficult to say as his French is not so good here).
340   Benito Amilcare Andrea Mussolini (1883-1945), leader of Italy's National Fascist Party from 1922 to 1943.
341   A character in "The Story of an African Farm" previously referenced.
342   Possibly a reference to Tsar Boris III of Bulgaria who was in talks with Hitler around this time?

Thursday November 21st

A long walk along the main road and saw a German motorised column company doing manoeuvres: no other traffic. The fields are well cultivated and we saw a lot of ploughing in progress: the ploughs here are drawn by two oxen and sometimes by a horse and an ox, a very strange sight. We did about 5 miles and I was dead tired: this diet is not a strength building one. I spent the evening giving Major Roberts my paper that I read to the Circle. We discussed my inglorious part in the war: the after months may not be amusing for me but attack is the best policy and I must adopt it. The Germans bombed Birmingham losing 7 planes! Italians now fighting in Albania!

Friday November 22nd

Beards are coming off fast: at present I am shaving every other day. I went to the dentist, two small holes, one in my front tooth which is rather worrying. I went with a guard and while waiting in the road outside the dentist's neat, modern, wood covered house, I practised some German with rather indifferent success. After 1 ½ hours of waiting, I was taken into the wood panelled waiting room and after a few minutes I went into the surgery. The dentist, large and dark, resembling Victor McLagen[343], was very quick with his electric drill and I felt very little. He filled both the teeth and in a mixture of English and German and French told me that it was finished: it was all so quickly done that I have my fears as to its efficacy. The house looked comfortable and well furnished: there was, of course, the inevitable photograph. I spent most of the day copying out the title part of "Capt Brassbound's Conversion" by Shaw[344], which I am to play in the New Year. No English air loss reported: this state of things is quite often reported. The Italians were repulsing attacks. Parliament was opened and Churchill and Halifax[345] made speeches. Halifax spoke of new and better relations with the USSR (my first note book arrived through the Canteen).

Saturday November 23rd

At last a warm shower. I went to Bibbings' shorthand class and learned some grammalogs (ie signs for words). Garrett spoke of the rise in Germany from the fights of the early Teuton Knights against the Heathens in Poland till 1870. All Prussia's success has been due to military action and in 1807, when the land was brought up to modern standards, the university and the army were very closely linked. Bismarck[346] was a diplomat and after the Diet[347] in which Austrian independence was discussed, he became so tired of all the Democratic talk that he vowed he would do without a parliament. He was an arch schemer and always let his opponent declare war viz Napoleon III and he altered a telegram with no nervousness or shame. Compare the rotten state of France in 1870 and 1940. Hitler must have studied Bismarck. A variety concert compèred in dynamic style by F Fielding: his best joke "Hitler has sent telegram to God complaining of his non belligerent attitude in the Bucharest earth quake" (These have been very serious). Conjuring tricks in which razor blades were swallowed. Connors gave us some songs with

343 Victor McLagen (1886-1959) was an English boxer who later became a successful film actor.
344 "Captain Brassbound's Conversion" by George Bernard Shaw, published in 1899.
345 Edward Frederick Lindley Wood, 1st Earl of Halifax (1881-1959), was Foreign Secretary 1938-1940 and then served as British Ambassador to Washington 1940-1946.
346 Otto Von Bismarck (1815-1898), a conservative German Statesmen who was responsible for unifying most of the German States into a powerful German Empire.
347 An English name for continental parliaments.

his Pierrot[348] show technique: two lovely tenor songs from Smith who has a very sweet voice. The enthusiasm is very great at all these concerts. The Italians admit retreating into Albania with losses and admit water shortage "difficulties" in U Africa. The King spoke of our faithful allies, Turkey and Egypt.

Sunday November 24th

An extra half hour in bed: breakfast is 8.45, lunch 12.45, supper at 6. A very heavy frost and thick morning mist. As MacLean was ill, we had no service as no one else has permission to take a service. Every woman should study the outspoken girl character of Olive Schreiner. A cold lunch of bully, pickles and Red Cross plums, which were very pleasant. I got out a fine new book: "Vanished Pomps" by a diplomat, Lord Frederic Hamilton[349], several extracts "Prussia is the only country that has made war pay". "Prussians worship brute force and brute force alone". Bismarck "never trusted an Englishman who spoke French too well!" "Words are useful to paper over cracks". The Italians are making a strategic withdrawal. The air losses are negligible.

Monday November 25th

The air was much warmer again: a temperamental climate of extremes. Very little wind and strange to say, no bird life at all except for the ducks and geese who live in the little brook that runs under the Speisesaal window. I usually do a passage in shorthand as well as my German. Hamilton regrets that Peter the Great made the mistake of trying to westernise Russia too quickly. Russians are essentially Asiatic and corrupt. A rehearsal of "Capt Brassbound" with Langham. A play is a network of climaxes and one character must hold the audiences' imagination: unnecessary movement by a subsidiary character can spoil the whole play by losing the focus. We lost 11 planes against 7. The Italians have a defence line within Albania.

Tuesday November 26th

This morning's walk was a new one, along the railway line for about 3kms. We passed some troops on field training, all looking very cold and bored: not very different from us, with the officer trying to look intelligent and interested but with his thoughts on his food and evening's entertainment. Any long walk is most fatiguing. There was no traffic on the road and very little on the railway. The last 1940 meeting of the French circle was a comic debate on the respective merits of the "café" and the "pub". The general conclusion, arrived at in English, I fear, was that the café combined a drinking with a social centre, even a family centre, whereas the town "pub", unlike the country one was entirely an alcoholic concern. Bristol and Southampton bombed and a long denial of our bombing claims 24th/5th.

---

348   A stock character of pantomime, a sad clown.
349   "Vanished Pomps of Yesterday; being some random reminiscences of a British Diplomat" by Lord Frederick Hamilton, published in 1921.

Wednesday November 27th

The weather was bright, cold and frosty. I was working hard on my German still and concentrating on the German into English: I want to be able to read the paper not only here but also when I take up foreign journalism. Hamilton was full of amusing incidents in Portugal and South America. What a wonderful life must be a diplomat's: I must find out more about a lecture by Capt Jackson, our Kitchen Officer on "The Day in the life of a Stock Broker". A jobber is a specialist in his particular branch: he quotes two prices a)to buy from a broker b) to sell to a broker. The difference is his profit. Quotations are in fractions of £1 "Either side" = a closing to 1/16: "under the figure" = 1/32: the figure and under = 1/64. "Arbitrage" = broker gets early price on provincial market abroad and then buys before price rises. "A bull"= shares bought but not handed over. "A bear" = seller of shares which broker does not hold. 1 air loss. Italians claim annihilation of expeditionary force on the Epirus front.[350] British diplomatic activity in the Balkans.

Thursday November 28th

Wet and dull. PT had by now become voluntary and the attendances became less and less numerous: I always did it because I have a horror of slacking off. Whether I really like doing it, or, whether I do it because I think I should, is a question that I always ask myself. Garrett dealt with Germany till 1914. Austria's violent war policy of extension in the Balkans and Russia's fear of a second outburst from her Slav population, an outburst that would have been more serious than that of 1910 on the occasion of Andrássy's[351] treachery, were instrumental in bring about an "impasse". Kaiser Wilhelm was a violent "wind bag" and was surprised to see his speeches taken seriously: it is certain that the GHQ's of Austria and subsequently Germany forced the war: Kaiser's sign or abdicate situation on his return from cruise. GHQ feared 1916 as year of Russian reorganisation. Did Hitler and the army precipitate this war knowing that our peak year was 1942? How unstable and dangerous is it to be a citizen: propaganda makes it worthwhile and gives that dynamic feeling of righteousness. The afternoon walk was as before and, though it was cold and damp, it was nevertheless invigorating, both from the physical as well as the mental point of view: barbed wire and mud get rather monotonous and the sight of so many of the same faces is almost unbearable: work is the only relaxation. I started, but soon put down "400 million customers",[352] a book full of admiration for the author's advertising ability which, if it were as good as his writing technique, would probably have difficulty in selling chocolate to POWs even though he seemed to have great success and this is rubbed in, in selling cigarettes, pins, safety and drawing, to ignorant Chinamen. An American from Ass Press is reported to have said that we are in great need of financial support from USA and that the U Boat menace was as acute as in 1917. David Feilding's war news: his only revolver ammunition was that one cartridge which he had won at poetry poker. He got to France on May 8th and never found his RE[353] unit.

350   A region in south eastern Europe shared between Greece and Albania.
351   Gyula Andrássy the Younger (1860-1929), Minister of the Interior of Hungary 1906-1910.
352   "400 Million Customers" by Carl Crow, published in 1937.
353   Military abbreviation: Royal Engineers.

Friday November 29th

This morning we had some snow but the wet slushy snow that does not stay. I broke my little red celuloid razor given to me at the Pionnier's[354] Camp but have gained a Gillette, as Colin is not shaving now and has a wispy beard. We got some dates at the Canteen, old and shop soiled, but most acceptable: it's more profitable for the Gs to sell them to us rather than throw them away. On a visit to the infirmary to see Barrie, I made the acquaintance of Antony Neave[355] a young Middle Temple barrister (Eton and Merton, where he knew Colin Sleeman[356]) and we talked over old friends: he thinks we may have to take our exams again! Talked about the bar with Bibbings, red nosed, true blue, North country middle class. I started A P Herbert's "Water Gypsies"[357]: a light hearted airy story of every day characters full of that spontaneous humour and tragedy that separates the true from the theatrical. Our 35 Scottish comrades had a St Andrew's night dinner. Italians report a naval action South of Sardinia. Plymouth bombed. A denial of Cologne raid.

Desmond after he qualified in 1939

354   French: Pioneer's (camp), known to the Germans as Frontstalag 133.
355   Desmond has made a mistake here with the Christian name. This was, in fact, Airey Neave (1916-1979), who was at Eton, Merton and Middle Temple, as Desmond confirms. He was a prisoner at Spangenberg until February 1941 and was then moved to Stalag XX-A near Thorn, Poland. In April 1941 he escaped from Thorn but was recaptured and sent to Oflag IV-C at Colditz Castle. He escaped from Colditz in January 1942 and made it to neutral Sweden. Airey Neave was the Conservative MP for Abingdon from 1953 to 1979. He served as Shadow Secretary of State for Northern Ireland under Margaret Thatcher. He was killed on 30th March 1979 as he left the Palace of Westminster by a car bomb planted by the Irish National Liberation Army.
356   Colin Sleeman (1914-2006) was a British Judge.
357   "The Water Gypsies" by A P Herbert, published in 1930.

Saturday November 30th

A very heavy frost and the wash house is so cold: I still strip to the waist but many wash fully dressed, one even in his overcoat: what price the dirty French? There are a few cold shower fanatics, hoping to get repatriated on a lunacy idea. Garrett was on pre-war internal politics. Conservatives till 1906 with Lord Salisbury[358] and then liberals under C Bannerman:[359] Asquith,[360] The Parliament Act 1911 and LG's insurance bills. Winston was against the large Navy but once in the cabinet proceeded to increase the Fleet. What a form of government for the honest man in the street: is the man in the street honest even though he tells himself that he is? Vol II of Nine A News[361] appeared which was quite fun. Two plays, "Man of Destiny" by Shaw[362], the costumes were really magnificent and Garrett was a very imposing and life-like Napoleon: he fortunately did not overact this dominating part. "The Monkey's Paw" by WWJ[363] was quiet and impressive. A newly arrived Padre gave us latest news from France and RAF. The same petrol burning story and invasion defeat of Sept 15th, we heard the story in August and it was heard here in July: these are known as Abort[364] rumours. Little damage in the East End and civilian morale is high. News of raids on Plymouth: 13 English 3 English lost. German destroyers in action in channel.

Sunday December 1st

The night had been terribly cold and shaving was almost impossible owing to the numbness of my cold hands: my circulation is very poor these days. MacLean preached a fine sermon: now is the time to ponder over the important and unimportant things of everyday life: how well this life of monotony tells us what we really need; work, thought and good entertainment. The day was bright and mostly clear. I spent a lazy afternoon reading the Water Gypsies. The new moon was worshipped: my wish was my constant one, that of receiving good news from home. The sunset was perfect: a sky intermingled with orange, red and a deep blue green above the pines. The cold in bed was intense and I dressed myself in long Czech pants and French canvas trousers as well. Raids on Plymouth and Bristol but only 2.2 losses. RAF shot down plane carrying Chiappe[365] the new French High Commissioner to Syria: he was préfet[366] of Paris in 1934 and he acted very high handedly: what consequences? I wrote to my American friend Kate of Rennes via the Belgian Red Cross.

---

358   Robert Gascoigne Cecil (1830-1903), known as Lord Salisbury, British Conservative Statesman and thrice Prime Minister.
359   Sir Henry Campbell-Bannerman (1836-1908), a British Liberal Party politician who served as Prime Minister from 1905 to 1908.
360   Herbert Henry Asquith (1852-1928), British Liberal Party politician who served as Prime Minister from 1908 to 1916.
361   Other sources confirm this was a POW camp magazine.
362   "The Man of Destiny" by George Bernard Shaw, published in 1897.
363   "The Monkey's Paw" by W W Jacobs, published in 1903.
364   German: latrines (i.e. latrine rumours).
365   Jean Baptiste Pascal Eugène Chiappe (1878-1940) was a high ranking French Civil Servant, Chief Commissioner of the Paris Police in the 1930s and high commissioner of France in the Levant. In Autumn 1940, the aircraft he was travelling in to Lebanon was shot down by mistake by Italian planes taking part in the Battle of Taranto.
366   French: Chief Commissioner of the Paris Police.

Monday December 2nd

It was very cold (-9) and the wash basins were full of ice. A few of us started reading Molière's "Malade Imaginaire",[367] amusing but blatant, written in very simple French. Garrett's lecture was on Jutland: his is the Anti Beatty[368] school and it certainly seems that he acted most rashly e.g. in not waiting for a signed receipt before his run South. The enemy gunnery was very good and we lost two ships from magazine explosions (this is impossible nowadays). The heavy frost produced a wonderful sky effect, this evening the dominant colour was mauve. A terrific table quarrel, the outcome of which was that Bibbings stayed with us and we were joined by Mac, Smith and Anthonie: old Shortman and Jacobson caused a lot of trouble. The Germans made a heavy press attack on Switzerland: is this the usual technique? Only 1 British Legion parcel a month now.

Tuesday December 3rd

It was warmer though still freezing. G finished Jutland: Beatty was brave, impetuous and born after his real time: he had the advantage of being supported by Winston and the journalists, though modern writers are rather inclined to support Jellicoe[369], whose command at windy corner was brilliant. A new walk in the afternoon, along the course of the brook, along a cart track which wound over the hills, always climbing, until we reached the altitude of the Schloss.[370] The sun was very warm but the snow still lay thick on the high ground. Our guards never let us near any woods and a pleasant walk is often spoiled by the bad pace. Our identity photos were taken and we also had a Guernsey group. Smith made a grand entrance by giving us a Brot pudding:[371] bread soaked in water, potatoes and a few figs, sugar and saccharin to flavour. These puddings take about 15 bits of bread, laboriously saved from other meals, a whole issue of fat and sugar, but they are worth it. I started Conrad's "Arrow of Gold".[372] He has fine descriptive power and makes the unseen heroine live, she is alive and full of mystery. The plot is of the Carlist[373] rebellions of 1870s. Heavy raid on Southampton, 2 British and 2 German losses! We bombed Italy hard. Goebbels[374] admitted that it would be sometime before England was defeated. I wrote to Aunty Wendy, J de Fontenay and Bh with a message for Aunty. Saving my other two letters to reply to home letters!

---

367 "Le Malade Imaginaire" ("The Imaginary Invalid") by Molière, published in 1673.
368 David Richard Beatty (1871-1936), a Royal Navy Officer who commanded the 1st Battlecruiser Squadron in the Battle of Jutland in 1916.
369 John Rushworth Jellicoe (1859-1935), a Royal Navy Officer who commanded the Grand Fleet at the Battle of Jutland in 1916.
370 German: castle.
371 German: Bread pudding.
372 "The Arrow of Gold" by Joseph Conrad, published in 1919.
373 i.e. The Third Carlist War
374 Paul Joseph Goebbels (1897-1945) was a German politician and Reich Minister of Propaganda in Nazi Germany from 1933 to 1945.

Desmond Mulholland, Captain Connors (Hash) and Douglas McCleod taken at Oflag IXA on 3rd December 1940.

Wednesday December 4th

A lengthy pay parade: we received 24 LGM[375] as the half pay reprisal has been lifted. My shorthand seems to be making some progress as does the German. I spent this afternoon on my new Italian grammar which had just arrived from Johannesbrunn: Valéry's tuition has been most valuable and I am concentrating first on learning words. Holland gave us a lecture on Books and their selling. Novel writing, regular output of 1000 words a

---

375   i.e. Lagergeld Marks (POW currency).

day is necessary. Financially, speed more important than style. Have MS[376] professionally typed. Submit to an agent who corrects and suggests a publisher. Sign MS with total number of words (Stanley Unwin book on publishing[377]). Learn correctors' proof marks. Libraries are most important customers. Book collecting Modern First, CONDITION counts. Old books, age is no criterion. Original bindings, wide margins and complete + blank pages. A good informal talk full of unconscious witticisms. Heavy Southampton raids: 1 German loss, 16 ships sunk in an Atlantic convoy and a merchant cruiser, Caledonia.[378] French Syrian army may stand with de Gaulle while Turkey is leading a Balkan group.

Thursday December 5th

Another good fall of snow and I postponed shaving till after Appell. A great treat with a square inch of beef! My book is most entertaining: the descriptions are colourful but always manage to keep a sense of mystery. I get very tired here even though I seem to do very little: perhaps it is the feeling of never ending monotony. I feel terribly sorry for the fellows who just sit at cards all day long: they look so miserable. The increase of pay has brought with it a great many gambling schools. I'm not gambling: firstly, I have too much to do and secondly I get rather bored with cards and gambling always makes me frightened and I don't enjoy it. Raid on Bristol and Southampton but no losses reported: the Italians are in the same positions.

Friday December 6th

There was a heavy fall of snow during the night. Our orderly brought up some tea and I shared a jug with my two neighbours, Arthur Watts, R W Kents, and Capt Duggie Harris, RASC.[379] They are both rankers[380] and extraordinarily good hearted fellows and I may say that their behaviour and especially their language makes me wonder what benefit a public school education is to the average young man. Their home life is most pleasant and they live on the best of terms with their families at all times: it has been a pleasure to be next to these two real soldiers. I received my first letter: it was from Zabette and had come from the Langendorf Camp: it was one of my class, a Jeweller from the Place St Pierre[381] who had written to her. News was good and the "copains"[382] are back at the "A". She is sending me a parcel a month. Smith got a letter from Jersey dated Oct 25th. We must hear soon. I wish mine had been from home. I got ink and paper from the Canteen and started writing up this diary. The Air losses were 3.3 with raids on London. The Italian news is now very limited. England has a trade agreement with Turkey and has called a Pan Islam conference in Egypt. France has made a levy of manpower in Tunis. I am suffering terribly from chilblains on my left foot. It must be due to undernourishment. I now sleep with socks on, or, what is left of them, for my only two pairs are almost unwearable for the holes.

---

376 Presumably short for manuscript?
377 "The Truth about Publishing" by Sir Stanley Unwin, published in 1926.
378 The Caledonia was converted to an armed military cruiser and renamed HMS Scotstoun, which was sunk by a German U-boat in June 1940, not December?
379 Military abbreviation: Royal Army Service Corps.
380 A Ranker is a Commissioned Officer who entered service as a recruit.
381 Possibly Place St Pierre in Guernsey?
382 French: friends, pals.

Saturday December 7th

We went through the Treaty of Versailles[383] at Garrett's lecture. Germany was humiliated (Bismarck never let this be his policy) and the economic purpose and the shortsightedness of the USA were perhaps the causes of this war (Bismarck always said that a defeated nation should be made to accept an indemnity and not pay one). A Variety Show at 7.30 with the Unterlager[384] singers in negro spirituals and sea shanties, the favourite "Mountains of Mourne"[385] by Capt Booth, this officer's life revolves around pig farming and it is his sole topic of conversation. Doc Gorrie put on a screamingly funny Eastern sketch. Smith gave us some charming drawing room songs and Barrie played a Chopin[386] Nocturne and Weber's "Invitation to the Waltz".[387] News: 10.7 air losses in Germany's favour. Only a mention of Albanian front. Empire conference to be held shortly. Four new arrivals came from Belgium with the usual rumours: that Italians have left Albania and that we have made a landing in Italy: 5 attacks on England and all repulsed. Announced on English radio not on Oct 15th. We are absolutely cut off and the war seems so abstract and this life so endless.

Sunday December 8th

MacLean gave us a sermon on Hope for a golden age to come, not always a golden age that has been. A race meeting was held in the afternoon. The race game is on in which horse moves are on cards and there is a rotation: each jockey is given a whip and with skilful use of it, that is by noting the cards, he can usually avoid the water jump. I was working on the Tote and we made 50 RMs profit. I read "Frederick the Great"[388] from my newly arrived book of Macaulay's Essays. The style is simple and clear: I always remember Grandpa's admiration of Macaulay and I concur with him: I wish he were alive still and we could discuss the essays. I read some of Jane Austen's "Pride and Prejudice":[389] full of charming conversations and so very true: it is all so very nice.

Monday December 9th

A number of doctors left us for work in a hospital: they were a very cheery crowd and we shall miss them: I don't think that they are to be repatriated. Paverner, a very intelligent and friendly man, gave me his German reader for which I was very grateful. Lovel lectured on Geography in relation to History, stressing the importance of the Balkan gates and how easy it was to enter and invade Italy but how difficult it is to operate offensively from within that land. I painted my feet with Dr Scholl's ointment which I think will be successful.

---

383 One of the peace treaties at the end of World War I, it ended the state of war between Germany and the Allied Powers. It was signed on 28th June 1919.
384 German: Lower Camp.
385 "Mountains of Mourne" written by an Irish musician, Percy French.
386 Frédéric Chopin (1810-1849), a Polish composer and virtuoso pianist. Chopin wrote several Nocturnes.
387 "Invitation to the Dance" (often known as" Invitation to the Waltz") written by Weber in 1819.
388 Frederick The Great and his times" by Thomas Babington Macaulay, published in 1842.
389 "Pride and Prejudice" by Jane Austen, published in 1813.

"Frederick the Great": notes. The King of Prussia had already determined to break his plighted faith "Ambition, interest, the desire of making people talk about me carried the day and I decided for war". Guarantees, he said, were mere filigree, pretty to look at, but too little to bear the slightest pressure. Great civil tolerance. Benevolent despotism. We could make shift to live under a debauchee or a tyrant: but to be ruled by a busybody is more than a human can bear.

Tuesday December 10th

Today it was the Geographical position of France in the History lecture. France's European and Colonial ties did not help France to perform either of them with unquestionable success. The sea is no barrier to ideas but the sea provides an inherent fear and people will only take to the sea if their land is not sufficiently fertile. Extracts from KRs[390] were read after lunch and I felt very relieved: a POW shall only be court martialled if captured through his own misconduct or neglect. A great meeting to re-elect the Entertainments Committee who had resigned owing to undercurrent opposition against their producing "Journey's End".[391] They were re-elected for they represent all the camp talent and the meeting was "Much Ado about nothing".[392] A walk along the main road with a bitterly cold wind. I sent two Christmas cards, one to Aunty and one to Mummy. I finished "Frederick the Great": the style is delightfully easy whereas the horror of the seven years war is fascinating in its awfulness. A heavy raid on London, 2 German losses. Italians retreating to prepared positions. A letter in The Times "I am a POW, have good food and good beds: tell this to my army, navy and marine friends, especially the Marines".

Wednesday December 11th

As there is no organised PT now I do some in the gym, that is a room set apart for ping pong! I started reading an old Frankfurter Zeitung[393] to pick up the style and the words. I read "Dr Johnson",[394] another of Macaulay's essays: a strange character suffering from physical troubles which embittered him but did not prevent him from working to overcome his hardships. We had a HAT night in the Speisesaal: that is six subjects placed in one hat and six names in another. Old Bishop, a dear old gentleman of the Salvage Corps[395] who was never told of the retreat and so became a Gefangener,[396] made us laugh by telling us "How I spend my days". Two other men disappointed us, one on "My profession", a clerk in the Rumanian Oil Coy,[397] and a typical one at that. The other on "My favourite Sport" Rugby Football: "it is grand", was all this articulate gentleman could say. Dr MacKay, with his charming Highland voice, told us of "Modern Dress" and two debateable subjects were taken, "Should women use cosmetics?" voted Yes. "Is birth control to be desired?" voted: Yes, so that returning POWs can have long waited

---

390   Military Abbreviation: The King's Regulations; a collection of orders and regulations in force in the Royal Navy, British Army and Royal Air Force, forming guidance for officers of these armed services in all matters of discipline and personal conduct.
391   "Journey's End", a drama by R C Sherriff premiered in 1928.
392   A reference to Shakespeare's comedy "Much Ado about nothing".
393   A German language newspaper that appeared from 1836 to 1943.
394   "Dr Johnson and his times" by Thomas Babington Macaulay.
395   The Salvage Corps came into existence in the 19th century and emphasised salvaging property after the regular firemen had done their job.
396   German: Prisoner, captive.
397   Abbreviation: Company.

fun without making themselves prisoners again. I continued "Pride and Prejudice" and felt like strangling the piously irreligious Mr Collins. News: the Italians still retreating.

Thursday December 12th

12 new doctors, including a French man, a Niçois[398] working in the Paris hospitals: he was captured in the Vosges[399] and has been sent from camp to camp, always to be sent back to France: the journey is long and almost unending. He was very impressed by the good organisation of the camp and he is very pleased and impressed to see how, unlike his own countrymen, we are able to live together without disputing violently over all problems, from Foreign policy to food (very foreign to us). He agreed that France had learned a hard but deserved lesson and he had some nasty remarks about Gamelin[400] and the French GHP.[401] His name is Lt Vissier and he has a Jewish, dark, appearance but as he is an ardent Catholic and anti Juif, his looks belie him. Lovel spoke about Spain: the Catholic intolerances can be put down to the continual crusade against the Moors. Spain also was hindered by having both a foreign and colonial commitment. The Catalans, due to their sea coast life and contact with foreign culture, were and are a democratic and tolerant people whereas the Castilians, cut off in their mountain pastures, are feudal and intolerant. News: The Italians retreated in Libya and lost a general. Rumours of Roosevelt compromise when he gives our War arms on Jan 4th?

Friday December 13th

Two letters came from Jersey, dated Oct 30th and Nov 5th, but still nothing from Guernsey. Red Cross parcels have been floating in: about time too, when we have had only 7 in 6 months for £5,000,000 subscribed. 10 orderlies left us, one, Dobson, very cunningly collected addresses. I wonder when we shall hear from him again. The rooms were impossibly cold as the central heating system had broken down. I attended the final talk on "Othello", slightly high brow for me but an interesting argument on whether a tragedy should finish at the top of its curve or on a downward curve? Italians still retreating in Libya.

Saturday December 14th

There are 120 parcels up now and we can look forward to Monday. A notice was read from the paper saying that Klippfisch[402], of which our fishcakes are made, can be kept for ten years and a note Red Cross, please copy. A flash back variety programme. Community singing. Barrie gave us an Aunt Jane radio talk. John Mansel, one of his dumb sketches, this time at the cinema with his girl, Langham, a pre-war speech in the Oliver Wakefield[403] manner, a skit on the Canteen: if you are a friend of the firm, you can be sure of beer! Pure singing and dancing in the best Tyrolean manner and two sketches by the new lads. A sketch must have smut to go down really well here and, if either of the usual conversation words (F G or B) are used, there are hoots of laughter: and here we are supposed to

398   French: a person from Nice, France.
399   A department in the east of France.
400   Maurice Gustave Gamelin (1872-1958), a French General remembered for his unsuccessful command of the French Military in the Battle of France in 1940.
401   I have not been able to identify the meaning of this acronym.
402   German: dried cod.
403   Oliver Wakefield (1909-1956), a popular British actor and comedian.

have the flower of English manhood. The moon was unnaturally bright, thrusting the Schloss upon us against its background of electric starlight. German raids on Sheffield. Italians retreating fast. A wire from Italy bemoaning the unpatriotic spirit of the wealthy.

Sunday December 15th

It was bitterly cold: shaving was almost an impossibility as my hands had swollen up and become red lumps of agony. The singing was very lusty in church as we had words written out. The Padre gave a fine quotation from Emerson,[404] when he addressed Dartmouth College:-[405] ***[406] Walking in the yard made my hands so cold that I could have screamed with agony: 16of frost and very little to eat. In the afternoon there was a reading of "Measure for Measure"[407] a bawdy but comic play. I took Lucio, a stupid, tactless courtier. I played some bridge with Major Roberts and two majors in their comfortable little room. I did not play too badly and managed to come away with 90 pfgs,[408] at 5 pfgs a 100. Our lights went out because of an air raid and I heard with a thrill the faint hum of an engine. We see and hear very little air activity in this region. The Italians are well behind the Libyan frontier and well on the run.

Monday December 16th

I passed a cold, uncomfortable night and found most of the taps frozen up. We received our parcels and it was heaven to eat milk chocolate again, my parcel had: cheese, condensed milk, Lingfold milk and treacle in mine. The whole camp atmosphere changed and smiles replaced those depressed worried looks. Still, I'd rather receive a letter from home than any parcel. 15 of frost but dry, clean cold. A deal of hot air was talked about the CO after the resignation of the Mess Committee on account of the CO's high handed action on the distribution of parcels: the fireworks are to come! The Italians admit the bombing of Naples and the hitting of two battleships. The Italians have retreated 130kms in Libya.

Tuesday December 17th

21 of frost this morning and icicles all over the taps. At 10 we went for a lovely walk along the railway and back through the village: this latter, with its narrow streets, old carved houses and little monster faced gargoyles, was absolutely deserted: no shops open and no shoppers: a wet Sunday could not have made it more deserted. We came back along the canal to see the little children in their brightly coloured pixie bonnets, skating and tobogganing on the ice. Would the whole world were children playing on the ice! Unfortunately, the older we grow, the thinner becomes the ice and periodically we fall into the cold abyss: the crack splits the whole structure and it is very difficult to repair the damage: only a hard frost can do the repairing. The evening sky was once again full of red green tints. Our bread supply was late and it was not till 8.30 that we sat down. "Pride and Prejudice" was nearly

---

404   Ralph Waldo Emerson (1803-1882), an American essayist, lecturer and poet who led the Transcendentalist Movement of the mid 19th century.
405   Dartmouth College, a member of the Ivy League founded in 1769.
406   Desmond leaves a space here obviously intending to insert the quotation at a later time.
407   "Measure for Measure", a play by William Shakespeare written in 1603 or 1604.
408   German: abbreviation of Pfennig, a minor coin of the Mark currency.

over and all was turning out happily in spite of the tactlessness of Mrs Bennet[409] and the foolishness of Kit:[410] what a common type is Mrs Bennet. The Mess Committee have withdrawn their resignation and all is well. Once again "Much ado about nothing".

Wednesday December 18th

A lecture on banking by Capt Edwards who is a big man in the Westminster Bank Head Office. He told us how banks dispose of their surplus money to brokers, how overdrafts and loans are regulated and gave us strong advice against acting as a guarantor. I had a walk with Beckwith, a great long streak in the Foresters: he is in Imperial Tobacco[411] in peace time. He drew my attention to a little house in the village which looks like the fairy tale sugar cake with its frosted windows and green and white colouring. The frost and the heavenly sky colours turned the whole village into a fairy tale and the old bow legged woman crossing the little bridge with a stick in her hand and a goose leading her completes the picture. David Feilding, a second son of the Earl of Denbigh, a qualified mining engineer, gave us a talk on mining and investments. This industry has made and lost a great deal of money for speculators. He told us of the frauds that can be perpetrated, especially in the taking of assays by syringing gold dust into them, dropping gold filled cigarette ash into them and even shooting gold dust from a shotgun into the mine face. The Canadian miners are not slow off the mark and make plenty of margin money by covering information. Very little activity but high praise of Sheffield's defences from an American source.

Thursday December 19th

I spent the morning translating a leader hinting that we should demand entry into the United States! It is long work but I must persevere. We had a long wait for Appell in the snow, our room was like an icebox so I had to sit in the corridor, smelling with damp clothes. I read Macaulay's essay on "Bertrand Barère": a great insight into the revolutionary character though it was written as an attack on a justification of Barère. I also started to read "Cranford"[412] by Mrs Gaskell: perhaps rather a sameness after "Pride and Prejudice": though rather more rural.

Friday December 20th

It was a glorious morning, biting cold and clear. The village is lovely in the sunny snow: the children tobogganing and skiing down the hill behind us have great fun: the milkman now goes his round in a sledge, his horse tinkling with little bells. I wrote to Nanny after supper and then read some Shelley which had just arrived. I love "Ode to a nightingale".[413] I read on "Cranford": it is rather tedious on the whole but occasionally gives quite an amusing anecdote e.g. the Alderney cow in his vest and pants and poor old Capt Brown's death caused by his earnest perusal of Pickwick. Italians are holding the attack: a French regiment fought very well.

---

409   A character in "Pride and Prejudice".
410   A character in "Pride and Prejudice".
411   Imperial Tobacco, founded in 1901, based in Bristol.
412   "Cranford" by Elizabeth Gaskell, published in 1851.
413   "Ode to a Nightingale", a poem by John Keats (not Shelley as Desmond believes) written in 1819.

Saturday December 21st

12 Gold Flake fetched 50 marks at an auction, 7/6 each. The cold was still just as intense. It was too cold to walk, a raging northerly wind swept the snow off the roofs in a blizzard. We had a rehearsal of a Nativity play written by MacLean and the music by Barrie Grayson. The words were few and impressive, the whole play relied on tableau and lighting. I got rather tired of "Cranford" and started reading "Private Faces" by Harold Nicholson MD:[414] it is the story of an imaginary crisis, of how the smallest details and delay can bring public opinion into play. It is a show up of Democratic muddling and is too appallingly true. The style is bright and amusingly descriptive, though rather journalese, a succession of qualifying phrases instead of a good simple adjective. We heard the RAF planes and the detonations were very heavy: I wonder if we have hit any hospitals!

Sunday December 22nd

The wind was cutting through, a real winter's day. I spent most of the day reading my novel, a book for democrats to read, learn and inwardly digest. Smith received a letter dated Nov 15th but still nothing from Guernsey, no papers but news that the Bank of England has been hit. It must be terrible for the women and children to have to spend their nights in these uncomfortable shelters: it is extraordinary and rather awful to think that we are still safe, though perhaps our daily living conditions are not so pleasant.

Monday December 23rd

I did not work today but spent my time writing up my diary and reading my book: it is excellent political satire and the moral to be drawn is don't put off any important decision, and if a decision is to be made, make a definite one. The weather is still very cold and the snow is thick, clean and crisp. The Italians are in serious trouble, two divisions covering their retreat into Bardia[415] which is now surrounded so it is just a matter of days.

---

414 Desmond has made a mistake here. The novel is called "Public Faces" by Harold George Nicholson and was published in 1932.
415 Bardiyah, a Mediterranean seaport in the Butnan district of eastern Libya.

Tuesday December 24th

30 of frost this morning and I set out on the walk with a borrowed Balaclava, a pair of gloves and a pair of mittens that Major Roberts very kindly gave me. I was wearing long pants now and also a very good Red Cross vest that I had got from a communal parcel. We went a new walk, through a snow bound little village and the village trough looked so cold, and up a steep slippery path to a plateau from where we got a wonderful view of the Schloss, shrouded in the morning mist: the castle is placed right on the pinnacle and gives me the impression of Mt St Michel,[416] the snow looking like a foaming sea. In the evening the Nativity play was produced in 4 scenes 1) An inn scene culminating in a tableau of the Inn Keeper and two citizens gazing at the supernatural light pouring through the doorway. 2) The shepherds in the fields and the visitation by the angel. 3) Herod's court with the visits of the priests and the Kings (I was the second King). The costumes were simple and most effective. 4) The Adoration, a tableau of the shepherds and the Kings. The lighting and lovely music made a most impressive and sincere production. We sang communal carols with great vigour and a quartet sang some lovely part carols, so passed a hearty, joyful evening: an attempt to forget loneliness and it was only when the quietness of the night fell upon me that I thought of those I loved: it has taken this war to make me realise how dear Le Paradou[417] is to me. It is terrible, this absence of news: I have just to hope and pray. The news brought back the war: Liverpool was heavily bombed and Bardia was in serious difficulties.

CHRISTMAS DAY Wednesday December 25th

We were all up bright and early and the wash places overflowed with unfamiliar faces. The air rang with cheerful greetings: the spirit of Christmas was upon us: whether because of better food or because it was Christmas day, the day symbolic of good will to all men: the day when the advocate of love and charity, the two cardinal thoughts of joy, was born. I like to think that we were moved by a real spirit of joy. The Speisesaal was decorated with mistletoe, Christmas trees and silver tangled greenery: its usual dirty sameness seemed to have given birth to a festive home and I kept expecting Santa Claus to appear and give us all presents: but no Santa and no laughing kiddies. Our breakfast was a sight for sore eyes, sausage, bacon and fried potatoes, better appreciated than all your morning eggs, kidneys and mushrooms. I spent the interim between breakfast and church, walking up and down the snow covered yard and looking at my first white Christmas.

Church was a joyful service, though I suddenly felt sad and homesick thinking of those mornings in St Martin's Church and then the drive up to the Paradou: I am sentimental and perhaps enjoy my sadness: that does not make me less concerned for the safety of those I hope for. I did so hope to have a letter by this Christmas day. Immediately after church I wrote to Mummy and told her how I missed them all: she must get the letter. Lunch was gargantuan, a whole tinned steak and kidney pudding each, peas, potatoes then a Brot pudding. The toasts of "The King", with musical honours, and "Absent Friends" were drunk in rather inferior Rhine wine (2 bottles between 3) but this made no difference to the

416   A rocky tidal island, a commune in Normandy, France.
417   "Uncle Mickie's house in Guernsey (see Introduction).

spirit in which they were drunk. There was nothing else to be done but go to sleep: this increase of heavy food had made me quite incapable of any movement. I walked hard after Appell and at 5.30 we sat down to supper, an hors d'oeuvre and a huge trifle made of bread soaked in jam and Ovaltine[418] and covered with whipped cream formed by beating margarine, sugar and condensed milk. It was Smith's triumph and I fear we were defeated. After supper came the Elbersdorf[419] fun fair opened by the Duchess (impressively played by Barrie). Here was Crown and Anchor races,[420] roulette, a treasure hunt, spot the Lady,[421] a jumble sale, darts and many other games of chance. I ran a dart game which I named Dart Geld,[422] it was necessary to pierce a 5 mark note three times to win 10 marks. I was all square on the evening: I should have been in hand but one of the orderlies got the knack with consequent disaster for my business. At 9.30 marmite and we all returned, noisy and weary, to our beds. A wonderful day under the circumstances and it is interesting to note that the Authorities had provided us with 7 slices of bread, 6 potatoes and a piece of Blut Wurst[423] for the whole day. The news was cheering. Bardia is about to fall and Graziani[424] has bemoaned the fact that England has put all her might into the field against poor little Italy. Churchill made a tactfully timed speech to the Italian people, saying that one man was to blame for their present position. So to the replete snores of 35 Gefangeners,[425] I fell asleep. So passed Christmas Day 1940. What shall I write in 1941?

Thursday December 26th

I spent my day, a wet snowy day, working as an orderly so that they might have the day free for their pantomime. 9 of us were working: after lunch I cleaned and washed the tables, swept the floor and dried the cutlery. The tables get filthy after every meal and it is impossible to get any form of oil cloth. After supper I washed up the dishes: it was a quick supper, for as well as handing out the tea, I had to clear out the room. The pantomime produced by 2nd Lt Kelso, a young Sheffield school master who was badly wounded in Norway, produced Dick Whittington, having the orderlies as his actors: the words were his own and the music and scenery was by Grayson. The highlight of the pantomime was little Titch (about 4ft high) as a very well disguised cat. The cast was of about 30 and the lines, said in a colourless cockney monotone, were killingly funny, "I won't, I won't marry that old man." Sergt Gray, as Widow Twanky, has a Scotch accent that must be heard to be believed. The singing of soulful songs was appalling to hear: sweet oozy sentimentality sung out of tune and with earnest passion. A huge success at troops' concerts. Still, we had a very good laugh and I thoroughly enjoyed the evening. We cleaned the room up when it was all over and then Capt Jackson gave us a treat of scrambled eggs, made from powder, but they tasted very good to me. The evening was much warmer as I left off my socks. No news as the papers did not come up.

Friday December 27th

We had a very long cross country walk, through snow bound fields and up ice covered roads made perilous by the children's tobogganing. The difficult walking conditions made us all very warm and I was most fatigued when,

418	A hot chocolate malt drink.
419	The location of the Lower Camp, Spangenberg.
420	An army gambling game.
421	Possibly "Find the Lady", a three card game.
422	German: (Dart) money.
423	German: Blood sausage (similar to black pudding).
424	Rodolfo Graziani (1882-1955) was one of Mussolini's military commanders in the Italian colonial wars taking place in Libya and Ethiopia before and during WW2.
425	German: prisoners.

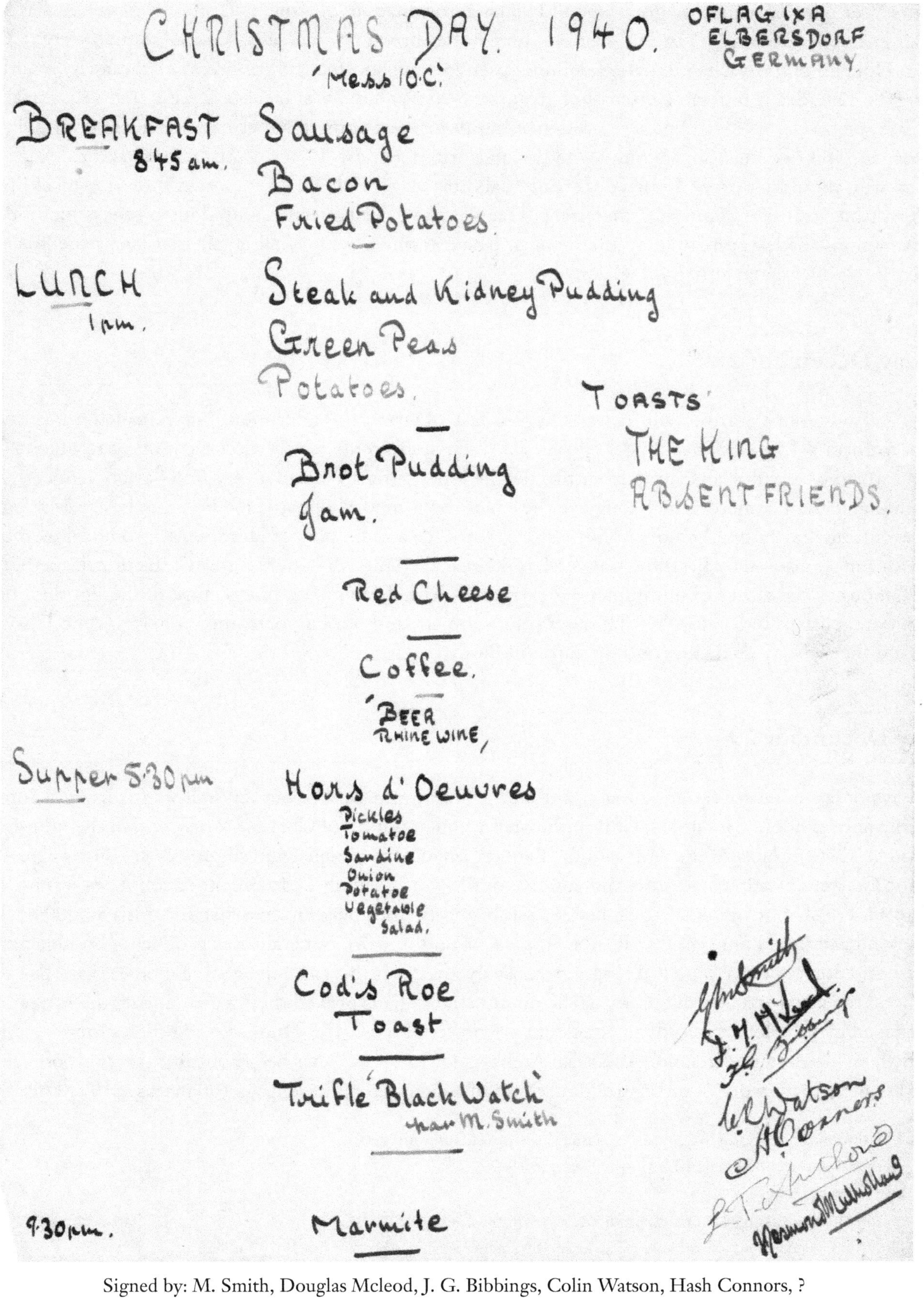

CHRISTMAS DAY. 1940.

OFLAG IXA
ELBERSDORF
GERMANY

'Mess IOC'

BREAKFAST 8·45 am.
Sausage
Bacon
Fried Potatoes

LUNCH 1 pm.
Steak and Kidney Pudding
Green Peas
Potatoes

TOASTS
THE KING
ABSENT FRIENDS

Brot Pudding
Jam.

Red Cheese

Coffee.
Beer
Rhine Wine

Supper 5·30 pm
Hors d' Oeuvres
Pickles
Tomatoe
Sardine
Onion
Potatoe
Vegetable
Salad.

Cod's Roe
Toast

Trifle 'Black Watch'
par M. Smith

9·30 pm.
Marmite

Signed by: M. Smith, Douglas Mcleod, J. G. Bibbings, Colin Watson, Hash Connors, ? Desmond Mullholland

two hours after our departure, we got home. I had been fortunate in borrowing Connors' gum boots as my shoes are leaking most consistently. In the evening, under the direction of Neave, several of us (Garrett, Grayson, Fielding, Holland and Strachan, a pale, feminine, pseudo sophisticated, full of literary superiority, youth) (came together[426]). The idea is to form a discussion group to talk over serious subjects affecting political, social, literary and artistic questions. Neave conducted the meeting in his best court manner and was most convincing. I felt rather lost and inferior but I must conquer these inferiority feelings: I have as many ideas and can express them as well so why should I worry. I started to read "Babbitt" by Sinclair Lewis,[427] which gives a cynical impression of modern American life, aiming for materialist ideals through dishonestly scrupulous business methods: that is dishonest actions made compatible by the modern business philosophy of all is fair that keeps the business man from becoming liberal and anti good fellow.

Saturday December 28th

The weather was much warmer and it was thawing fast. During the afternoon, Neave called a meeting of law students to form a Lego Political and Lego Social discussion group: a very necessary thing to take us out into the living world of great events, away from this detailed, petty life. We had a very fine Variety Concert, a topical monologue and then some original songs at the piano by a new Medico, Capt Fox: his best was "Gefangener Blues",[428] cutting and catty: Connors in his best Pierrot style: a radio play of Horatius as produced by the NBC[429] of America and sponsored by Brattling pullvers! A sketch called the "Prisoners Return": the tragedy is that he finds himself famous as the father of quintuplets. I carried on with "Babbitt": a fine picture of the fighting, fiery, four flushing, evangelist Bill Monday.[430] The descriptions are apt and not cumbersome. There was no Christmas air activity and the artillery duel still continues around Bardia.

Sunday December 29th

It was thawing fast and consequently much warmer. I went to the service but left half way as it was a communion service: my faith is not in Sacraments: it is in the mercy and goodness of Christ as a man and in the infinite truth of his teachings. I spent most of the day reading "Babbitt", cynical materialist and slightly depressing. The American hero is the Go-getter with his greatness personified in the word "selling". "In the other countries art and literature are left to a lot of shabby bums living on booze and spaghetti. In American the artist draws his 50,000 bucks as any captain of industry and I am proud of it". "Europe is one lot of worn out countries producing bootblacks, scenery and booze and don't know a loose leaf ledger from a slip cover". Is this to be the goal of modern Europe? A raid on London and the usual artillery duel! An article on how the Italians proved their worth during the retreat, an army can be gauged by its valour, not only in attack but also in retreat, c.f. with Dunkirk and articles therein. America is to convoy her ships as far as Ireland. American Ambassador to Vichy[431] has been consulting with Roosevelt on how to assist Pétain[432] in his work of reconstruction. A tin of condensed milk went for 100 marks (£10). This milk habit

---

426   The sentence does not make sense. I assume this is what Desmond means.
427   "Babbitt", a novel by Sinclair Lewis, published in 1922.
428   i.e. "Prisoner Blues".
429   National Broadcasting Company, a radio network in the 1940s.
430   Desmond has made a mistake here. The character's name is Mike Monday, not Bill Monday.
431   Vichy was France during WW2 from the German victory in the Battle of France in July 1940 to the Allied Liberation in August 1944.
432   Philippe Pétain (1856-1951) was a French General and Chief of State of Vichy, France from 1940 to 1944.

is getting beyond control: I no sooner pierce one of my tins (we have had 3 recently from the International Red Cross who have taken over the work of the British Legion) but it is all drunk, this sweet, sticky, smooth liquid runs with slippery ease into my ever demanding body. I have no control on this passion, however innocent it may be.

Monday December 30th

The snow had all gone and it was very wet under foot. I was nearing the completion of this diary after several days of hard work. The day was devoid of anything special except for an interesting conversation that I had with Laing on literature and its appreciation: a great deal of my appreciation has been taken from phrases proposed to me by text books. A real appreciation of style must come from real study and not from dilettante reading, backed up by the ideas of publicists and critics. I am reading a number of books that should be read not entirely to get the style, but also to learn new characters and to compare styles and characters, classical and modern. I finished "Babbitt": the American democrat does not want equality of wealth but does want a wholesome sameness of thought, dress, painting, morals and vocabulary. The news was an anti American tirade and warning them of future ship losses. A German ship attacking an island off New Zealand.

Tuesday December 31st

This New Year's Eve was a day of blizzards, fine powdered snow and bitter cold winds. I was lucky to receive three letters, a copy of a wire sent to Aunty by the BL,[433] a letter, full of love and hope, from Geneviève and a card from Verstraeten, a real "Copain's"[434] card. The day's festivities began at 10pm when a second supper was served of bacon, sausage and scrambled egg, some beer and some very inferior wine, which seemed to render your men both intoxicated in that noisy aggressive manner and also, when bed calls them to its bosom, they accept its tender mercies by being violently ill. A Smoking Concert was set in motion by some stalwart songs from Connors: his voice could be heard even above the laughter and noise of broken glass that accompanied the other items. Fox at the piano, Smith with two attractive, pretty Victorian drawing room songs and a clarinet, flute and accordion trio. The guard appeased and gave us a mouth organ recital and their enthusiasm was only quelled by the striking of 12 on the camp gong. "Auld Lang Syne"[435] was alcoholically intoned and then perfect attention for "The King" in which our visitors joined enthusiastically. The New Year was represented by the 60 year old sailorman who potters about the kitchen. As Lights Out were at 12.45 the remains of the Speisesaal were put together and the noisy crowd, in New Year's Eve tradition, staggered to bed. So 1941 came to Oflag 1X A, full of song and laughter and hope that next year would see an end to this terrible war. We were all glad to say farewell to 1940, a year that augured so well and ended so badly.

---

433   British Legion presumably.
434   French: friend's/pal's (card)
435   "Auld Lang Syne", a Scottish poem by Robert Burns, written in 1788 and set to the tune of a traditional folk song.

1941

Wednesday January 1st

There was a heavy fall of snow during the night and the intense cold did not assist the sore and sorry heads. I went back to work on Italian, which I intend to take more slowly and thoroughly. I spent the evening talking with Laing on my diary. I am trying to concentrate on quick colourful descriptions, searching criticisms and useful ideas. I wrote to Daddy, Geneviève and Claude and from now on am keeping copies of my letters. I started reading "A Tale of Two Cities"[436] but am finding it difficult to get into the story: the characters are elusive and the descriptions are not so minute as Dickens' wont: it is this change of style that keeps me a little outside the story. The best description is that of the starving citizens grovelling for the wasting wine. News of a very heavy raid on London, between Waterloo Bridge and the city.

Thursday January 2nd

It was terribly cold and our walk, which we took in the afternoon, was not made very pleasant by the ice sharpened wind that cut more skilfully than a jagged knife. Poor Col Gibbs received the sad news that his wife and little boy have been interned but he has no details: she is, of course, a British citizen. I do wish we could have a letter from home to set my mind at rest. I wrote to Alma Brady care of her old school, Wellesley College, Boston. We spent the evening discussing Psychology and Prison: Neave very ably took the chair and very cleverly moved the discussion from one member to another, at the same time uniting the threads and keeping them within bounds. Barrie gave a well thought out introduction (see note book[437]). I spoke two or three times and am recovering from my nervousness of being laughed at. We dealt with Herd Instinct and Mass Suggestion. I was becoming more interested with my book and seemed to be falling in with this new Dickens: the usual no-good hero was showing himself and the sweet, sympathetic young girl so beloved by D was showing how good and kind she was. Does D give us a wicked character from the female sex at any time? I have never met one. His aristocrat speaks the view of the Englishman when he speaks of the old French aristrocracy, "Detestation of the high is the involuntary homage of the low". Raids on English airports. Roosevelt in fireside talk attacked Nazi philosophy and exhorted the industrialists to give all to Britain. He will fight to the last Englishman. A report from the States says that the Ass. Press building was destroyed on the 30th and that dance music is de rigueur in the tubes. (I am now reading my own Frankfurter, the Times of Germany).

Friday January 3rd

The cold in our room was insufferable: tea left at 8am was frozen stiff by 10. It was a strong blizzard of powdered snow carried along by a high wind and walking was almost impossible. I spent a long time on the paper as translating is a question of much reference to the dictionary. A vocabulary is the most essential asset in the study of any language. I finished my book which became a thrilling boys book with some differences: the writing was for an artist's eye "the furious sounding of the living sea" outside the Bastille and the psychological study of Dr Manette,[438] of his intense reasoning and sanity at one moment turned into harmless, tragic insanity by the effects

---

436   "A Tale of Two Cities", a novel by Charles Dickens, published in 1859.
437   Desmond is referring here to his own notebook.
438   A character in "A Tale of Two Cities".

of a return or of a reminder of his old environment. I began Hilaire Belloc's "Napoleon"[439] (I am now keeping a note book in which I am noting my reading). I shall give here only my general impressions and those statements that I consider of constructive interest and importance. Belloc speaks of Napoleon as one who sought and nearly succeeded to bring everlasting peace to Europe by a great unification built on conquest. Does Hitler intend this? Humiliation and defeat of a people will never bring peace: only sane terms granting complete freedom, vigilantly watched freedom and this watching backed by force, only to be used to back up a warning: a warning that has been given clearly and has been given through the rulers of the defeated race. Belloc has an easy style, simple sentences and phrases, to the point and strongly bound. Unity and purpose are as necessary in writing as in any other sphere of art: say what you want to say so that it is easily understood by the simplest intellect: the great intellect will understand you as well: he will also see that you are genuine and are not acting with words to cover over the lapses in your work. But it is so attractive to coin long sounding difficult phrases. Remember that someone has to read your work: you, as the writer, are the servant of the reader: if you try to make the reader your servant, he will very soon see that you are consumed in that ever burning fire that is made for the bad writer, the fire of public boredom and contempt. As an athlete tries to do impossible things with his strength so does the young writer with his words. The athlete realises that these fantastic essays into spectacular nonsense are harmful. The young writer learns as well and soon his impressive desires fall into a more sober channel. These thoughts came over me as I tried to write a short story. My work was long winded and unnatural and I felt like tearing it up: but I will continue and try and put into effect what I have so glibly written here. The Times correspondent has been expelled from Portugal. Moscow reports upon the new English enemy, loss of sleep.

Saturday January 4th

It was decidedly warmer in the room, though the temperature outside was still about -10C. Some Italian in the morning: it is very similar to French, in fact the similarity is rather confusing especially in the translating into Italian. I spent the afternoon reading Belloc. He spends a long time dealing with the religious phase in Napoleon's character: also he lays great stress on the factor of bad health. He was absolutely certain of himself and took no other advice: this was successful until his health began to fail. He never realised the religious differences, the strongest of all differences from which all cultures arise: he was not farseeing enough due to this religious oblivion. I am of the opinion that Napoleon never thought of religion: he was eaten up with himself and his own power. It was his desire to show his power and that of his war machine that lost him the day after so much success. It was a physical impossibility for him to keep up the strain of war, in his march into the vastness of Russia. It made no difference whether his opponents were Catholic or Jew: they merely waited for the first signs of weakness and seized on them: Napoleon lost them when he could not hold them down, not when they realised their religious beliefs and decided to assert them. Napoleon believed himself led by fate "No Poet is Atheist in the matter of his Muse". This may have been true for his physical safety but it was not a safeguard of this strategic success. "Energy is the well spring of intelligence" (Napoleon). "Journey's End" was produced in the Speisesaal. The simplicity of the scenic effects gave a stark realism and fear to this dreadfully true picture of moral degradation. Stanhope[440] is afraid, he drinks to cover his fear and this puts upon him a veneer of cynical austerity that covers cruelly his own sensitive and delicate character. Capt Mansel gave a brilliantly nervous schoolboy ardour so much admired by "Uncle", the quiet, peacefully happy, second in command. Charles Edie had the unsympathetic coward role, which he portrayed with intense realism, making the young Hibbert[441] into the despicable, but naturally frequent

---

439   "Napoleon" by Hilaire Belloc, published in 1932.
440   A character in "Journey's End".
441   A character in "Journey's End".

character in any demoralising war. The whole play followed the climaxes in the most expressive manner and the final scene, the destruction of the dugout, was a master piece of productive skill and stage managing foresight. 5 German officers who attended, expressed their appreciation in glowing terms. A heavy raid on Cardiff, as a reprisal for the Bremen raid. Italians welcome to German airmen. Denial of English report of a Stalin[442] declaration of Jan 1st! A new War Production Ministry: Beaverbrook[443] named Raider in the Pacific: 10 successes.

Sunday January 5th

This morning MacLean preached his usual good sermon using the parable of the barn, well stocked, and the soul empty. He begged us to put into life that which would live on and withstand the physical blows. Culture, thought and education will always stay with us and now is the time to put into the world our receptive and reasoning talents to accumulate a store of knowledge for future happiness and enlightenment. We are more fortunate than those free people who can devote their time to the accumulation of wealth and amusement, not essentials in themselves. I spent a great part of the day writing, or rather copying articles into "The Fragment", a production of Neave, Holland and Strachan. It is full of intellectualism and long words, rather school boyish if it did not have good ideas, if perhaps rather cynical. It was tedious work and I had the feeling of being the poor fool who should do the dirty plodding work so that the great minds might work. In the evening we were privileged to hear a piano recital by Barrie Grayson Mus Bac. LRAM.[444] This pianist fills his execution with youthful joy, making his playing not a work, but an amusement. He draws the melody from the piano, asking the music to express his own feelings. He began his programme with a light, lilting "Impromptu" of Chopin.[445] The melody rose from the right hand as the musical sounds coming from a clear, swift moving brook as it leaps among the water smoothed stones. Suddenly it quietened and a peace settled over the little stream: the pool that it had reached was deep and the rippling brook had time to take its breath. But not for long, for soon it was cantering on singing for the very joy of life. The pianist's second piece was another of Chopin's, his "Nocturne in E flat",[446] a quiet softness filled the common and dirty room and we all followed the composer, taking his way through the darkened wood, the brittle twigs cracking sharply beneath his steady tread: suddenly he broke from this encircling gloom, his eyes beheld a vast green meadow dimly visible in the morning light; he heard the greetings of the waking birds and was at peace. Such was the spell cast upon me and it was with an effort that I brought myself back from my ramblings to listen to Grayson's explanation of the "Capriccio" by Scarlatti,[447] an early 17th C piece written for the harpsichord: this instrument having no sustaining pedal, and having plucked and not struck strings, required a swift moving, technically executed type of composition. If Grayson's useful explanation had not roused me from my reverie, this galloping, swift moving fun certainly made the air rush against my face and my ears sing with the brilliantly reproduced runs. After this visit to the old school, we moved into "Melody Consolation No 3" by Liszt.[448] Here was a quiet seashore sunset, ripples gradually climbing up the beach until they reached the high tide rocks, then their softness suddenly changed into violence, beating heavily against these obstacles: the climax rent the air but could not hold itself and the sounds fell till they gradually died into the distance exhausted by their efforts. "Lieblich"[449], a piano arrangement of a song by

---

442   Joseph Stalin (1878-1953), de facto leader of the Soviet Union from the 1920s until his death.

443   William Maxwell Aitken, Lord Beaverbrook (1879-1964), Minister of Aircraft Production May 1940 to April 1941 and then as a Minister of Supply until February 1942.

444   Bachelor of Music. Licentiate of the Royal Academy of Music.

445   "Fantaisie Impromptu in C sharp minor" composed in 1834 by Frédéric Chopin.

446   "Nocturne in E flat" from Op. 9 No. 2 composed in 1830 by Frédéric Chopin.

447   Domenico Scarlatti (1685-1757), an Italian composer. Scarlatti composed several Capriccios.

448   "Melody Consolation No. 3" composed in 1849 by Franz Liszt.

449   "O wie lieblich ist das mädchen" ("Oh, how sweet is the maiden") from Op. 138 composed in 1849 by Robert Alexander Schumann.

Schumann, that wonderman of song writing. This striking air was quicker and had a more modern, sophisticated savour of a young man coming through youthful excitements into powerful manhood. Grayson's playing was unaffected: he was playing his instrument and making it do his will: he was not using it, as so many of our amateur pianists use it, to show off his finger technique and his decorative posture. Pascalle,[450] Handel[451] took a melody and worked into this ground base a variety of tuneful variations, the melody always remaining prominently in the treble clef. The piece was rhythmic and had a safe quality. I mean by safe, a personal safety, a feeling that the music was going to do what I was hoping it would do: it did do so: it was safe. Following this came some variations by the same composer, "The Blacksmith Variations".[452] This was as happily conservative, a scamper between the two hands to vary the pleasing air. A little Arabesque by Schubert[453], the most melodious of all composers, was as Grayson said "A little patchwork quilt". The great feature of the evening was Bach's "Organ Prelude and Fugue in A minor".[454] A fugue, Grayson told us, was mathematical, a voice, or melody repeated by a 2nd voice lower, a 3rd voice ¼ higher and a fourth voice on the original key. A prelude, on the other hand, was a ramble up and down the instrument. Liszt had transcribed this organ piece for the piano and his transcription has managed to capture all the power of the organ key boards. The word to describe this Fugue is Magnificent. Imagine a giant on his mountain top gazing into the valleys at his feet and watching the efforts of the mighty armies struggling to gain possession of the vital town lying between these valleys. So each voice strove to gain the mastery of the instrument and that room of ours rang with the struggle. To finish off his programme, Barrie played us "Consolation" by Liszt.[455] The whole evening had been a consolation to us, it had taken our souls and shown them other worlds. It was only left for us to applaud the man who has created for us this musical miracle. I went on reading "Napoleon": I was at his battles of Italy: his victory over Piedmont[456] in the Ligurian hills: though his forces were half of his opponents, his energy and quick action won the day: he split the enemy into small portions and crushed them in turn. The mans[457] of the battles are very clear: just essentials and drawn in square design. Colin got his first letter from home, dated 16th Dec.

Monday January 6th

I had a wonderful parcel from Zabette: it is kind of her, especially as France must be very short of food: a pullover, socks, slippers, towel, flannel, two slabs chocolate, 2 tins of jam, 2 cheeses, 2 patés, 2 tobaccos, 4 paquets jaunes[458] and a pain d'épice[459] which was delicious. Lovel introduced his new course of History lectures beginning with Kant's[460] Maxim "Geography is the Foundation of History". He followed with several examples of Geographical conditions on Population e.g. the Andes Indians. Then the island position of England: Physical unity brings political unity and nationalism: Italy is the exception that proves the rule. The Influence of the sea on England. Energetic, temperate climate. Good fishing and natural harbours have made a nation of seamen: the sea is no barrier to ideas. Three questions 1) Is splendid isolation possible? 2) Environment is more important than race? 3) Geography

450   I am not sure who Desmond is referring to here.
451   George Frideric Handel (1685-1759), a German born, British Baroque composer.
452   "The Harmonious Blacksmith" by George Frideric Handel, published in 1720.
453   Franz Peter Schubert (1797-1828), an Austrian composer.
454   "Organ Prelude and Fugue in A minor", composed in 1708 by Johann Sebastian Bach.
455   Listz (previously referenced) wrote several Consolations.
456   A region in Italy.
457   Abbreviation: manoeuvres.
458   French: yellow packets (a brand of Gauloise cigarettes).
459   French: spiced bread (more like a cake).
460   Immanuel Kant (1724-1804), a German philosopher.

lies at the foundation of History. Law Discussion on "Crime and Punishment". General conclusion:- Law must be strongly interpreted and psychological treatment only in certain cases, these cases to be at the discretion of the judge. Juvenile criminals must not get impression that they are heroes and distinct from the ordinary criminal. Modern J Cts[461] very often help the children to dramatise themselves. A good sordid whipping, administered summarily would be more effective. News: Raids on Bristol and Avonmouth. Thunderbolt sunk by Italians.

Tuesday January 7th

We had the usual main road walk: the road was very slippery and there were huge snow drifts. A very striking sight was a train emerging from the snow bound woods, its smoke resting immobile on the gaunt trees. Pope began his German conversation class; he does not speak in English and it is a good hour to get into the language. A German NCO was giving the Niemand method, a series of questions and answers, progressively harder. A system that is rather absurd with this vast class and also when he has not got the illustrated key. However, it enables those who do not like work and have a guilty conscience to pretend that they are learning German. In the evening Lovel's Discussion Group met, practically the same formation as Neave's. Lovel began the discussion by talking around the theme "Desire for security is the prime motive of social organisation". Discussion arose on three of his points 1) the origin of human society 2) Priests as law givers 3) The growth of Autocracy (Talk is noted). Ethics is not religion. Ethics are a rule of conduct coming from a belief in an ideal. There are two codes, a physical and a mental code. Ethics are rules for the conduct of the mental life: personal ethics is one's own moral code. Religion is the sanction behind ethics. News. Raids on London. Bardia advance posts taken. Excuse letter from the Telegraph, avalanche of tanks. Brain four, Alexander,[462] Beaverbrook,[463] Bevin,[464] Duncan[465] in Inner cabinet. (Must read Frazer[466]).

Wednesday January 8th

Weather much warmer and a slight thaw. History: Rome was always tolerant, except where the practice was political or indecent to Roman ideals. There was little nationalism and most nations were conquered by the Roman tradition. Augustus gave 250 years of peace. Steppe[467] mentality is to destroy enemies "Peninsula Europe" by Leidt[468] (a comment on Germans). "A Capital city must be sufficiently near its most vulnerable frontier", e.g. Constaninople. Rome remained spiritual heart of the empire. Mediaeval nationalism in "St Joan" (Shaw).[469]

---

461   Abbreviation: Juvenile Courts, presumably.
462   Albert Victor Alexander (1885-1965), British Labour Co-operative politician and First Lord of the Admiralty in the wartime Coalition Government.
463   Lord Beaverbrook, previously referenced.
464   Ernest Bevin (1881-1951), British Trade Union Leader and Labour Politician and Minister of Labour and National Service in the wartime Coalition Government.
465   Sir Andrew Rae Duncan(1884-1952), a British businessman brought into the wartime Coalition Government who served as President of the Board of Trade and then Minister of Supply.
466   I have not been able to identify this person.
467   I think Desmond is referring to Russia?
468   I have not been able to identify this work.
469   "Saint Joan", a play by George Bernard Shaw, published in 1924.

R G Collingwood's "Roman Britain".[470] A letter from Aunty in reply to Red Cross notifications: sent on Nov 6th. My card sent on Oct 31st. A lecture on East Africa by Lt P Maxwell. An irregular lecture by a regular officer. E Africa is a country for damn good shooting and a damn fine life and the N-----s make excellent porters. The excitement was given to this inspiring address by the minute description of two enemy raids: during these vital incidents our lecturer was not present. Bardia has fallen. England lost 50 planes and many men. A raiding party of 50 on the French coast. BBC hit twice.

Thursday January 9th

We went for a lovely walk along the course of the river, climbing later up a snow covered icy path to the altitude of the Schloss standing gauntly cold in its coat of leafless trees. The sky, peeping through the snowy clouds was blue but the effect of its light on the distant hills was electric: soft yellow light somehow warming the clean, icy snow. We had an influx of new officers from hospital where the food was not very good and many of the wounded could make no progress towards better health on this unsustaining diet. I started Russian: it is very hard, having about 36 letters in the alphabet and, though their sounds and their alphabetical positions are different, they bear a distinct resemblance to our characters, which adds to the confusion. L Cook is a very good teacher and he gave us a number of well known Russian words whereby we could associate the Russian alphabet with our own letters and pronunciation. At the Discussion Group we carried on with prison psychology and discussed "Self Assertion: a good thing when combined with a real incentive". Complexes: the only good discipline is that engendered by a desire to emulate or do something that is really worth doing e.g. in Oflag IX A there is no desire to become the best Gefangener: there is no standard to attain, nor any discipline. Lack of discipline is the key to prison psychology. Conclusion: this life is good for constructional thought and philosophy. The Life, as any type of life, is entirely what you make it. My own feelings on my captivity are rather strange. I have learnt much from the study of others: in normal times the good and the bad in us is not very apparent against the diverse activities and entertainments that occupy us. Here these diverse factors are not apparent and a man must fall back upon himself. I have realised that I am very ignorant: for the first time I have been tied down to argue and discuss and my knowledge has been faulty. I could not turn the subject to the Saturday night dance, to the merits of Miss A on the appallingly unsocial conduct of X when he goes about with Miss Y. Here is the one opportunity, free from worry and material pleasure, when I can work and learn. I can realise that what seemed to be vital is quite unnecessary for a happy and useful life. Knowledge is the key to a useful life: the attaining of knowledge is the key to a happy prison life. With this learning, new fields of thought open themselves before me and I feel myself becoming more competent to step through my life and to make it a success, not only from my one side but from the side of those about me. The time must not be wasted: The life of a POW has taught me to see: it has taught me the meaning of silent thought: it has made me see and this is most important, those things that are vital and those that are just form. Study of myself, coupled with a careful study of others, has taught me the meaning of the old adage "it is never too late to learn". I like to think that my motto will always be, "It is never too early to learn". (These discussions are most useful a) for making the participants think deeply and also for keeping their thoughts within limits). I went on with "Napoleon" and his decisions and rapidity of action absolutely astound me. His confidence is almost supernatural "It was necessary that I should win. But any other man would have retired". His return to France and his adoption of the throne were excellently portrayed and his character was amply shown in his shortness with the Papal Nuncio.[471] He wished to be Emperor: it would be useful to have the Papal sanction, therefore the Pope must give his sanction. Nothing

---

470   "Roman Britain" by R G Collingwood, published in 1924.
471   A Papal Nuncio is the equivalent of an ambassador from any other country.

is too difficult when it was needed in his personal advancement. News. Fighting between Bardia and Tobruk.[472] Scorn on Roosevelt from Italy. De Gaulle and Gen Spears.[473] A rumour of 100,000 Italians dead and prisoners.

Friday January 10th

Lovel gave us an insight into the old Norse men. The Normans came from the Norse strong strain and the Franc intelligent strain and the Norman invasion was of infinite value to us. Shorthand was becoming much more interesting, almost a new language. I did some washing, though I am still most unsuccessful at this useful art! Great joy at the arrival of Bulk stores. Jam, chocolate, cheese, biscottes[474] and cigarettes, which I swopped for cheese and chocolate: there is a very fluctuating market and exchange prices are never even; I am now after chocolate as my jam store is well stocked. Holland gave a criticism of "Journey's End" as a Play. He treated himself as a closet critic as opposed to an auditorium critic. He said he was a pedant and, on these grounds, he said that no play was great that is lasting, if it was not written in verse. The play followed the Aristotle[475] unities of time, place and theme. As a picture of the war, it would serve as a reference in so far as it would show the feelings of certain individuals. It had no real historical value. Was not the play enhanced by the hysterical post war audiences? A discussion followed on entertainment value. My opinion is that art is created as the public demands it: greatness and entertainment value are to be viewed separately. The entertainment value depends entirely on the general feelings of the audience, during war they like amusement, during peace they like war to show them how brave they are. The greatness must be judged by one who has not been carried away either by the actual play or by the feeling of the audiences: perhaps a foreigner is the best critic, certainly if he lives at a later period. My own feelings are that "Journey's End" was very moving and interesting in that it asks you how you would behave under similar conditions: it is a personal play. I could never criticise it because I was too moved by it. The author successfully "put it across": time alone can tell if it is a great play. News. Raids on Coventry, London. RAF hit churches in Cologne[476] and Dusseldorf.[477] Italians SW of Tobruk. Naples[478] and Palermo[479] bombed. Hospital ship bombed. Roosevelt War Budget. Food scandal at home.

Saturday January 11th

Very cold and fine. Glorious pink colouring of the snow and the smoke from the Schloss stood out as a pink design against the blue background. Russian went quite smoothly and it now looks a little less like double dutch. Am getting more attuned to German and paper reading is much quicker though still a lengthy tiring process. A Smoking Concert: not as well organised as usual. A laughing sketch went quite flat. Major Garrett gave a very amusing imitation of the German class. Fox was full of dirty digs, true and piercing, in his song "You wouldn't know your son, Mrs Lagergeld". And then a cynical piece "Susannah was an Intellectual girl". The best story of

---

472   A port city on Libya's eastern Mediterranean coast.
473   Edward Louis Spears (1886-1974), a British army officer and MP noted for his role as liaison officer between British and French forces in the 2 world wars.
474   French: light, soft bread, toasted or crisped in an oven.
475   Aristotle (384BC-322BC), a Greek philosopher and polymath.
476   Germany's 4th largest city.
477   Capital city of North Rhine-Westphalia.
478   Capital city of Campania, Italy.
479   Capital of Sicily.

the evening was the "Mills of God"[480] story. News: nothing new except the German Russian Trade pact[481] and the Bahrain Island affair[482] though I am not very sure as to what happened. The temperature was about -15C and it was bitterly cold. I saw a lovely sight, a big sleigh with two pixie capped children drawn by a big dapple grey horse, two coloured plumes waving over its back and the little bells tinkling in the still, cold air. No letters for us at the Kommandantur.[483] What has happened at home?

Sunday January 12th

Once again I was in darkness for my bed was covered by its top bunk: it is most annoying because I can no longer read in bed. The weather was clean and cold and I had a fine walk. MacLean gave us the story of Jairus'[484] daughter, bringing out the point that nothing was too insignificant for God to look at and to help. I wrote for some time and then finished Belloc's "Napoleon." I enjoyed it very much and became fascinated by the battle descriptions so very clearly laid out and showing the rapidity of movement and decision of this great man. The literary work made these facts more delightful: the end of a battle always brought some colourful word picture and all the way through the ageing of this man, who conquered and then wishing to conquer, lost all his last hours at St Helena are the greatest tragedy: the man who could decide whether he would be King or not was to die in what was little more than a stable, cut off from all glory and cut off from his greatest friend, the humble soldier of France. Will the words "The Army will not march" bring about the downfall of another would be world conqueror? In the evening Barrie Grayson gave us another concert and the Speisesaal was very full, though I fear that not all those who came desired to listen, as their whispering and shuffling, their bottle rattling and page turning, made quite clear. However loud the music may be, the rattling of a chair or the faintest whisper will stand out and the whole sequence of the melody will be lost. So few people realise this and now I can appreciate how Grandpa must have felt when we used to chatter and giggle while he listened to a "Promenade", lying well back in his chair, the red glow of his pipe alone marking his presence: but we were very young and he was very tolerant, how little did I appreciate him. Barrie began with a "Chromatic Fantasia and Fugue" by Bach;[485] he explained that it was essentially a performer's piece. In writing it, Bach[486] was 200 years ahead of his time and his chromatic scheme, a new type of writing, was severely criticised. Before Barrie began playing this work, he took a little air of Handel's and treated it without its trills and runs, "without its frills" and then with them, to show us the structure of this early harpsichord and spinet music. The work itself was very inspiring; its high technical standard, combined with its precise never ending rhythm, made it live, not as a human being lives, one moment happy and the next moment sad, but as some perfect machine never hesitating and all the time producing: the piano was producing note upon note with not a pause, and the whole air was alive. What a difference from last week's strafe:[487] this time a flowing straightforward, perfect Bach: last week a striving, fighting Bach. Two moods of one great man. From this early Mathematician we moved, or rather must I say Barrie led us, to Brahms,[488] no less a mathematical composer though living some 200 years later. This was a "Ballade" and the composer intentionally, with multitudinous chords, put

---

480 The meaning of the story is that retribution is slow but certain.
481 German-Soviet Commercial Agreement signed in February 1940.
482 Possibly a reference to the bombing of Bahrain by Italy which forced the Allied Forces to upgrade Bahrain's defences which further stretched Allied military resources.
483 German: Oflag Headquarters.
484 Biblical story of the resurrection of Jairus' daughter by Jesus.
485 "Chromatic Fantasia and Fugue" by Johann Sebastian Bach, composed around 1720.
486 Johann Sebastian Bach (1685-1760), German composer, organist, harpsichordist, violinist and violist of the Baroque period.
487 German: punishment.
488 Johannes Brahms (1833-1897), a German composer and pianist.

an amusing imitation of the German class. Fox was full of dirty digs, true and piercing, in his song "You wouldn't know your son now Herr Gröls". And then a cynical piece "Susannah was an Intellectual girl". The best story of the evening was the Wills of God story. News: nothing new except the German Russian Trade Pact and the Bahrein island affair though I am not very sure as to what happened. The temperature was about -15°C and it was bitterly cold. I saw a lovely sight a big sleigh with two fur canvas covered children drawn by a big dapple gray horse, two coloured plumes waving over its back and the little bells tinkling in the still, cold air. No letters for us at the Kommandantur. What has happened at home?

Sunday 13th: Once again I was in darkness for my bed was covered by its top bunk. It is most annoying because I can no longer read in bed. The weather was clear and cold and I had a fine walk. Maclean gave us the story of Cyrus' daughter bringing out the point that nothing was too insignificant for God to look at and to help. I wrote for some time and then finished Belloc's Napoleon. I enjoyed it very much and became fascinated by the battle descriptions, so very clearly laid out and showing the rapidity of movement and decision of this great man. The literary work made these facts more delightful, the end of a battle always brought some colourful word picture and all the way through the aging of this man, who conquered and then wishing to conquer, lost all. His last hours on St Helena are the greatest tragedy. The man who could decide whether he would be king or no was to die in what was little more than a stable, cut off from all glory and cut off from his greatest friend, the humble soldier of France. Will the words "The Army will not march" bring about the downfall of another would be world conqueror. In the evening Barry Grayson gave us another concert and the Speisesaal was very full, though I fear that not all those who came desired to listen as their whispering and shuffling, their bottle rattling and page turning, made quite clear. However loud the music may be the rattling of a chair or the faintest whisper will stand out and the whole sequence of the melody will be lost. So few people realise this and now I can appreciate how Grandpa must have felt when we used to chatter and giggle while he listened to a 'Promenade'; lying well back in his chair, the red glow of his pipe alone marking his presence. But we were very young and he was very tolerant; how little did I appreciate him. Barry began with a chromatic Fantasia & Fugue by Bach; he explained that it was essentially a performers piece. In writing it Bach was 200 years ahead of his time and his chromatic scheme, a new type of writing, was severely criticised. Before he Barry began playing this work he took a little air of Handel's and treated it without its trills and runs, without its frills, and then with them to show us the structure of this early harpsichord and spinet music. The work itself was very inspiring its high technical standard combined with its precise never ending

The actual page from Desmond's diary. Note the Geprüft (approved) Stamp at the top.

a whole orchestra into his single instrument. Here was a busy London Dickensian day, the carriages rumbling, the horsemen clattering and the pedestrians hurrying. Suddenly a lull and a gilded coach bearing some noble gracious lady passed across the scene: just time to catch a glimpse of her as she smiles and then she is lost in the mad, pulsating turmoil of the crowed street. Brahms, in a more peaceful mood, was shown us in a "Romanze".[489] This was a simple melody, enclosing a pipe pastoral melody, as if a little boat was floating down a sluggish stream, over hanging fields dimly visible in the evening glow, the little boat comes upon a clearing in the trees and from the meadow comes the shepherd's call, "Oh, if I could but wait and hear you play" but the slowly running stream carries its little burden into the tree darkened glades. "The Impromptu" of Schubert[490] was a piece full of perfectly controlled runs rising to a swift climax, then came the chord contrast but the itching fingers would not tarry long and were once again scampering up the instrument until tired and weary, though no less active, they stopped to rest. A song, a chromatic song from Wagner,[491] arranged by Liszt. The treble took the song answered by the crescendoing arpeggio base and all the while the melody lived on inside its decorative frame. Slowly but surely, the sound rose to a mighty crescendo and, when once again the melody softly answered this wealth of sound, it remained hanging in the air, absurdly beautiful in the smoke filled dirty wooden room. Then came Mozart's "Fantasia in D minor".[492] This was typically Mozartian: airy and not ornamentally complicated. The piece was full of contrasts: chromatic runs with perfect timing: so it ran its airy way, finishing with the charming little melody that we always expect of Mozart. The finale of the evening was the famous "Moonlight Sonata",[493] that sonata of which we hear so often the first gentle, rippling movement: the second, minuet movement, augured the harsher third movement. The stormy sea crashed, with heavy chords, against the mighty rocks, never ending, never tiring. Even with the final chords this mad, melodious storm went on even into the cold, snowy night. Just to round off this evening's pleasure, Barrie played us a tuneful Grieg[494] piece which brought me back to my old school days of MacDowell and his "Eine Wilde Rose".[495] So were we taken from our normal dreary day, taken to the realms of a musical Kingdom.

Monday January 13th

There was a heavy fall of snow during the night and I can hardly imagine our yard without its white covering. Lovel lectured on the Norman invasion which was good in that it put England in touch with European culture and also gave us a real central government. William was "stark and fierce but he did good justice". The Normans were the best stock in Europe. At this time, many of the Northern Saxons were driven into the Scottish lowlands, which is very amusing when one hears the lowland Scot praising his own qualities, different from those of the rather inferior Englishman. In the evening Grayson began a series of lectures on Music. He commenced with an explanation of the old Modes and plain song leading up to the discovery of the modern scale. With the "Ash Grove"[496] he showed us Musical form: the full staves, commas and phrases. This delightful little piece is in pure symphonic form, ABA, and is perfectly written. The clefs for viola and cello were new to me and I found it all most interesting. When I was too young to appreciate music I was made to learn, when I was too busy to practise and now, when I long to play and am understanding the musical lesson, I am not experienced enough to play. I do not

---

489   Johannes Brahms composed several "Romanze".
490   "Impromptus" are a series of 8 pieces for piano, composed in 1827 by Franz Schubert.
491   Wilhelm Richard Wagner (1813-1883), composer, theatre director, polemicist and conductor primarily known for his operas.
492   "Fantasia No. 3 in D minor", a piece of music for solo piano composed by Wolfgang Amadeus Mozart in 1782.
493   "Piano Sonata No. 14 in C sharp minor", commonly known as "Moonlight Sonata", composed by Ludwig Van Beethoven in 1801.
494   Edvard Hagerup Grieg (1843-1907), a Norwegian composer and pianist.
495   "To a Wild Rose" from "Woodland Sketches" composed in 1904 by Edward Alexander MacDowell.
496   A traditional Welsh folk song.

regret my music lessons, I only regret that I did not try to understand and not merely play what I was told. News. Raids on London. German air attack in the Mediterranean. Denial of English report of raid on France with 50 bombs and 500 fighters in which we suffered no loss.

Tuesday January 14th

We went for a long walk along the railway: it was very much warmer but as my shoes leak, walking is not very comfortable, especially as I have no second pair. We began rehearing the "Dover Road" by A A Milne.[497] I have the part of Nicholas, a young man who has been trapped by a married and tiresome woman. I have this part instead of that of Capt Brassbound. In the evening Lovel gave a very fine lecture on the Augustan age in which the citizenship of Rome was the highest honour to which a man could aspire. Roma and Augustus became the citizens' creed. The Government in Rome had broken down and men wanted a leader who would bring them security. The Princeps (Augustus) used the old forms of Government but he governed 1) with the army and the Civil Service: 2) he realised the necessity of spiritual regeneration. 3) his own moral conduct was most important in leading people. 4) As far as Morals can be regulated by Law, Augustus regulated them; but he seems to have realised that this too wanted some spiritual sanction. This spiritual regeneration was the key to his 200 years success. News. A Malaya Class battle ship hit. A Naval officer court martialled. Dalton[498] speech on the blockade header in the Times article about regenerating Democracy on National Socialist lines. Today I made my first pudding Recipe. About 18 pieces of brown bread cut into little squares, 4 potatoes mixed with Ersatz fat then mixed with the bread. All this soaked in a tin of orange juice and sugar then put in the oven. The result, a very palatable dish.

Wednesday January 15th

Lovel's lecture course went on with the History of England and I was astonished at how little I knew. William Rufus[499] followed his father and though a strong King, he lacked his father's good qualities. On his murder Henry I[500] seized power: he was a very competent King but not competent enough to leave a son. His daughter Matilda succeeded him though Stephen soon seized power and God and his angels slept. During this time the barons grew in power and on Stephen's death, Henry II,[501] Matilda's son came to the throne: he has been called the English Justinian. His latter life was marred by his affair with Becket.[502] He was succeeded by Richard I[503] and his reign 1188-1198[504] was a terrible reign for England for Richard spent his whole time away on Crusades[505] which have been called the Papal Foreign Policy, that is to say the Papacy encouraged them to use up the baronial surplus energy. The bishops at this time were also great temporal princes. The advantage of the Crusades was that men's minds were opened and the knowledge and culture of the East gradually filtered through to our island home. On

---

497   "The Dover Road", a comedy play by A A Milne, published in 1921.
498   Edward Hugh John Neale Dalton (1887-1962), a British Labour politician and Minister of Economic Warfare in the wartime Coalition Government.
499   William II (1056-1100), King of England from 1087 until his death.
500   Henry I (1068-1135), King of England from 1100 until his death.
501   Henry II (1133-1189), King of England from 1154 until his death.
502   Thomas Becket (1118-1170), Archbishop of Canterbury from 1162 until his murder in 1170.
503   Richard I (1157-1199), King of England from 1189 until his death.
504   These dates are incorrect. Richard I's reign was 1189-1199).
505   The Crusades were a series of wars that took place in Asia Minor and the Levant from 1095 to 1291.

leaving the lecture I glanced into the shower house window and, to my utter amazement, I saw Jim Symes[506] and Nicolle.[507] I was nearly knocked down by the shock and my mind was filled with the most terrible forebodings; had they been taken at Jaonnet[508] on account of information received? It was with a beating heart and a worried mind that I waited till after lunch when I got the opportunity to speak to them. I then heard the awful news, which I had always prayed against, that Mums had been taken. Their news was that she was at St Lô and that she was being well looked after. The only good piece of news was that the other families had been returned and there was every possibility that Mums had also gone. How terrible for her to have left home. I wonder what happened to Uncle Mickie. I feel that home will never be the same and I do so feel my responsibility for this misery. I have worried and worried and have come to the conclusion that worry will do no good. I have prayed for Mums and she must be safe. She, I know, will realise our terrible predicament and all I can ask is her forgiveness and hope that she and everyone will forgive. A letter must come soon and tell me that all is well again. Meanwhile, I just wait in an agony of suspense. I also heard that one of my Langendorf letters got home. The most unlucky news was that Ferbrache[509] came a day too late! We took Pete's advice. The whole business was completely bungled. The raid itself went to Herm,[510] at least 6 miles away! These two new arrivals have had an even more unhappy time than I: and all to no purpose. Stupid but amusing lecture on how to farm when your living does not depend upon it by John Jessup.

Thursday January 16th

I continued with Russian and have now mastered the alphabet and we have begun a few easy nouns and verbs. It is terribly difficult. In the afternoon we went for a very long walk, under the railway bridge, through the village and up the hill, past our usual halting place until the snow clad Schloss was almost lost in the cold, late afternoon light. I received a letter from Zabette posted on the 20th of November telling me that she had dispatched two parcels: I have received the second one. I wonder if the first will ever appear. In the evening Neave gave us a very highbrow lecture on "Prison Philosophy": Gentlemen next door, hearing odd sentences now and then were under the impression that Neave was setting himself up as God! He dealt first with the Metaphysical side, having as its basis the transcendent power of the mind. The second half of this paper was of the Ethical side of prison life and his Conclusions were: It is our duty to subordinate our desires to our wills – seclusion is the time to contemplate. The perfect prisoner is the one with a will to perfection: it is he who creates the greatest good and gives and receives the greatest happiness. God is the perfect mind. God is simple perfection. The power of thinking shows the mind its defects. News. Another big flight over Northern France.

---

506 James Symes, also involved in a scouting mission to Guernsey (see Introduction).
507 Lieutenant Hubert Nicolle, Royal Hampshire Regiment, also involved in Operation Anger, Desmond's scouting mission to Guernsey (see Introduction)
508 Le Jaonnet Bay, Guernsey.
509 Sergeant Stanley Ferbrache took part in the botched raid on Guernsey on 3 August 1940. The intention had been to attempt to rescue Desmond and Philip Martel during the raid.
510 One of the smaller Channel Islands. See map at beginning of the book.

Friday January 17th

I spent a long time copying out my part which is a job I hate. Lovel went on with England's History and went through the Edwards especially with Edward III[511] and Crécy[512] and Agincourt[513] when our superior fire power won the day. Effect of Great Plague on England causing much land to be put to sheep as there was insufficient main d'oeuvre.[514] It was Henry III[515] who brought in Flemish weavers. The Magna Carta[516] was forced on John by the barons and though it was a statement of the subjects' rights it was only the rights of the Barons that were envisaged. The day was very uninteresting though the Shorthand periods are always quite fun. I am not sleeping very well as I can't get my mind off the news I had. News. HMS Southampton[517] sunk and the Illustrious[518] damaged.

Saturday January 18th

I got up in a furious temper. There are now showers in our building though they are only heated to prevent the taps from freezing. It is customary for us to go down about 8.15 when the water is beautifully warm. This morning, however, the members of room 15, led by Hash, decided to avoid the Hoi Polloi by taking their shower at 7.30: consequently when I arrived about 8, the water was almost cold. I was livid: I shouted about being public spirited and not considering other people. I had every reason to be angry, for there are about 20 sprays and ample room for room 15 and the other rooms. This early morning grouse rather coloured my morning and that, on top of a worried, sleepless night, made me feel very out of sorts. I had also been overtaxing the old brain, what with usual work, preparing lectures, and learning a part. On the advice of Col Gibbs, I took it easy, getting much mental relaxation is the making of a trifle. Recipe:- 7 pieces of bread, spread with jam, then placed in a Dixie forming layers with tinned figs and little plums that I got from France. The whole covered with cocoa, sugar, dried and condensed milk. The proof of this trifle will be in the eating. At last I was able to obtain another note book which I shall keep for my book of Essays which I am going to call "Prison Talk", basing it on "Table Talk". The subjects well be infinitely various. The greatest drawback to this life is the impossibility of peace and quiet. From the early hours of the morning till late at night the sound of human voices fills the cramped rooms. Politics and smut, religion and love, metaphysics and food, every known subject and three well known and well worn words reach one's ears at all times. When I am tired, I feel as though I must be in the famous Bedlam:[519] when I am not tired, I contribute to the Bedlam. No chance of real study for no sooner have I settled down to work than I must go to the Canteen or go on Appell: always this part life. At last, no one here. I spoke too soon. "Working?" "Yes." "What's for lunch?" "I don't know" and so it goes on until I could scream. But self discipline and concentration are what I am striving for and soon I shall be able to work in the middle of the most heated argument!

---

511   Edward III (1312-1377), King of England from 1327 until his death.
512   The Battle of Crécy took place on 26th August 1346 and was a major English victory and one of the most important battles of the Hundred Years' War.
513   The Battle of Agincourt took place on 25th October 1415 and was a major English victory in the Hundred Years' War.
514   French: labour.
515   Henry III (1207-1272), King of England from 1216 until his death.
516   The Great Charter of the Liberties of England (1215).
517   HMS Southampton bombed 11th January 1941 by German Stuka dive bombers south east of Malta.
518   HMS Illustrious bombed on 10th January 1941 by the Luftwaffe east of Sicily.
519   The Bethlam Royal Hospital, commonly known as Bedlam, a hospital for the treatment of mental illness in London.

Sunday January 19th

It was much warmer and the thick white snow was quickly becoming a wet, dirty slush. The Padre made one of his excellent sermons. He is such a convincing speaker: not that he is imbued with great oratorical powers, but his voice is soft and natural. His text was "Believe in the Lord thy God and love thy neighbour as thyself". This was Christianity in its true sense. "Nothing is more unpleasant than the man who lives a life made up of stulted rules: a man who meters out charity in terms of personal advancement, both physical and spiritual". A man once asked St Augustine what he must do to be a good Christian, the answer was "Love the Lord thy God and the rest will look after itself". I spent the afternoon reading "England their England" by A G MacDonnell.[520] This is English social life as seen by a young Scots journalist who is employed to get data for a book which is to be written on English character. I do not often laugh at what I read but this was an exception. The dinner party at which Mr Huggins " fixes the bloody butler" and then suggests to a Major General that Australia should be given to the Japanese, made me rock with laughter. The style is one of great contrasts: cynically funny at one moment then tragically beautiful, the cricket match and then the conversation in the Aylesbury pub. It is a book that any flyleaf would describe as "a cure for the blues". In the evening Barrie gave us another of his recitals. He began with the "Italian Concerto" of Bach,[521] no programme of his is complete without a Bachian Interlude. This piece was written in a jocular mood with a simple theme followed by a slow movement and finishing with a return to simple theme, which predominated as a ground base. Strangely enough this concerto was written for the piano alone and not for the piano as a solo instrument. From the start the mood was light, a wealth of continuous sound like the little bubbles rising from the bottom of a glass filled with sparkling champagne. The second movement was slow, the methodical base melody standing out against the tripping, delicately fingered right hand. The third movement brought us back to merry laughter and I had the opportunity of watching the pianist's fingers: perfectly controlled, they flashed, almost invisible, so fast did they move, up and down the keyboard and every note came from the instrument as crystally clear as when a piano tuner strikes each individual note. This piece of Bach was much more colourful than the usual Bach and helped me to appreciate this stupendous producer. I had so often thought of him as dull and highbrow. Now I am learning that his work is not entirely composed of quick three noted trills. His crescendos and his chords, his diminuendos and his finger play are as full of interest as his successors'. Barrie followed this with an "Air and Variations" by Beethoven.[522] This piece was full of melody, brought out by the flowing Arpeggios. It was as if a sharp breeze had come upon the peaceful sea, which answered immediately to this violent visitor by rising up and demanding its accustomed quiet. The fight was short and soon the sea was moving gently to the little ripples. Some pieces of Schumann followed "Other folks and other hands"[523] a piece of rhythmic little melodies full of delicate cadences: a picture of country loving people living in a world of sunshine and green fields. "Cradle song"[524]: as melodious as before showing us that Schumann lived a life in which song must have played a predominant part. This delicate air was more sophisticated by its employment of more modern chord intervals. It finished on a note of absolute quiet. "Novelette"[525] was a 'jack in the box': mighty crescendos made with strident chords and then delicate finger filigrees followed by a martial ending. Schubert, that other composer of the Romantic School who taught us the meaning of a song, was shown us with "Moment Musical"[526] which is a pretty tune dealt with in three or four ways. The effect was one of religious slowness; a picture of monks walking within

---

520 "England, their England", a comic novel of 1920s English urban and rural society by A G MacDonnell, published in 1933.
521 "The Italian Concerto", a 3 movement concerto composed in 1735 by Johann Sebastian Bach.
522 Ludwig Van Beethoven (1770-1827), a German composer and pianist, composed more than 20 sets of Variations.
523 I have not been able to identify this piece of music.
524 "Cradle Song", a piano solo from Op. 124 composed between 1832-1845 by Robert Schumann.
525 From "Noveletten", from Op. 21 composed in 1838 by Robert Schumann.
526 From "6 Moments Musicaux", a series of 6 short pieces for solo piano from Op. 94 by Franz Schubert, published in 1828.

the walls of a monastery garden. Great chords answered by a delicate repetition. The clouds crossed the sky, the air was filled with foreboding but nothing stopped the religious tread. "Variations" by Mozart[527] followed. Here is a composer whose good humour never seems to change: youth cries out in all his work, a youth that only seems to see the fun in life and this feeling took me right through to the playful ending. Haydn,[528] Mozart's contemporary, but his elder both in years and style: though he is light when he wishes, that spirit of youth does not stand out: it seems more the pleading of a young man who loves a serious life but watches with tolerance the games of his fellows. "Gigue in F"[529] was a gay dance which was so fast that it was tiring to listen to. The bright dresses flashed before our eyes until the individual colours were lost in the bright vortex. "Capriccio"[530] was also very fast and was a performer's piece; our performer did not fail. His two hands seemed miraculously to finish a phrase together, so fast did they travel up and down the keyboard. The great item of the programme was "Andante"[531] and "Rondo Capriccioso" by Mendelssohn.[532] This first movement had a striking treble melody supported by thrilling chord runs. The "Capriccio" was as if the pianist's hands had been let loose on the piano and seemed to fall in the right place. It was powerful and exciting. Here the base took the melody and the right hand ran with increasing speed into chromatic runs. Perspiration of excitement was pouring off me when at last this riot of sound died away. As much demanded encores, Barrie played "1st Prelude" of Bach,[533] which composition was the basis of Gounod's "Ave Maria"[534] and then he played a Chopin Waltz which he always calls the "Green Waltz"[535] and it is the ideal name. So ended yet another evening of sheer enjoyment. It has wetted my appetite and I long to hear an orchestra: when I return to civilisation, I shall sit for hours listening to Yehudi Menuhin[536] playing that wonderful Max Bruch[537] concerto. My prayers were that such an evening would come and that, in spite of all the terrible things that have happened, we shall sit in the comfortable lamplight and listen to the violin rising above the waves of the orchestra.

Monday January 20th

Instead of snow, mud was covering the yard and the rain was streaming down in torrents. Walking for me was out of the question for my long suffering shoes were like the proverbial sieve. Lovel dealt with the uncivilised period of English History that culminated in the Wars of the Roses leading to the seizing of the throne by Henry VII[538] and 1485 may be considered as one of the key dates of History. I spent the afternoon translating a Belgian Officer's report on his Army's conduct during the Blitzkrieg.[539] In the evening I rehearsed and then went to Barrie's music lecture. We are most awfully lucky to have Barrie here and he is responsible for most of the cultural activities here for as well as music, he also gives lectures on art, furniture and kindred subjects. His lecture this evening was principally devoted to Bach who he calls the father of Music. He started life as a church organist and his

---

527 Wolfgang Amadeus Mozart (1756-1791) wrote many Variations.
528 Franz Joseph Haydn (1732-1809), an Austrian composer of the Classical Period.
529 I have not been able to identify this piece of music.
530 Haydn composed many Capriccios.
531 Felix Mendelssohn-Bartholdy (1809-1847) composed many Andantes.
532 "Rondo Capriccioso in E Major" from Op.14 composed in 1834 by Felix Mendelssohn-Bartholdy.
533 "1st Prelude", composed in 1722 (?) by Johann Sebastian Bach.
534 "Ave Maria" composed in 1890 by Charles Gounod.
535 Frédéric François Chopin (1810-1849), a Polish composer and virtuoso pianist, composed many Waltzes.
536 Yehuni Menuhin (1916-1999), an American violinist and conductor.
537 Max Christian Friedrich Bruch (1838-1920), a German Romantic composer and conductor.
538 Henry VII (1457-1509), King of England and Lord of Ireland from 1485 until his death.
539 German: lightening war.

early composing was setting elaborate chorales to the simple hymn tunes of his day and, in doing this, he came in for much criticism from the congregations who did not wish their singing to be complicated. He produced an incredible amount of work and in all of it there is not a single harmonic fault. He started using the syncopated type of writing and managed to employ successfully the discordant dominant seventh. His fugues are his greatest contribution and they are the most difficult piece of music to write. Barrie's example was the "Three blind mice". A subject, filling in piece, then back to subject. Four voices but all must be in different keys. The rules must be obeyed. 1st voice starts in the subject key, the 2nd is 5 notes higher, the 3rd 4 notes lower and the 4th takes up the subject key. In answer to a question, B advised how to listen to and appreciate music. "The only way is to hear a piece over and over again: at first you take it as a whole and then you pick out the intrinsic beauties or in the case of an orchestra, the individual instruments." Music, like any art, must be studied and the result of any study is a complete knowledge and appreciation of the subject. Appreciation and Knowledge must run hand in hand. News: Meeting of Hitler and Duce.[540]

Tuesday January 21st

The rain was still pouring down and walking was absolutely off. I devoted a lot of time to learning my German words: I have been putting them down but have been too lazy to learn them and I am convinced that a vocabulary is essential to the quick understanding of any language. In the evening Neave gave us, that is Lovel's Group, a very interesting survey of Plato[541] and Aristotle 490BC-323BC. Plato, a pupil of Socrates,[542] was a Utopian: his ideal state is one in which the best shall rule and the others shall be educated. The philosopher is disinterested and it is he who must rule: the people who do the philosopher's order must do good. Can we compare this to the English 18th Century? A leader must be found who is disinterested, or rather who lives for his ideal and can retain his position by example and energy. Aristotle was concerned with facts and may be called the world's first real scientist. "No more: classify and serve the King". He set men on the track of "Man is a political animal". Man always looks to things that will help him most. Neave's conclusion was that the Greeks began the art of thinking and we are still trying to answer their problems. Is it possible to form an intellectual aristocracy by a system of grading children and sending the highest grades, both intellectually and in character, to a form of electoral college from where the rulers would be drawn? Should a man whose sole desire is to get drunk on Saturdays have the right to call upon the State for the assistance that the State will give to us useful, intelligent members of the community? "Prison Talk" must take this question. News. Suez Canal bombed. Malta bombed. Compulsory fire service between 16 and 17.

Wednesday January 22nd

It was still very wet and I was beginning to ask for the return of the frost. We were very lucky to have some Red Cross food. Two boxes of Knäckebrot, a crisp whole flour biscuit, and a bar of Portuguese milk chocolate. Any idea of saving this chocolate has absolutely left me: once open it is finished for my feeling is, as regards this matter, "What you haven't got, you can't have". Not a very wise philosophy but one must have a moral excuse. I started reading John Buchan's "Augustus":[543] it is going to be hard work and is not a book that can be skipped through for Lovel told us Augustus' system was one that lived and that is what we are looking for. In the first chapter, we find a

---

540   Il Duce, Mussolini's title for himself during WW2, meaning "The Leader".
541   Plato (427BC-347BC), a philosopher in Classical Greece.
542   Socrates (470BC-399BC), a philosopher in Classical Greece.
543   "Augustus" by John Buchan, published in 1937.

saying of great import "The world demanded(s?) peace and law not liberties and privileges". In the evening I gave a lecture in the Speisesaal on the Channel Islands. I had little Smith in the chair. I managed to speak for about 1 ½ hours and found it no difficulty at all though it became much easier as the lecture progressed. I spoke from a few notes under the headings of 1) Geography 2) Historical 3) Population 4) Organisation (a) legal (b) political Id. parochial 5) The islands today 6) Sark 7) Alderney. It was a success, so the audience would have me believe, and I think I shall get it down in written form. News. A German flag was pulled down in San Francisco. Ward Price[544] had an article, otherwise not great news. Illustrious hit again.

Thursday January 23rd

The weather was still very unpleasant and our usual walk was cancelled. I went to a Russian class and found it very difficult, the language is pleasant sounding and not too difficult to read. The most difficult part is the learning of a vocabulary but I don't intend to become really proficient: if I can do all the exercises in the little grammar, I shall feel very pleased. I went on learning my German words, a very dull occupation but the only possible way of getting a fluent grasp of the language. I hope in a month to be able to read almost anything. I find the print of the paper very tiring to read and I often suffer from violent headaches. If I stop working and walk for some time, these soon pass. Not having much food will account for this. I wake up very frequently during the night and my brain whirls about with German, shorthand, thoughts of home, worries and fears. No chance of taking a long walk by myself, or going to a cinema where, to be amused I have only to sit and watch. Here my reading is always serious and I make my pleasure from it. Another extraordinary thing is the fact that I seem to be picking up Grandpa's ways. I never move a step without a pencil and note book and a penknife and, if I could, I would carry a pair of scissors. I hear and read so much of importance that I must put it down. I seem to see Grandpa now sitting in his upright chair, his Times laid on his knee and a little note book in his hand: his pipe sets up a little curl of smoke. I never thought about it then but now I wonder what he was thinking about. Probably a world where he could read good books and where he would not have to meet uninteresting people. I want peace to read and think. I know I must make that peace. I must learn by working and reading what are essentials. I must know before I talk and then I will be listened to. Knowledge, coupled with constructive personal thought, is the only way to teach: the past must be used to help the future, but an enlightened future profiting by the faults of the past. News. A German officer was shot in Bucharest. 3,793 killed, 5,000 injured in England during air raids.

Friday January 24th

The yard was slowly drying up and walking for me was much more pleasant for I wore Hash's Wellington boots and sent my leaky shoes to be mended. Lovel gave a quick survey of 1066-1485. The most interesting economic phase was the 'Law of the just price' whereby Christians could not charge more than the guild price, nor could they under charge. Money could not increase and must not be lent at interest. The Jews, however, were not bound and in this way they amassed great wealth. Nationalism grew with the Reformation, for before this Catholicism took its place: this latter religion (we can almost call Nationalism a religion), however, became increasingly secular and Leo[545] even said "Christianity is a popular superstition for Popes". I must read Pollard's "Factors in Historical

---

544   George Ward Price (1895-1961), Daily Mail journalist.
545   Pope Leo X.

Development".[546] Henry VII, the Tudor Despot, reined on the consent of the people: they wanted security: they were tired of wars and Barons and so-called peoples' charters. Henry VII is most interesting for his experiment in using middle class lawyers to reap his taxes and enforce his laws: from these bourgeois sprung the modern aristocracy, the 19th Century politicians. This day was taken up with rehearsing and learning German words, not very thrilling. Great joy was in the camp. The Greek Red Cross, for the second time, had sent us 50 cigarettes each: I managed to get 2 bars of chocolate and some sweets. I am the real Shylock when cigarettes are in the camp. I had another laundry session and am getting quite the expert and the clothes seem to be quite well washed. I am enjoying "Augustus" very much. It is mostly historical and one cannot but be amazed by the strength of character of this young, frail man who commanded a vast army and with this power was able to appreciate the situation in such a way that he could realise the importance of retaining old, peaceful forms. "The world demanded peace and law, not liberties and privileges" c.f. with the Tudor period. Augustus won through on his 'auctoritas':[547] a successful leader, and a tribune. Tobruk had fallen. One division of Italians was taken: 3 Australian divisions, 2 tank divisions and a free French division under General Catroux.[548] Vissier left us but showed us an amusing letter before he went.

Saturday January 25th

We did some Russian sentences: I managed to struggle through them with very few mistakes. I received a Christmas card from a Miss Christine Knowles, some member of the Red Cross, a very attractive picture and some words by Burns.[549] We also got some garlic sausage and some goose from the Yugoslavian Red Cross. I hope the men at Stalags get these too. At Shorthand we had a speed test and I just managed to get 40 words a minute. In the evening we had a sporting review, rather feeble except for one or two highlights. Barrie and Fielding put on two marvellous ballet dances, one based on "Les Cignes",[550] the other a real "Apache dance". Barrie in a magnificent, black, rather risqué dress and David in the usual "Mec"[551] attire. An all in wrestling match and a real bout of boxing, Crawford against Private Jones, which was quite good. It was fought on the stage with no ropes and was very dangerous: we were all quite glad when it was over and declared a draw. News. Very little German activity. Colonel of an OCTU[552] wrote a very tactless letter. Bevin strongly opposed for his demands to conscript labour. One more week gone by and still no news from home. A letter went to the US Ambassador on our behalf last Sunday and I hope it has some good result. This suspense is terrible. Smith had a December 17th letter from Jersey but it went to VIII H. Perhaps our letters from here have never been sent home. I find that, though I have ambitions in work, I cannot feel settled. When I get home will I find the door closed? I feel so terribly guilty about it all. If only I could have waited another day. The whole thing is so awful that I try not to think about it.

---

546   I have not been able to identify this work. Possibly "Factors in Modern History" by A F Pollard published in 1907.

547   Latin: the general level of prestige a person had in Roman society.

548   Georges Catroux (1877-1969), a French army General and Diplomat who served in both WW1 and WW2.

549   Robert Burns(1759-1796), a Scottish poet and lyricist.

550   French: The Swans (either Swan Lake or The Dying Swan).

551   French: Fellow/bloke.

552   Military abbreviation: Officer Cadet Training Unit.

Sunday January 26th

Ld Acton.[553] "The combination of different nations into one state is as necessary a condition of civilised life as a combination of men in Society". Padre MacLean gave us his usual good sermon, this time stressing the importance of contemplation and keeping the door open for quiet thought. No great man has ever been able to do without his retreat into the wilderness when he was able to put everything into its real perspective. Everyday life is too full of excitement and haste: the unimportant, because it is exciting, becomes important, solitude and silence prevent the imagination from picking up and retaining, to the exclusion of all else, those sensual factors of everyday life. Thoughts can be taken from their normal context, the frame of life, and put into a clean, fresh background, the background of the mind, of the free clear thinking mind. This day was not very enjoyable because I was suffering from a splitting headache: I find that I am not able to concentrate on anything difficult for any length of time without feeling very tired. One hour of Russian and I feel dead tired; that is why I am letting that language take its own course. I lay down after lunch for about an hour and dozed to the accompaniment of the burble of nonsense that usually pervades our room: today I like to hear it, for my mind had no difficulty in following the meanderings of prisoners as they told for the nth time the exciting story of their individual war achievements. As Barrie had injured his foot during the Apache dance and, as the piano was also hors de combat[554], I went on reading "Augustus". The great point of Augustus' policy was that he retained the ancient functions and put his own personal "auctoritas", backed up by the weight of his army, to execute new purposes. He never put himself as infallible and his idea was "The council to which time hath not been called, Time will not ratify". His people followed him; his own personal example and his paternalism endeared him to his subjects. After anarchy came hierarchy: a hierarchy of function and expertness. Nothing was allowed that would undermine the dignity of his office and to unite his country he gave it a cult built up on his own example and genius. He refused to be treated as a God but he wished the spirit of his work, the forming into a union this great empire, to be worshipped as the religion of Roma and Augusta. The Romans were not interested in philosophy and abstract beliefs: they desired concrete rules for human conduct and government and Roma and Augusta was not merely an ethical aspiration of the few. It was a cult formed with the specific intention of uniting this vast empire which, with its tolerance and laisser faire,[555] could only hope to survive by a central example. Augustus as an "être politique"[556] realised this: he made himself the example and the citizenship of Rome the ambition of all. I was struck by a passage in this book: "No great country was ever saved by good men because good men will not go to the lengths that may be necessary", c.f. this with "Violence is justifiable if the ideal be good". But only good men can have ideals?

---

553   John Dalberg-Acton (1834-1902), usually known as Lord Acton, a historian, politician and writer.
554   French: out of action.
555   French: i.e. policy of inaction.
556   French: political being.

Monday January 27th

The weather suddenly turned cold again, and though this was not advantageous to the facial extremities, it was certainly more agreeable to the caged pedestrians. Lovel dealt with Henry VIII.[557] His reign began with great reforms and he was a very popular monarch: somehow the British public are very fond of a full blooded ruler. They were tired of impersonal Kings who only wished to war with their neighbours. The church was in a very corrupt state and Rome was not reverenced by the people. It is a fallacy to believe that Henry wished to reform the church. On the contrary, he wrote a book against Luther[558] and, right to the end of his reign, he was intolerant of any reform of the services. He wished an annulment of his marriage and not a divorce: he even begged the professors of Europe to study the question and they held that his marriage was null. He broke from the temporal power of the papacy and, with the spoils of the church, he created the class of squires, "the backbone of England". He was farsighted and made himself safe with the people. The rest of the day was taken up with rehearsing. I have found that to enjoy amateur theatricals, one must be in the mood. There are days when I feel like screaming, especially when I have to go over a piece 2 or 3 times. A play from the inside is often very thin. If I ever write a play, I shall have it acted by my friends and attend all rehearsals. If I still laugh or weep after 3 weeks, then I shall think that it still has a chance of success. News. Very encouraging from the Italian front. Tobruk had fallen and 20,000 prisoners taken by 3 Australian divisions. A long article on the rat plague in London and a long account of Bevin's nationalisation of the armament industry and the intense opposition?

Tuesday January 28th

We went for the walk under the railway bridge. I was able to see what an icy road looks like. The surface was solid ice and even the drains were frozen. How cold the ducks looked floating about in the swift flowing streams: they owed their salvation to their speed. The slow coaches were frozen solid, no longer did their rippling voices call: they were dead, dead as a great city lost beneath the hard, once molten lava steam. When I got back I was very pleased to find two letters from England, one from Herbert Stephenson and the other from Wendy. Wendy's letter was full of gaiety, dances and parties, weddings and engagements. It carried me back to those days when I used to rush home from the Inn, just pausing to buy a crimson carnation from the little shop on the corner of Lamb's Conduit St, and leap into a steaming bath. Then the careful tying of my bow and the laying in its place of each individual lock of hair. A taxi, then the sound of the band and the last minute glances in the mirror to see that the tie was still as nonchalantly well tied: at last the blaze of light of the ballroom and the sight of lovely dresses forming kaleidoscopic patterns on the polished floor. Then the search for hostesses, the smiles of familiar faces and the grasp of soft, sweet perfumed hands. It all came back to me and I felt very sad. I did love having these two letters but how much more happy would I have been to see Mummy's almost unreadable scrawl across the envelope, telling me how much work there was to be done in the greenhouse. The American Consul who visited the camp was given our names so a letter must come soon. I pray that it will be good news and that no news is good news, that supremely optimistic catch phrase derived for the benefit of those who are too lazy to write letters. We had two new doctor arrivals whose news was very encouraging and we heard about the battle of Taranto[559] and of de Gaulle's

---

557   Henry VIII (1491-1547), King of England from 1509 until his death.
558   Martin Luther (1483-1546), a German monk, former Catholic Priest, Professor of Theology and seminal figure in the Protestant Reformation.
559   The Battle of Taranto took place on the night of 11-12th November 1940. It was the first all aircraft, ship to ship, naval attack in history. This was an attack on the battle fleet of the Regia Marina in the harbour of Taranto, Italy, and was the beginning of the rise of the power of naval aviation over the big guns of battleships.

Dorothy Michael (Desmond's mother) as painted by Uncle Mickie (Arthur C. Michael).

brilliant work in Central Africa. In the evening we discussed Pilato[560] and Aristotle and came to the conclusion that we needed in our world a highly trained body of directors of public thought who were disinterested. The crown must be used to appoint them, for in the crown can be built up that idea of spiritual power that must drive the masses. Equality of opportunity must be given in education and those most promising, both intellectually and in character, must be given the opportunities of what we may term a "Leader school". The first men to learn must be the educators. News. The British were now S of Derna[561] and advancing well. Threats of the attack on England.

Wednesday January 29th

The temperature was about -15 and it was most bracing. I was keeping to my early shower and was now shaving every day. I think it is more economical in blades and cold water gives a very excellent shave: my face, except for the rather weary growth on my upper lip, is as smooth as the posterior of the proverbial infant. In History we dealt with Edward VI[562] and Mary.[563] The former's reign was important for the actual church reforms. The attack on

560   Pontius Pilate.
561   A port city in eastern Libya.
562   Edward VI (1537-1553), King of England and Ireland from 1547 until his death.
563   Mary I (1516-1558), Queen of England and Ireland from 1553 until her death.

papal lands and servants combined with the increase of sheep farming, led to a dangerous growth of unemployment. Mary was very well received by the population for she was Henry's nomination and the Tudor tradition was very strong in the hearts of the people. This early goodwill was soon lost by her great religious intolerance and from this date springs the English hatred of the papacy and perhaps the beginning of Nationalism. The loss of Calais, though much regretted at the time, was a good thing for England, having no European claims, was able to devote her whole attention to the colonies; France, on the contrary, was torn between the fight for the Rhine and the desire of an Empire. Pitt,[564] by his supporting of the German Princes was able to make true his famous words "We shall win Canada on the banks of the Elbe". I received a letter from Geneviève: she had a miserable Christmas but the letter was full of hope. She asked me for camp labels so that she can send me more parcels. I received one of hers today which had been badly damaged. It contained a hollow scarf, one end over my head and the other round by neck giving me the appearance of a violent "sans culotte":[565] there was also a pot of delicious butter, some chocolate, a few lumps of sugar and a small 'pain d'épice'.[566] I think it is very good of her to send me anything, for I am sure they must be very short of food. A new series of lectures began given by a 2nd Lt Spink B Com[567] on Economics and my old knowledge was reawakened. He dealt with Elastic curves, that is to say curves of products that vary very much in quantity when the price is decreased and inelastic curves, curves of products, e.g. bread, that the quantity remains the same whatever the price. It was rather difficult to follow but this is probably because the lecturer was new to the platform and his difficulties were increased by certain Mr Know-alls, all of senior? rank, who gave little lectures at the same time. I spent the evening writing to Aunty and to Uncle Mickie. It is a great art putting everything on to one piece of paper. Let's hope this letter home will receive an answer. News. Our troops are still S of Derna but action in East Africa would seem to be more intense and some Australian troops had been captured. The Empress of Australia[568] was reported to have been badly damaged. I had moved into Harris' bed as he and Arthur Watts had moved into an old soldier's room. I have now a top bunk with Colin underneath. It is much more pleasant because I can now read in bed and also we have a cupboard each just by the window: 2 cupboards on their own. I have put up some prints that I cut from the Frankfurter and life has taken upon itself a much more civilised air. I was struck by two quotations in my book, one which would make an excellent Epilogue to a man's life and it is what I should like.

> *"Since well I've done my past, then gentles pray*
> *Applaud and send me with your thanks away"* (Greek play)

And also a remark of Augustus, *"We also must be soldiers and in a campaign where there is no intermission and no discharge"*.

Thursday January 30th

It was a lovely morning though still very cold (-14) and we went for a new walk. Over the level crossing and to the right, instead of along the railway track. We had to walk in the shade of a wood for some distance and then came

---

564 William Pitt, the Elder (1708-1778), British Whig Statesman and Prime Minister.
565 French: without breeches(meaning the urban lower class).
566 French: spiced bread (more like a cake).
567 Bachelor of Commerce.
568 RMS Empress of Australia, an ocean liner converted into a troop ship during WW2, was torpedoed off the coast of Africa in January 1941 but survived.

out into the sunlit, glistening white country, the grey, icy road weaving its way through woods and snowy fields. I walked with Oldman and we talked of Harry Cantan and the days before this war. I wonder what Harry is doing now? I wish I could see little Sally and hear her talking away to herself, happy as a little bird on a sunny spring day. No letters for me today. I did a Russian class: I am taking it very easily and now I can read it quite easily, the first difficulties seem to be over. A long rehearsal in the evening, which was brightened by a Battle Royal[569] between FF and Beckwith. FF without his beard must have EGO written on his face. Having been prompted the whole time, he turned to us at the end of the rehearsal, and beaming seriously said "the trouble with you fellows is that you miss your cues". Had he a sense of humour, it would have been one of his better remarks But as it was said in all seriousness, I felt that I must be going slowly mad. I began reading Clive Bell's "Civilisation".[570] The Author is an art critic and this is his basis of Civilisation. He takes an original line: he takes the generally acknowledged Civilised periods, the Athenians, Italian Renaissance and Voltaire's France. With these he compares the savages. Any factors that are common to both societies he takes as uncivilised and, by a process of elimination, he arrives at two factors that distinguish the Civilised states. Sense of values which comes by reflection and not instinct, and the enthronement of reason, when everything requires a reasonable explanation and justification. Civilisation is artificial. Now our standards have failed for we do not reflect, we like what we get, not get what we like. Civilisation is cosmopolitan "whenever a learned man takes his seat, there is home", it is tolerant and free from Taboos. A civilised man can talk on anything. "Il n'existe de grand dans ce monde que l'amour des arts, l'amour des choses de l'esprit, l'amour de ceux qu'on aime."[571] News: an article on England's inner cabinet using Lloyd George[572] as the leader of this. Denials of riots in Italy.

569	i.e. a row.
570	"Civilisation" by Arthur Clive Heward Bell, published in 1928.
571	French: There is nothing greater in this world than love of the arts, love of spiritual things and the (reciprocal) love of those you love.
572	David Lloyd George (1863-1945), a British Liberal politician and statesman.

Friday January 31st

Lovel went on with the Tudors, dealing with Elizabeth's[573] astute political sense, which she had learnt in those perilous days during Mary's reign. She played Hercules Francis[574] (Frog he would a-wooing) off against Philip of Spain.[575] He spoke of the Elizabethan seamen and the Armada denying the common belief that Elizabeth was too mean to let her ships be fully armed: rather the ships were too small to carry 7 days supply of munitions. Europe was beset by Loyals and the Counter Reformation. The Jesuits, being confessors of all the great Kings and rulers, were able to wield a vast political power. It was interesting to learn that though the Elizabethan seamen practised slaving and other particularly vicious trades, they were intensely pious and their expeditions were backed by the most religious , or should I say, most religious to the onlooker, business men. Civilisation is not based on religious faith. We were fortunate in receiving 20 cigarettes from the Bulgarian Red Cross. We get smokes from every Red Cross but our own. During the week we had received some chocolate, both eating and drinking, from Geneva. I had increased my supply by judicious swapping of cigarettes. I saw a very interesting sky effect. It was a very bright and cold day and an aeroplane flying at a very great altitude left behind it a long thin cloud of exhaust smoke made much denser by the intense cold. At moments one had the impression of a cloud climbing vertically into the sky. In the evening there was a reading of "King Lear":[576] I had a very small part. I very much enjoyed the play, though I found concentration very difficult. Shakespeare's English is as difficult to me as it ever was. Kent[577] has a very fine character and old Gloucester[578] is indeed tragic, especially when he has lost his sight. I learnt the origin of 2 quotations: "I am more sinned against than sinning" and "Ripeness is all". Hitler made a speech with no startling facts. A Germam Flieger[579] escaped from Canada.

Saturday February 1st

It was much warmer and in the late afternoon the snow began to tumble down so that the yard once again became a blanket of Irish lawn and our cage became quite romantic, except for the dirty Abort[580] corner. Russian was quite fun and Shorthand was a Dictation when we were able to reach 45 words a minute. Connors received two letters from England. Still nothing from Guernsey though a Jan 17th letter has come from Jersey. The highlight of the day was the "Nine A Review". The songs were written by Fox and the production was by Dross whose imitations of Max Miller[581] and Flanagan[582] were masterly. There were 10 plays in 10 minutes. A travelogue of Spangenberg, set in a grassy glade with b----- all livestock. An old time melodrama, "It's alright chaps, he's only tying her to the lines". A tour of London theatres with Gert and Daisy,[583] Flanagan and Allen,[584] Max Miller and a screamingly

---

573   Elizabeth I (1533-1603), Queen of England and Ireland from 1558 until her death.

574   Hercule Francis (1555-1584), Duke of Anjou and Alençon.

575   Philip II (1527-1598), King of Spain and Portugal (as Philip I) and King of England and Ireland during his marriage to Queen Mary I and pretender to the kingdom of France.

576   "King Lear", a tragedy by William Shakespeare, first performed in 1606.

577   A character in "King Lear".

578   A character in "King Lear".

579   German: airman/aviator.

580   German: latrine

581   Max Miller (1894-1963), a British comedian who was very popular in the 1920s, 30s and 40s.

582   Bud Flanagan (1896-1968), a popular English music hall and vaudeville entertainer.

583   Gert and Daisy played by Florence Elsie Waters (1893-1990) and Doris Waters (1904-1978), a British female comedy act remembered for their entertainment in WW2.

584   Bud Flanagan (referenced above) and Chesney Allen (1893-1982), a comedy double act in the WW2 period.

funny Eastern dance. A new crooner, Bing[585] Hunter, absolutely made "Gefangener Blues". Fox himself gave us a very personal song which roused quite a stir in certain circles. Napoleon's farewell to his troops was very well put on and the "Cads of the RAF" were as good as anything heard in London. One great joke: a huge crash "Is Dr Gorrie here?" Silence and consternation. Then "Hiya Doc." The curtain came down on a first class entertainment with a tuneful finale "In Spangenberg again". Every movement was studied and the show had a universal appeal. The "Insignificants" had won a success over the "Highbrows". News. Derna had been evacuated.

Sunday February 2nd

There was a heavy fall of snow during the night and the courtyard was covered with a carpet, about 6 inches deep. It was that crisp clean snow which flattens securely under the weight of a shoe: it does not creep surreptitiously into the shoe and insidiously wet the foot, nor does it form a treacherous surface more befitting to the Pickwickians at Dingley Dell.[586] That feminine word which covers English conversation to the exclusion of more forceful words, nice, can be used without fear of criticism, to this snow: nicely clean and fresh. The Padre was as sincere as ever but I'm afraid my thoughts were straying and the subject was not a vital one. I have had no news from home and it is now 6 months since I left Guernsey. It is terribly worrying having to live on rather flimsy rumours, not knowing whether Mummy is safe; I feel so terribly guilty about it. I just hope and pray for forgiveness and spend my time working hard so that if the trouble I have caused is as great as I think, I shall not waste the opportunities that are given here to use. I spend about 3 hours a day on German and my vocabulary is now pretty comprehensive. Exercises are much more interesting now, for I don't have to keep returning to the back of the book for words: also, constant reading is impressing phrases and sentence formations into my head. My method for learning a future language is:- First to take a few lessons with a competent teacher to learn the correct accent and any alphabetical difficulties. Then work on a grammar to get a grip of the language, hard at first then slacking off. Then buy a dictionary and wade through a newspaper, noting down the words; it is fatal to do spasmodic reading, a certain time must be allotted every day and also the words must be learnt after every day's reading and revised the next day. The usual journalistic words soon become very familiar and then it is time to take up a novel. This should be one of the recognised classics and of a serious nature. Now is the time to return to the grammar and work through certain exercises. It is also the moment to take up conversational lessons. With a good vocabulary, conversation soon develops. This is the method I have followed in learning German and I shall adopt the same method for Italian and, in a lesser degree, Russian: the grammar of this last language is greatly simplified by the fact that there are only two tenses and no articles. The difficulty is the case declensions and the different adjectival endings; the prepositions require a great deal of study. With a vocabulary, not easy to learn for new sounds must come into play, I should be able to make fairly good progress. As the war does not look in the least like coming to a speedy end, I hope to tackle Spanish! I spent the afternoon reading "Elizabeth and Essex"[587] and am fascinated by Elizabeth's character "a beautiful negation": never would she come to a decision and ever was she ready, like all the Tudors, to use a worker for her own ends and then, rather than be thought in the wrong, she would cast her servant to the crowd and sacrifice him. She understood the majesty of Monarchy but, at the same time, she fortunately understood her people and gauged their feelings. She vascillated to keep England out of war, which was to her a wasteful thing. She desired no criticism from Parliament and when it came she crushed it. In crushing it, she never closed her ears to it and put it from her, as so many Monarchs have done, thinking, as did James I, that "as it is blasphemy to dispute the word of God, so is it treason to dispute the word of the King in the height of his power". Rather did Elizabeth keep

---

585   A reference to Bing Crosby, an American singer and actor (1903-1977).
586   "The Posthumous Papers of the Pickwick Club" by Charles Dickens, published in 1836. Dingley Dell is a farm.
587   "Elizabeth and Essex" by Lytton Strachey, published in 1928.

it in her heart for, though she knew that she was Queen, she also knew that England was a country full of human beings who were prepared to support her if she was queenly, that is majestic, true to her country and just to her people. Elizabeth kept criticism in her heart and pondered over the justness of her people's demands. If they were fair comment upon her and she would lose nothing by submitting to them, she would graciously thank her people for bringing their claims to her notice and she would grant them. She had not given way, she had deliberated over good advice: her audience, grateful to have their wishes granted, were even more flattered to realise that their advice had been taken. The Queen, by her dignified understanding, or so it appeared, had, by acquiescing, enhanced the majesty of her position and men were prepared to brave the greatest perils for a word from her. She knew when to give way and how to give way graciously. Her strength was prodigious, as the Spanish ambassador realised, having been compelled to stand for 3 hours in her presence, for she did not sit down during audiences, and this mannish strength, combined with her feminine intuition of danger, learnt by years of painful watching during Mary's reign, combined to make the Greatest woman of England inhuman in her majesty, and yet so very human in her vacillation and her little romantic parries with her courtiers. A splendid body, holding an understanding mind: great as she was, was she not perhaps the outward form of Cecil's[588] brilliant state craft. I fully realise the important role that the peace loving Cecil played and how he was able to curb the Queen's impetuosity but I feel that with no other being could his policy have been so successful. She was the actress, not merely acting her role as she was told by the producer, but the actress who listened to her producer, realising his skill and putting her own greatness and thought into this part. But what of Essex[589] in this book? He was a romantic, living for honour and glory, imbued with a fanatical hatred of Spain that governed his whole life. A servant of Royalty in those summary days had to curb his thoughts. Essex could never do this and though Bacon,[590] that cynical Renaissance figure, advised Essex to play a more subservient role, the spirit of the Middle Ages would not be suppressed and his instructor's dissimulation was never maintained by him, for the steel of verity soon showed its face: his military taste, not his military genius, took command: he threw himself into wild expeditions and weakly listened to his wilder friends. The Queen stands before you with a throne, she is surrounded by your enemies. How could Essex, that full blooded boy cut off from this great Majesty who looked upon him with such desiring eyes, resist the opportunity of making himself into a public idol? He forsook Bacon's advice and failed. His treachery was open. Bacon, who had been so often with Essex when he, Bacon, suffered from that painful disease, consumption of the purse, did not think twice before he prosecuted him before the Queen. Did he remember that he himself had written "Mean men must adhere but great men that have strength in themselves were better to maintain themselves indifferent and neutral." How easy for him to have betaken himself to the country when the trial of Essex was held. But the positions of the State were to be his in future if he proved himself to be a great prosecutor. Why not take this opportunity: do we always say what we mean? In Bacon's case, at any rate, words were not justified by deeds. News. 27% increase in Irish trade. Economic agreement with USA envisaged.

---

588   William Cecil (1520-1598), also known as Lord Burleigh, an English Statesman, Chief Advisor to Elizabeth I, twice Secretary of State and Lord High Treasurer from 1572.

589   Robert Devereux, 2nd Earl of Essex (1565-1601), an English nobleman who led an abortive coup d'état against the government in 1601 and was executed for treason.

590   Francis Bacon (1561-1626), an English philosopher and Statesman who served as Attorney General and Lord Chancellor of England during Elizabeth I's reign.

Monday February 3rd

The snow was still very thick. In History Lovel dealt with the period after the Armada. He made it clear that History cannot be divided into water tight compartments and periods must give birth to movements in following times. The Stuarts had all the Tudor despotism but lacked their understanding and tact. The external danger, which had helped to keep Elizabeth on the pedestal of a unified, safe country was no longer there and the population could turn its eyes to the study of internal problems. Parliament, under Elizabeth's tactful handling had gained self respect and also it had become very Puritan,[591] being composed mostly of wealthy business men who were usually Puritans, the wool trade, the great source of wealth, being in the hands of the Puritans. Elizabeth, in this age of youth and enquiry, had walked delicately along the middle path. Her age had been one of scientific, geographical and artistic enquiry full of vibrant characters and yet, in spite of all, it was a crude age. Great religious belief combined with hateful cruelty. Beautiful plays interspersed with vulgarity. Can one compare it to Germany of today full of scientific and artistic development yet always a streak of brutality? Art and History are well shown in a book "Poetic Procession" Roxburgh.[592] I was very pleased to get two letters from Aunty, Dec 1st and 24th, in which she spoke of having had no news from home. I hope Russell got through his exam. What fun to see them all again. We received some sheets from the Hungarian Red Cross and we drew lots for them. I was fortunate enough to draw a pair: they are sown into a sleeping bag and are of very good linen. One advantage is that they simplify bed making. I am up regularly at 8 and my bed making is quick but effective. I roll my blankets to the end of the bed, straighten the sheet bag, pull back the blankets, tuck them in and voilà.[593] I don't touch the mattress because the wood wool is settled into a very comfortable hollow and I'm frightened of making it lumpy: a good excuse anyway. <u>News.</u> Derna has been evacuated.

Tuesday February 4th

I missed the walk, unfortunately, as I have trouble with my left foot again. This time it is a type of active eczema between the toes, caused by some germ that lives on the floor of the shower room and assisted by improperly dried feet. I have had some ointment on and I must give up my daily shower for some time. Also very slow in healing. Instead of walking I did a German exercise with some success. More rehearsing and FF has been given the sack, which is a great relief. Gilder, one of the MOs[594] has his place. We had another issue of Bulgarian cigarettes (every Red Cross but the British) but cigarettes are at a huge discount and have no swap value: still the time will come. A letter from Zabette was quite encouraging, though she was rather sorry not to have heard from me. News. Siam and Indo China Armistice.[595] Times article on menace of Japan.

---

591   The Puritans were a significant grouping of English Protestants in the 16th and 17th centuries.
592   "The Poetic Procession" by J F Roxburgh, published in 1922.
593   French: that's that.
594   Military abbreviation: Medical Officer.
595   A formal Armistice between Indochina and Siam was signed on 31st January 1941.

Wednesday February 5th

The weather was much warmer and the yard was gradually becoming a sea of dirty mud. If England has the most variable climate, it is closely followed by Spangenberg. Today was a great day for the stomach. In November, George L J Cook had sent my name to a friend in Belgium who had the job of readdressing Medical Comforts parcels sent by the Red Cross to British soldiers in hospital. As all these soldiers are now in Germany, the parcels are sent on and in time we should all receive one. They are wonderful parcels; tinned meat, margarine, chocolate, sweets, Bemax,[596] marmalade, fruit, milk and Horlicks,[597] also bandages, dressings, aspirin and Epsom salts![598] This stomachic day was made even greater by the distribution of a Red Cross parcel each. I ate a vast amount of chocolate and I can't understand how I ever refused this delicious invention. Lovel's lecture was on the two first Stuarts. James I[599] was a 'shambling pedant', the wisest fool in Christendom. His reign opened with trouble with the Puritans for James' maxim was "No Bishops, No King." The feeling against Spain was very great and James was foolish enough to pander to Spain by sacrificing Raleigh.[600] He was, from 1608, advised by worthless servants who pressed him to ask for money: in reply, Coke,[601] the staunchest of Parliamentary lawyers, discovered the Magna Carta and used it to support his claims of "No supply without redress of grievances." Unlike Elizabeth, James did not act tactfully with his people and he had not the Queen's insight into their grievances and her ability to give way gracefully. He antagonised his people by not sending aid to his protestant daughter Elizabeth.[602] He was unprepossessing and, though intellectually competent, was practically stupid. His son Charles,[603] on the other hand, had a regal presence and was a good family man, so necessary for a Monarch in Puritan England, or even in any land as Augustus discovered; but Charles was unfortunate enough to have married a strong willed Catholic, Henrietta Maria,[604] who was always looked upon with suspicion and disfavour by his subjects. He was always led by favourites of whom Buckingham[605] was the worst. Wentworth,[606] on the other hand, was an unscrupulous sound administrator and, during the 11 years tyranny, there is little doubt that the common people were better off, though the upper and middle classes suffered by the impositions of forest laws and baronetcy monies. When at last Parliament was recalled, they put forward the grand remonstrance which, in the opinion of the mass, was too forward. Had Charles not hastily tried to arrest the five members, there is little doubt that the people would have reacted in favour of the King. The rest of the day was taken up with rehearsing which gets rather dreary. In the evening Lovel gave us a lecture on "Educational Reform". The trouble with modern education is the dangerous influence of parents. "Even a young black beetle is a gazelle to its mother" and also the "Fetish of the Certificate". The great weakness is the weakness of Teachers. Discipline must be enforced but with reason, not with blind force. Secondary education from 14 should be apprenticeship for life, with a cultural background. Greek would stimulate enquiry and specialisation must only be undertaken with a cultural background, which amounts to education for leisure. Civies should be taught History, Geography, Economics, good citizenship and Logic. Discipline was his keystone: boys should fight problems with reason and not be coddled. Major Gee held that when Greek has been

---

596   A vitamin tonic food.
597   A malted milk hot drink.
598   Used as a topical treatment for aches and pains and in solution as a laxative.
599   James I (1566-1625), King of England and Ireland from 1603 until his death.
600   Sir Walter Raleigh (1554-1618), English aristocrat, writer, soldier, courtier, spy and explorer.
601   Sir Edward Coke (1552-1634), an English barrister, judge and politician.
602   Elizabeth Stuart (1596-1662).
603   Charles I (1600-1649), King of England, Scotland and Ireland from 1625 until his execution in 1649.
604   Henrietta Maria of France (1609-1669).
605   George Villiers (1592-1628), 1st Duke of Buckingham, royal courtier and favourite of Charles I.
606   Thomas Wentworth (1593-1641), 1st Earl of Strafford, English Statesman and supporter of Charles I.

abandoned, the cultural life becomes stereotyped for the Romans were not mentally imaginative. <u>News.</u> East African losses are severe on the Italian sides.

Thursday February 6th

My foot was rather troublesome so I could not go on the walks: I do like to get some exercise and when I get home I shall love the long cliff walks alone with nothing but the sea below me and the windy sky above. In the afternoon I addressed the Naval Study Group with "A Voyage on a submarine" in which I tried to give the psychological life of a seaman in one of these craft, the intense discomfort, coupled with the strict discipline. Not a discipline of red tape and saluting but real discipline that is a realisation that safety relies on the implicit obedience of command. It is not a discipline of rank, but of knowledge. I had prepared no notes and I just talked of the voyage as it came to me. I managed to talk for a whole hour without much difficulty. I seem to have got 'the gift of the gab' as Grandpa used to say. At Neave's group we discussed medicine and development of Civilisation. One theory raised was very interesting. It was that racial development follows a Cultural ideal. That is to say that when a race has an ideal, those who most nearly fulfil that ideal will become the popular heroes and will be the most attractive to women and from them the best stock will come. The example of this is that of the old Norsemen who, as their land was a barren one, turned to the sea and created an ideology of valour. Their race was full of magnificent men and women. The application of this theory to modern life would be possible if marriage were made an ideal, an ideal to beget strong and mentally superior people. A man would not merely marry for sexual pleasure; with the ideal in his mind of a betterment of mankind, he would choose someone who fulfilled his ideals. Those not chosen would in time die off, just as wolves have left our shores. They would be outcasts and, though they should not suffer physically or mentally, they would be merely unproductive because their capacities would not fulfil the marriage ideals. <u>News.</u> Denial of a Turco Russian secret pact. Col Donovan's[607] secret mission?

Friday February 7th

The History lecture was on the Civil War.[608] Parliamentary discipline in the Model Army backed up by a fanatical religious ideal made the troops invincible. The Royalist Armies were very loath to leave their home counties whereas the New Model was not a territorial army. Cromwell[609] was a great tactician, as Preston[610] in the 2nd Civil War shows, as well as a diplomatist; he was the only Parliamentarian in the Army, therefore was the natural link. Charles, who was a great believer in his own rights and the maxim, the end justifies the means, played a double game too often and so his life came to an end. The Parliamentarians were unwise to behead him for he at once became a martyr: it was impossible to keep him in the country but would not exile to America have been just as effective and on the Restoration the powers would have been united? Cromwell was a great foreign administrator and his Navy Acts[611] were the basis of our merchant fleet supremacy. His ideas were far seeing and his colonial vision was one

---

607 Colonel William J Donovan (1883-1959), a US soldier, lawyer, intelligence officer and diplomat best remembered as the wartime head of the Office of Strategic Services during WW2.
608 The English Civil War (1642-1651).
609 Oliver Cromwell (1599-1658), an English military and political leader and later Lord Protector of the Commonwealth of England, Scotland and Ireland.
610 The Battle of Preston (17-19 August 1648) resulted in victory for the New Model Army under Cromwell over the Royalists and Scots.
611 The Navigation Act of 1651.

of the ideal of collaboration, not the materialistic belief in the 'sponge' system. "Cromwell" by Buchan.[612] Letters by Carlyle. I attended a lecture by Symes and Nicolle which opened my eyes to the incompetence of the DCO.[613] The lunch of today was splendid, a piece of tender pork the size of a postage stamp: still, one could imagine a juicy piece of white meat, fringed with crisp brown crackling, served with roast potatoes and spring cabbage and apple sauce. How well I remember Grandpa mixing his mustard and sugar and vinegar into a 'bittersweet' sauce. More rehearsals as the play is on Saturday week and Eustasia, my lady friend, is laid up with flu, which is very prevalent here at this time. <u>News</u>. 17 of our planes shot down over France as against 3.

Saturday February 8th

It was very much warmer. Appell was at 9 o'clock and Capt – was taking it. He had a lot of complaints about standing still and hands in pockets and we had to produce our identity plaques, most of them have been lost which did not please him. His fate will not be pleasant judging from conversation. I struggled with Russian but I must do more work to make use of the classes. Shorthand is going quite well and my outlines are not bad. I have managed to get the knack of the soft and heavy lines. I translated some German History, the 1918 push and one thing that took my notice was the fact that, during this time, the German troops were allowed to plunder and this had "irreparable effect". That is probably why discipline has been so strict. No mention is made of opposition in this History. The fact is merely stated that some Army began retreating! History has caused much harm because it has been treated as a National subject. If it had been always kept as an international science would we have learnt more. Even medicine is made national with War? I have been reading a book called "The Great Victorians",[614] short essays by various authors. "George Meredith"[615] by Sir W Beach. The writer of "Ordeal of Richard Feverel"[616] was a great stylist who used ten words when one would do: his belief was that life was essentially worthwhile "The flame of the soul burns upwards (true idealism) but we must allow for atmospheric conditions (Victorian common sense)". "J S Mill"[617] by Sir Arthur Salter. Mill received an intensive education when young and was always "sérieux".[618] Knowledge must be attacked as an enemy before it is embraced as a friend. He held that False doctrine was fatal to reform in opposition to the Inductive school which held that truths external to the mind may be known by intuition or consciousness independently of observation and experience. His life was one of Integrity, Honesty and Courage in which, for him, reason was enthroned: reason should control art and not suppress it. "William Morris"[619] by Middleton Murry. Here was a Marxian socialist who came to his conclusions by regarding History through an artist's eyes, consciousness of the past was necessary to the true living of the present. To him inspiration was a matter of craftsmanship: and art was not God inspired but the pleasure of a man at his work as Ruskin[620] had said. What men wanted was fearless rest and hopeful work and as art was only for the rich, he was prepared to throw it away, feeling sure that it would live again. He was a supreme socialist and his life's work was to make popular the simple work of the individual man. His life was not comprehensive and never dealt with his

---

612 "Oliver Cromwell" by John Buchan, published in 1934.
613 Military abbreviation: Defence Coordinating Officer/Office (?).
614 I have not been able to identify this collection of essays.
615 George Meredith (1828-1909), an English novelist and poet of the Victorian Era.
616 "The Ordeal of Richard Feverel" by George Meredith, published in 1859.
617 John Stuart Mill (1806-1873), a British philosopher, political economist and civil servant.
618 French: serious.
619 William Morris (1834-1896), an English textile designer, artist, writer and libertarian socialist.
620 John Ruskin (1819-1900), a leading art critic of the Victorian Era, a prominent social thinker and philanthropist.

own financial position. So important in the study of a socialist! "Florence Nightingale"[621] by L Housman. This was very elaborately written and from it one could see that the famous nurse's motto should be "Blessed are the masterful". We must create a public opinion which will drive governments and this she did. Some notes from Bell's "Civilisation". Civilisation is a characteristic of societies and for any state to become civilised it must have a nucleus of civilised people. A civilised man is one who appreciates art, respects truth and knows how to behave himself. He demands a state supported leisured class. He fears that, at present, the connection between rich and poor is too strong: the rich man's desire is to become richer, the poor man's is to be as rich as the rich man. He holds that Despots can endow and protect a civilising class and that Athens was merely a state of oligarchy. What a civilised state must be based on is the desire to be civilised. Do we desire that end or are we content to rest with the means and not carry through to the end? <u>News.</u> Italians S of Benghazi[622] and hard pressed in Abyssinia. Crisis in France between Vichy and Germans.

Sunday February 9th

The weather was almost spring like in its warmth though it was very wet under foot. Our breakfast tradition was changed for we sat down to a very delicious fishcake. The new cook, a soldier (as opposed to the last rather dismal and insolent sailor who got very tired of his culinary pursuits and made the great mistake, prevalent in easy going and undisciplined communities, of thinking himself indispensable, and so lost his job), made a very good impression with his fishcakes which were well bread crumbed and a warm luscious brown. It was a wonderful achievement if one thinks that the basis of these cakes is a salty, high smelling piece of cod cats' meat in normal times. These fish have now been installed in the shower room in our building and apart from their nasal propensities, they are very obstructive when one is going to take a bath. However, we can't eat our fish and bath in it as well, and at present, owing to Pte Magee's 15 years cooking experience, I would rather eat my fish. Padre MacLean gave us his usual good sermon. He is a consistently good preacher, not one who occasionally gives utterance to a master piece of composition and intuition which is counter balanced by many weeks of commonplace copyings which are not worth the hardness of the seat: he speaks as one who has studied his intimate subject and as one who means and believes what he says. This week he dealt with the betrayal of Jesus and gave the interesting theory that Judas was actuated by a political motive, that is to say that he betrayed Jesus hoping that his master, on finding himself in danger of death, would preach a stronger form of conduct and incite his followers to overthrow the Roman rule. Our Lord knew that Judas was going to betray him and he let Judas into this knowledge but he did not try to stop him. If Judas knew this and went on with his betrayal would not his conscience suffer more? MacLean drew his conclusion from this: it was that God gave us this example and, if we did not wish to follow, he would not save us from ourselves: he was not to be treated as a benevolent old gentleman but as a living spirit which we could follow or not; if we did not follow, we should know that we were straying and that knowledge would be our punishment. I spent most of the day writing up my diary and reading "The Great Victorians". I am very interested in this period, so morally and mentally disciplined yet productive of fine characters, both political and literary. The moral and stylist limits forced a writer or an artist to crystallise his work into conventional themes and with this his characters are fuller and more minutely portrayed. "Lord Palmerston"[623] by H Nicholson. The bluff character, imbued with a supreme egoism and aristocratic mentality carried on his foreign policy with a spirit of reckless

---

621   Florence Nightingale (1820-1910), social reformer, statistician and founder of modern nursing.
622   Second largest city in Libya.
623   Henry John Temple (1784-1865), commonly known as Lord Palmerston, was a British Statesman who served twice as Prime Minister in the mid 19th century.

sportsmanship: "The law of nations must sometimes surrender to the law of Nature": his law of nature was one, not of a peaceful loving nature but of a violent, destructive, strength imposed nature. He admitted once that he liked power whereas Canning[624] believed that security and stability make the world safe for constitutional Democracy. The maxim that good diplomacy means certain diplomacy was replaced by Palmerston by the word violent. Foreign policy should be intelligible and popular: Palmerston's was popular, as a professional football win is popular. The end justified the means. "Walter Pater",[625] an aesthetic Victorian whose work was essentially sensual with a corpse like Victorian refinement. His most famous works are "Marius"[626] and "Renaissance Studies".[627] C Patmore,[628] a poet, gave us love and poetry mingled in a super sensual form. "Angel in the house".[629] The predominating feminine mind can say anything but has nothing to say. Robert Peel[630] was a politician who knew when to give way and his strength lay not in his discovery of principle but in his technique of application. His changes were carried out in his fullest conviction but they were not political successes because he did not prepare his party for them, feeling that he was indispensable and that his party must just do as they were told. Bagehot's[631] words sum up Peel:-"A Constitutional Statesman is, in general, a man of common opinions and uncommon ability." C Rhodes was damned by the unfortunate Jameson Raid, it is difficult to go deeply into his character if one does not know the facts of this fiasco (I must look them up). His character of a worker is summed up in his own words "A civilised man is anyone who is not a loafer." From a boy, he saw his goal, race union not ascendancy and with this ideal in mind he worked his way to Oxford and, at the same time, made himself a fortune. Rossetti[632] was a poet who stood for the Aesthetic lover. Lord Cecil who wrote this biography makes some interesting remarks on the 18th and 19th Century poets. Those of the earlier century occupied themselves with living needs and problems while in the latter they divorced themselves from life and became independent, taking their ideas not from worldly standards and situations, but from spiritual and intangible ideas. John Ruskin: here is a man whose whole style was relieved of its individuality by his early upbringing. During his young life he was compelled to read and learn the scriptures and this early drudgery permeates his whole writings. He was a Utopian connoisseur and lived in a muddle of our criticism and economic reform. He was one of the prime movers in the pre Raphaelite movement set afoot by a number of Victorian artists and writers who realised that art was losing its real position, that of portraying beautiful things and, with this realisation, they coupled a desire for moral stimulation and set about portraying ideas with a religious or moral significance. Lord Salisbury[633] was a social and intellectual aristocrat; a high churchman whose beliefs were cynical and fatalist; a politician aloof from all and sure in his creed, admitting of no alternative. His social aloofness is shown by one of his remarks "To be stewed and bored at dinner parties is the destiny of we unfortunate White Slaves." Swinburne[634] was a Revolutionary against the Victorian principle of permanent employment and satisfaction and the will for physical and mental comfort. His revolution was deep not as an undergraduate's present unconformity which is only part of his future conformity. A Trollope[635] was essentially honest "every author wants money and it is humbug to say that he doesn't"; this truth struck home and led to his unpopularity. His books are all very long and this is due, as it is with many other Victorians, to the habit of serial

---

624 George Canning (1770-1827), British Statesman and politician who served as Foreign Secretary and briefly as Prime Minister.
625 Walter Horatio Pater (1839-1894), was an English essayist, critic of art and literature and writer of fiction.
626 "Marius the Epicurean" by Walter Pater, published in 1885.
627 "Studies in the History of Renaissance" by Walter Pater, published in 1873,
628 Coventry Patmore (1823-1896), an English poet and critic.
629 "Angel in the House" by Coventry Patmore, published in 1854.
630 Sir Robert Peel (1788-1850), a British Conservative Statesman who twice served as Prime Minister.
631 Walter Bagehot (1826-1877), a British businessman, essayist, Social Darwinist and journalist.
632 Possibly Dante Gabriel Rosetti (1828-1882), an English poet, illustrator, painter and translator.
633 Robert Gascoyne-Cecil (1830-1903), British Conservative Statesman and thrice Prime Minister.
634 Probably Algernon Charles Swinburne (1837-1909), poet, playwright, novelist and critic.
635 Anthony Trollope (1815-1882), an English novelist of the Victorian Era.

writing. His work is based round the same characters and he uses the novel to tell his story and not to portray his own psychological idiosyncrasies, as so many of our modern authors are in the habit of doing. Tylor,[636] an anthropologist wrote "Researches into the early history of mankind"[637] and his maxim was that the Past is needed to explain the Present, the Whole to explain the Part. In the evening Barrie gave us another concert. He began with Mozart's "Eine Kleine Nachtmusik":[638] light and an ideal expression of the idea behind its conception, music to send Mozart's patron's little boy to sleep. "Sonata Op 10 No 2" by Beethoven[639] was one of his lesser known ones and was particularly enjoyable for the beautiful second movement, very tuneful in slow rhythmic time. Some little pieces by Haydn[640] followed a minuet and a dance that was almost Gaelic its breezy, fresh tinged happiness. "Nocturne in D flat" by Ralph,[641] a young, modern composer who died when still young, was packed with romantic melody, much more like Schumann[642] than like the composer's contemporaries who are fond of artificial mechanical monotony. Two pieces of Liszt, a transposition of a Polish song from Chopin and an arrangement of Mendelssohn's "On wings of song"[643] which was interesting because the melody was bounded by arpeggios carried from one hand to the other. His final piece was a "Prelude and Fugue in A minor".[644] This was the usual mechanically perfect Bach and I appreciated its mechanical perfection as I admire a huge, polished locomotive but it did not inspire me: the Prelude was a few chords and then it went into the breakneck Fugue with the voices very distinct. As an encore he played MacDowell's "An Eine Wilde Rose":[645] its peaceful song completed a fine evening.

Monday February 10th

The weather now was almost summer like, a fresh spring day and it is on days such as these that the life here becomes so irksome. The trees and the green fields call; the only answer they receive is a grumbling, noisy crowd of men hemmed in by grey forbidding barbed wire. Lovel dealt with the Restoration and portrayed Charles II[646] as an attractive, moderate King, tolerant in religious matters and enjoying life to the full. Even in Cromwell's day the country had been preponderantly Royalist, so much so that the Protector had always feared to hold an election: he had been "balancing a wig on the point of a sword". This period was the beginning of large scale political corruption which reached its culminating point in the 18th C. Clarendon Code[647] and Shaftesbury[648] discovery of

---

636 Sir Edward Burnett Tylor (1832-1917), an English anthropologist.
637 "Researches into the Early History of Mankind and the Development of Civilisation" by Edward Burnett Tylor published in 1865.
638 "Eine kleine Nachtmusik" composed in 1787 by Wolfgang Amadeus Mozart.
639 "Piano Sonata No. 6 Op.10 No. 2", composed from 1796 to 1798 by Ludwig Van Beethoven.
640 Franz Joseph Haydn (1732-1809), an Austrian composer of the Classical Period.
641 Possibly "Nocturne in D flat major" composed by American pianist Ralph Votapek (?)
642 Robert Alexander Schumann (1810-1856), a German composer.
643 "On Wings of Song", composed from 1833 to 1834 by Felix Mendhelssohn.
644 "Organ Prelude and Fugue in A minor", composed in 1708 by Johann Sebastian Bach.
645 To a Wild Rose" from "Woodland Sketches" composed in 1904 by Edward Alexander MacDowell.
646 Charles II (1630-1685), King of England, Scotland and Ireland from 1660 until his death.
647 A series of 4 legal Statutes passed between 1661 and 1665 which effectively re-established the supremacy of the Anglican Church after the interlude of Cromwell's Commonwealth and ended toleration for dissenting religions.
648 Anthony Ashley Cooper (1621-1683), 1st Earl of Shaftesbury, a prominent English politician during the Interregnum and during the reign of King Charles I.

the alleged Romist[649] Plot of Titus Oates[650] show the intense religious feeling. Then the Rye House Plot[651] was manufactured by Danby,[652] the first real Tory leader and the most unscrupulous of men, put the feeling against the Whigs, and so the ding dong went on. The afternoon was taken up with rehearsals and in the evening I became hors de combat:[653] my foot had gone septic and was most painful. The sore place between my toes had grown considerably and there was a gaping hole. I had it bathed and bound up and retired to bed. Dr Gorrie, our bearded Scotch MD,[654] advised me to stay in bed. It was only with great difficulty that I managed to find him at all for he was buried in one of the rooms playing poker for all his worth. There are many here, Mac and Colin among them, who play this game from 9 in the morning till Lights Out – vast sums of lagergeld change hands and it is nothing to hear of 200 RM going on one hand. I will admit that life is somewhat monotonous here and some excitement is needed but I do not think that a young man has nothing to do. I said to a friend the other day that one could not have enough knowledge: he replied that he did not want to know anything. If that is the desire of "leaders of men" what can the men be like? It makes one rather depressed to see one's fellows with leisure to learn and opportunities of learning, just sit and play cards for 12 hours a day. Perhaps Plato was right when he advocated a leisured class who studied and used their intelligence and others who had no desire of knowledge could do the menial work. The news was full of denials: one that we had shot down 90 Stukas[655] out of 125.

Tuesday February 11th

I spent the day in bed and it did my foot a great deal of good and the swelling soon went down. The treatment is boracic powder. My new bed is near the window and I have plenty of light to read by: the only snag is the fact that wood wool is very hard on certain portions of the anatomy. I spent most of the day reading Philip Guedalla's "100 days",[656] being a story of Napoleon's progress, both military and political between his departure from Elba[657] and his defeat at Waterloo. The style is very brisk and readable and the writer takes great pains to stress the importance of Brussels[658] upon Napoleon: he dreamed of it in Elba and even at Waterloo it had such an effect on him that he never stopped to consider a detour. The character of Fouché[659] is one of a despicable man who willingly sold himself. The book not only brings out Napoleon's character but also shows his influence on the hysterical masses. I began reading a German novel called "Seydlitz",[660] the story of an 18th C page boy: it was full of very hard words and I did not make much progress. The News was full of Far Eastern tenseness: also there was a raid on Genoa[661] which killed many civilians and hit no military objectives!

649 I think Desmond means 'Popish Plot'.
650 Titus Oates (1649-1705), was an English perjurer who fabricated the 'Popish Plot', a supposed Catholic conspiracy to kill King Charles II.
651 Rye House Plot of 1683, a plan to assassinate King Charles II and his brother, James, Duke of York.
652 Thomas Osborne (1632-1712), known as the Earl of Danby.
653 French: out of action.
654 Abbreviation: From the Latin Medicinae Doctor, Doctor of Medicine.
655 German: dive bomber.
656 "The Hundred Days" by Philip Guedalla, published in 1934.
657 A Mediterranean island in Tuscany, Italy.
658 Brussels, capital of Belgium.
659 Joseph Fouché (1759-1820), French Statesman and Minister of Police under Napoleon.
660 "Seydlitz" by E Von Naso, published in 1932.
661 Genoa, capital of Liguria, Italy.

Wednesday February 12th

My foot was much better and I stayed in bed till tea time. I made a point of getting up for supper because Smith had made us a very fine trifle, flavoured with figs and topped with custard and peaches. I spent the day reading a novel by Carola Oman "Henrietta Maria".[662] I was a little disappointed in it. Though giving an intimate and femininely inspired character of Charles II's unfortunate Catholic spouse, it did not include enough data on the political situation that led up to the Civil War. It was very charming and very skilfully portrayed the effect of HM's French and Catholic suite upon the rapidly increasing Puritan element in England. I am more fond of ordinary straightforward biography, giving facts and character, than the historical novel full of attractive but unimportant incidents. In the evening I prepared my talk for Neave's group. News. Another big flight over France and general increased activity. A rumour came through that the Renown[663] had shelled Genoa to prevent the embarkation of a German expeditionary force to Tunis to deal with Gen Weygand[664] (Clout discovered this in the Beobachter:[665] but this gentleman is very full of rumours and can predict the end of the war by the expression on Herr R's face. I did not get a chance to read this report).

Thursday February 13th

The weather was still holding and it was beautifully warm in the sun. I have optimistically ordered a deck chair and some sun glasses. My foot was much better but still walking was difficult. We had a new camp officer while Herr R goes to the Kommandantur.[666] The new officer seems very polite and salutes with great profuseness. I did some Russian and now feel that I have got inside the crust of the language. I am going to start learning words, which is not a very gay prospect. In the evening I gave my talk on France which seemed to go down quite well. I made my plan and spoke from a few consecutive notes. I have much more command of myself and am able to digress from my subject and return to it without having lost myself completely. I used an Introduction: a Historical survey with stress 1. on the social changes and characteristics 2. on the artistic side, stressing feminism and "salonism".[667] The second part dealt with modern France stressing Religion, Education and the attitude to sex and then a conclusion. I used a number of Voltaire quotations and I find an apt quotation most helpful. It is for this reason that I keep a note book by me in all my reading. <u>News</u>. A big attack on a convoy W of Portugal in which 14 ships were sunk. Willkie[668] and La Guardia[669] spoke, the latter saying that America would be absolutely ready in 1945! I can read the paper almost unseen and I study it fairly carefully. There is an enormous amount of information to be gleaned from the articles and I am astonished at the amount of news that is given. The Frankfurter is almost entirely filled with reports from England and Washington and the union between England and USA is always stressed. The

---

662 "Henrietta Maria" by Carola Oman, published in 1936.
663 HMS Renown bombarded Genoa on 9th February 1941.
664 Maxime Weygand (1867-1965), a French Military Commander in WW1 and WW2. He initially fought against the Germans during the invasion of France in 1940 but then surrendered to and collaborated with the Germans as part of the Vichy France regime.
665 Völkischer Beobachter – German: People's Observer, a daily newspaper published by the Nazi party in Germany from the 1920s until the fall of the Reich in 1945.
666 German: Oflag Headquarters.
667 Desmond has invented a word here but I think he is referring to the salons of Early Modern and Revolutionary France which were seen by contemporary writers as a cultural hub for the dissemination of good manners and sociability, the centre of intellectual and social exchange.
668 Wendell Lewis Willkie (1892-1944), a US corporate lawyer who was the Republican party nominee for President in 1940.
669 Fiorello Enrico La Guardia (1882-1947), Mayor of New York from 1934 to 1945.

letter from Rome would lead one to believe that Italy was finished in N Africa "but this would make no difference to the course of the war, no, not even if Tripoli fell." One gets the habit of always believing anything that has been denied. War time propaganda gives great scope to closer examination.

Friday February 14th

This morning was as pleasant as ever and I was very sorry that my foot would not permit me to go on the walk. An American came to inspect the camp but I had no chance to ask him about letters from home. I am convinced that they are being withheld deliberately; but that conclusion makes it all the more worrying. I spent the afternoon at my German. I had given up 'Seydlitz' as too difficult and had begun a book called "Todesurteil",[670] the story of a German POW in France in the last war. It is full of violent words about a French bombardment and written in a rather loose, staccato style. The Schloss looked particularly attractive from our bedroom window. The blue sky, spotted with white wisps of cloud, formed the background while the foreground was made by the rich green of the pines. Above them the grey, cold stones of the castle mingled with the barren brownness of the leafless trees which cloak the hillside. Now I begin to wish that I was a painter: at least I shall write some poetry before I leave here. After tea we went right through the play and it seemed to go quite well. News: the paper was again full of the nervousness in Australia. A report from Rome which gives the American interpretation of the meeting between Franco[671] and Mussolini. It is that Italy is suing for peace. This is strongly denied, with the assertion that Italy will fight to the last, the fact that they have shot 75 of our planes down in the last few days proving this statement. Why do they publish such a report; is it that the foreign radio is much listened to or is it that they feel that their position is so strong that it is a case of "water off a duck's back"? I beg to believe that the latter is not the case. I wrote to Victor Carey[672] today and asked him to exert his influence to get us news. I know he has been relieved of his official position but I take it that he must have some influence in German circles. Great joy was felt by many of the Gefangeners at the arrival of 150 Players cigarettes. I fear that these "tabbies" have now lost all swapping value: still, the time will come. One of the orderlies tells me that a parcel of books for me is at the K;[673] I can't think that it can be from England. Perhaps it is from Geneva, either the students' bureau or the Society of Friends.[674] They will be up in about 6 months.

Saturday February 15th

I had to miss my shower as my foot is not quite healed up. I had a tub down in a bucket which was very cold and uncomfortable. I am very grieved to see that my piece of lifebuoy is coming to an end. I am very fond of its fresh smell and it gives an excellent lather, and as Vic Oliver,[675] that King of wit, said "I can get next to myself". Most of today was taken up with a dress rehearsal of the play which was produced at 7pm. The costumes were excellent and I got quite a kick out of making love to Consley, rather an unattractive young man who had been made up to look as though he had just left Roedean.[676] My part of a gigolo, I much enjoyed and I felt very pleased when

---

670 "Todesurteil" (Death Sentence). I have not been able to identify the author of this novel.
671 Francisco Franco y Bahamonde ((1892-1975), a Spanish Military Leader and Statesman who ruled as Dictator of Spain from 1936 until his death.
672 Victor Gosselin Carey was Bailiff of Guernsey from 1935 to 1946.
673 Abbreviation: Kommandantur (Oflag Headquarters).
674 The Swiss Quakers.
675 Vic Oliver (1898-1964), an actor and radio comedian.
676 Roedean School, an Independent School for girls near Brighton, founded in 1885.

someone said "My God, you are a cad." I wore a pair of grey flannels, a light grey wind cheater and a very lovely paisley scarf; with my face powdered and my apology for a moustache well corked, I looked the real lounge lizard and would have been a credit to any dowager duchess. The play went very well and had a good reception; though the rehearsals had been rather wearying, it was well worth it. My only regret was that we were not playing more times. I have no feeling of stage fright and enjoy every minute of it. It is rather thrilling to look out at the smoke wreathed audience, the first few rows barely visible, and realise that they are all looking at you, not as yourself but as a character woven into a plot. We had collected signatures for beer and so managed to get quite a reasonable quantity. I had enough and indeed very soon fell asleep after a few rather whirly minutes. Another member of the cast, however, did not have quite such a peaceful night as I did. <u>News</u>. The Americans are evacuating their Far Eastern possessions. We dropped parachutists into the toe of Italy who were all captured; their principal task was to destroy water supplies. The denial of a rumour that Germany was selling Italian art treasures in the USA. An Italian general was killed in Cyrenaica.[677] I am reading Bacon's "Essays":[678] they are delightfully composed and are the work of a worldly man with a rather cynical outlook. I keep them by my bed and read one or two before I get up in the morning. They are full of useful advice "A place showeth the man: and it showeth some to the better, and some to the worse". "A man who hath no virtue in himself ever envieth virtue in others – for men's minds will either feed upon their own good or upon other's evil".

Sunday February 16th

The weather was delightfully warm and I felt very homesick at the thought of walking to St Martins though this was offset by the knowledge that MacLean's sermon would be infinitely better than dear old Coulthard's and I was not mistaken. He took his text from those lovely verses "Consider the lilies".[679] These verses have always pleased me in their beautiful simplicity and their encouraging meaning. Though we only see dirt and people here, these verses bring back the fragrance of the meadows and their very scent is hope; life will go on, flowers will always be beautiful. If we can appreciate the beauty there is still hope for us. I spent the morning writing up my Diary and after lunch I was invited by Holland to listen to him lecturing on the "History of the Novel." The Novel proper was a book which figured a hero and heroine in a domestic setting. Before the novel proper were a series of romances and Addison with his "de Coverley papers"[680] gave the idea to the Novel. "Robinson Crusoe"[681] combined a story with the ideas for reform and it is an adventure story for the young and a source of thought for the old. Swift's "Gulliver's Travels"[682] was a satirical picture. It was with "Pamela"[683] that the first English novel appeared and the Critics were very impressed by its moral tone (Richardson). As complacency is the death of creation, the exceedingly dull and moral tone was rather dispensed with and we have more life portrayals as Henry Fielding's "Tom Jones",[684] Smollett[685] and Sterne[686] and then the "Vicar of Wakefield"[687] which quite put the Novel on its feet. In the evening Barrie gave us another recital. This was more varied than usual, as he forsook his favourite and, I

---

677 The eastern coastal region of Libya.
678 "The Essays" by Francis Bacon, first published in 1597.
679 Biblical quotation, Matthew 6:28
680 "Roger de Coverley Papers" by Joseph Addison, published in 'The Spectator' in 1897.
681 "Robinson Crusoe" by Daniel Defoe, published in 1719.
682 "Gulliver's Travel" by Jonathon Swift, published in 1726.
683 "Pamela or Virtue Rewarded" by Samuel Richardson, published in 1740.
684 "The History of Tom Jones, a Foundling" by Henry Fielding, published in 1749.
685 Tobias Smollett (1721-1771), a Scottish poet and author, best known for his picaresque novels.
686 Laurence Sterne (1713-1768), an Anglo-Irish novelist and Anglican clergyman.
687 "The Vicar of Wakefield" by Oliver Goldsmith, published in 1766.

must confess, rather dully difficult Bach and gave us more Schumann. His recital included 4 songs by Schubert sung by Hunter who has a delightful bass voice, his deep notes being particularly resonant. "Ave Maria"[688] was a very balanced song and the melody moved easily over the lilting accompaniment. His second group of songs were two arias from the "Messiah"[689] and suited his voice ideally. The second, "They walk in darkness"[690] full of crescendos and quick unaccompanied parts. From these it was easy to see that Hunter was no beginner. He has been hiding his light for it was only in Fox's review when he crooned some modern nonsense in rather an attractive way that we realised he could sing at all (Incidentally Fox, Gilder and Davidson (Aberdeen) have left us but they hope to return in some 3 months time). Barrie's recital began with a "Novelette" by Schumann[691] which was a jack in the box little piece which did not please me as much as the usual melodic flow of this composer: I must be getting conservative in my musical taste; melody and lilt, strength and climax are what I like. His programme was all Schubert and Schumann, those song writers of the Romantic school. Some of the "Scenes from Childhood",[692] I especially enjoyed "Traumerei"[693] and the Schubert was well represented by the "Soirées de Vienne",[694] tuneful dance melodies which seemed to create for us the swish of silks and the colourful patterns swirling over the polished dance floor. Another delightful hour which took us home in spirit and it was in this mood that I went to the padre's meeting. I was particularly struck by one of his prayers for our loved ones at home "Prevent their feet from falling, their eyes from tears and their soul from death". All my heart goes into these thoughts and may they reach Mums. Still I have no news and it is five weeks since we wrote to the US embassy. It is quite certain that letters are being withheld from us, for what reason I cannot say. It is terribly worrying after what I heard from Nicolle and Symes. <u>News</u>. The report of the parachutists is given great prominence and the number is said to be 18 with a Captain and a Lieutenant: they have caused no damage.

Monday February 17th

This morning was perfectly lovely, a light frost and the sun streaming down from a cloudless sky. The very small garden behind the main block had a small row of reeds which seemed to have withstood the hard winter; they were very thickly planted and I remembered the days of thinning which I spent crawling along on my hands and knees, the hot sun beating down on my bare back. The village seemed full of children and the rumour is that they are evacuees. The little girls are sometimes very pretty, with little round pink faces and lovely fair curls, one little one especially who often sits by herself. She wears little boots and long woollen socks and on her head is a woolly pixie hat from under which peeps her face. This morning they were playing games and they had "Oranges and Lemons", "Nuts in May" and "Ring of Roses." All over the world little children are playing games while the educated adults are devising schemes for the destruction of all. I wonder what effect a prison camp must have upon the outlook of little children. They stand and pity chickens as they prance up and down their run. What must they think when they look at humans who perform antics and walk endlessly up and down the run? It would be interesting to speak to the Children of Spangenberg on this subject. Lovels's History was on the effect of the Restoration in Scotland. These Scots were energetic and their energies were devoted almost entirely towards a religious end; being intensely

---

688 "Ave Maria" from Op. 52, No. 6, composed in 1825 by Franz Schubert.
689 "Messiah" composed in 1741 by George Frideric Handel.
690 "The People that walked in darkness" from Messiah by George Frideric Handel.
691 From "Noveletten", from Op. 21 composed in 1838 by Robert Schumann.
692 "Scenes from Childhood", a set of 13 pieces of music for piano composed in 1838 by Robert Schumann.
693 "Traumerei" (Dreaming) from "Scenes from Childhood" by Robert Schumann.
694 "Soirées de Viennes" (Evenings in Venice) was actually composed by Liszt in 1852 and was inspired by Schubert.

Non Conformist, they suffered terrible persecution under James II.[695] Ireland was mostly Catholic and after the Treaty of Limerick,[696] which was not kept, most of the leaders left to take service on the continent and the power fell into the hands of priests and peasants. The protestant succession was well supported by the City of London because of the tie that the War Loans made between King and City. I finished "Henrietta Maria" which I found a little tedious. Written by a woman, it gave a very detailed and minute description of the standard of life of the Royalty but left out the factors that made this life possible sometimes and impossible at others. <u>News</u>. This spoke of shop thieves in England and the great food shortage. A long article on "Union Now" by Clarence Streit[697] which now is based entirely on Union between US and England; this union receives great prominence in the Frankfurter every day. I was sorry that I had not read the book which is sitting in the book case in the dining room at the Grange, waiting to be read when I get home: that is if I am accepted after all the trouble I have caused.

Tuesday February 18th

This day was dull and occasional snow blizzards swept down from the surrounding hills. Today I had an opportunity of watching the little boys at play. Their games were not so gentle. One young man, with epaulettes on his shoulder, drilled with noise and firmness a rather undisciplined squad, the leader of whom carried a wooden gun strapped across his back. The rear of the squad was brought up by a self willed young "fantaisiste[698]", wearing a blue ensemble consisting of blue woollen stockings, blue shorts and jersey and a blue wool beret pulled well over his ears. His hands never left his pockets and though he followed, out of step, his prancing companions, his thoughts were miles away as was shown by his occasional disappearances into the little shop "Kolonial Ware"[699] which can be seen from the dining hall. His return called for a general cessation of activity while the Fuhrer gave a severe reprimand to the delinquent and then proceeded to issue verbal orders with much accompanying gesticulation. Each of his squad saluted and went on his mission, except our little friend who ambled up to received his orders with his hands in his pockets and a sneer on his lips; "Of such stuff are democrats made". I am now doing an hour of Russian a day and find the exercises not too hard though full of very stupid sentences. I would much sooner learn "What is for dinner today" than "The step daughter of the blacksmith talks with the father in law of the carpenter". Who is the literarary genius that compiles phrases for grammars? In the evening Lovel's group developed into a discussion on busy bodies and the general apathy of the public for matters which are not within their own ken. Let political planks be home affairs and not vague international policies that colour a policy. <u>News</u>. Giarabub[700] has just fallen.

Wednesday February 19th

The morning was raw and wet and no sooner had we fallen in for Appell than we saw about 5 German officers and some 50 soldiers appear. One of the English speaking officers informed us that they had orders to search the camp. After some hanging about we were allowed into the Speisesaal, where we were compelled to wait for the whole morning. The search was very thorough. I was glad that I did not have anything taken, though many note books were taken and also slacks which have to be dyed. The companion in my room had quite a lot taken. The rooms were left very tidy. I expect the search is a matter of routine with the warm weather coming along. We had

---

695   James II (1633-1701), King of England and Ireland from 1685 to 1688 when he was deposed.
696   The Treaty of Limerick ended the Williamite war in Ireland and concluded the Siege of Limerick in 1691.
697   "Union Now" by Clarence Streit published in 1938.
698   French: joker, clown (pejorative).
699   German: colonial goods.
700   Italian spelling of Jaghbub in the eastern Libyan dessert.

a great disappointment. A ton of bulk stores arrived at the camp "Don de la Croix Rouge",[701] dates, biscuits, milk and chocolate. After the rather dreary morning, the view of food raised all hopes and excitement grew as the horse and cart (two lovely brown horses driven by a cheery, round faced soldier) swung into the gates. The rattle of a cart brings everyone to the window here and the only words addressed to red nosed Bibbings is "Any parcels." "Four men have gone down." From this moment it is an anxious wait. As the cart comes over the stream, the window rush begins and, until the cart enters the gate, speculation is great. The parcels are always given out at the steps leading into the main building and it is a great sight to see the orderlies staggering up the steps with their arms weighed down with Senior British Officer parcels. These parcels come from the station either in the hand cart or in the horse drawn cart, this latter being used for large quantities. I attended a lecture on "The Gold Standard"[702] by Spinks and, when it was over, I was surprised to see the depressed looks on the faces of my fellows. The reason was not long hidden; the bulk stores had all been taken back to the station; they had been wrongly addressed. This was a great blow, though I must admit that it had been almost too much to hope for food from starving France. I had a headache in the evening and went to bed fairly early after having started my "Prison Talk" book with an essay called "Night". I took two aspirin and was soon asleep. <u>News</u>. The paper was full of the new Turkey Bulgarian non aggression pact[703] which was announced as a defeat for our diplomacy.

Thursday February 20th

The weather is really most temperamental and the ground was today covered in a three inch coating of snow. The parcels did arrive today and there were about 200 Red Cross. A flying Officer who tried to escape from the Baltic Camp, (he was out for an hour and was recognised by the Dolmetscher[704] when he was going to catch a train) was brought down to a cell here as the top camp 'cooler' was full. He had seen a man brought down in February who said that the attack on England was expected every day, coupled with a Balkan attack. I spent the evening reading Vol I of "The Great Victorians" and I made a few notes. I hope to copy these notes out when I get home and I feel that they will be most useful to me, both in writing and in speaking. I do not think it is 'cribbing': I think it is learning from others and not only is it useful as memoranda but also book reading becomes a much more intelligent pursuit: the words stop before my eyes and my memory is impressed. I was amazed by the life of Booth[705] who set himself as a General of the army that waged war on Sin; his was a real army and, as a General, he spared no one. His army was to enjoy God, that sin was to be combated by a hot religion. "I like my tea as I like my religion – hot". F H Bradley was a philosopher famous for his "Ethical Studies".[706] Reality is the sole perfection, realisation of the spirit". Charlotte Bronte:[707] her sentimentality is due to her early life of always trying to impress Carlyle. He held a philosophy of action led by great men in an optimistic age. The great man theory has some disadvantages 1) It is difficult to find a man great enough. 2) The question of a successor is difficult. 3) Often a failure to recognise great man. Cobden:[708] had a large view of politics and world sympathy but he had an illusion as to the good will of the middle class. C Darwin:[709] "some are born great, some achieve greatness and some have it thrust upon them." His evolution theory was based on natural selection which is too easily explained. Hypotheses nowadays must

701 French: Gift of the Red Cross.
702 The Gold Standard is a monetary system in which the standard economic unit of account is based on a fixed quantity of gold.
703 Turkey and Bulgaria signed a non-aggression pact in February 1941.
704 German: interpreter.
705 William Booth (1829-1912), a British Methodist preacher who founded the Salvation Army and became its first General.
706 "Ethical Studies" by F H Bradley, published in 1876.
707 Charlotte Bronte (1816-1855), an English novelist and poet.
708 Richard Cobden (1804-1865), a British Manufacturer, and Radical and Liberal Statesman.
709 Charles Robert Darwin (1809-1882), an English naturalist.

live dangerously if they are to live at all. Dickens (GKC[710]). He was of the comic servant tradition "The English populace had lived on laughter – its substitute for religion, property and sometimes food". Dickens wrote better rhetoric when he was trying to be funny e.g. Buzfuz.[711] Disraeli: "Society capable of improvement by judicious combination of private and public effort (Real Democracy)". The Greeks valued – balance, sanity, sobriety of mind. Disraeli's aims were "Maintenance of institutions, preservation of Empire and improvement of condition of people". Gladstone: singular vivacity of his oratorical impulse. Speech making "Collect facts and figures as accurately and conclusively as you can and drive them home as if all the world must irresistibly take your own eager interest in them". A very useful and well planned book which shows the Victorians in all their phases: "they wanted money and power but liked to believe that it was as manna from Heaven". During the afternoon Neave gave a lecture on Divorce and the new APH act.[712] He went through the causes for divorce 1) Adultery (Thompson ve Thompson for Adultery in law). 2) Desertion for 3 years. 3) Insanity 5 years. 4) Cruelty, physical. 5) Bestiality and unnatural practices. <u>News</u>. Very full of Far East and Japan's speech to Butler.[713]

Friday February 21st

The weather was clear and cold. Lovel dealt with Marlborough[714] who he calls our greatest man of action who has never been praised till now for he hated both Whigs and Tories. Defoe's Diary for the character of Harley.[715] The parcels were given out and I got a very good one with some cocoa for the first time. We also had an issue of Portuguese chocolate. I cannot keep chocolate and I easily finished a pound, knowing that I should have kept if for a rainy day. A Doctor tells me it is because we are very short of sugar. We had 200 French cigs and 46 Portuguese. The rumour today is that we are leaving this camp, though it is not known where we are going or when. I shall be sorry to leave here as it is such a business getting books censored etc and we may be split up: still, I have at last got a suitcase, though I shall not forsake my old sack. About 7 poor old merchant seamen came in to be deloused; they had been in a convoy in which 13 ships were sunk by the Von Hippa[716] off Portugal. They were convoyed by one cruiser and had a cargo of oranges. They were taken to Brest[717] and on their way through France they were given civilians' rations which hardly kept them alive. This was confirmed by 4 Indian RIASC[718] Viceroy Commissions who have just come in. The seamen were very weak but quite cheerful. In the evening we had a Lantern Lecture[719] given by a German NCO. The first half was all about the German customs of Alsace, though one accidental remark was made about French – er.. Franconian architecture.[720] The second half was occupied with some quite good slides of the Black Forest.[721] The news was not very important, mostly about the Far East. Wrote to Nanny. Funeral of Gooch.

710 "Charles Dickens: A Critical Study" by G K Chesterton, published in 1906.
711 A character from Charles Dickens' "Pickwick Papers".
712 A reference to A P Herbert who lobbied for reform on divorce. His lobbying eventually lead to the Matrimonial Causes Act 1937.
713 Richard Austen Butler (1902-1982), a British Conservative Politician, chair of the War Cabinet Committee for the Control of Official Histories.
714 John Churchill (1650-1722), 1st Duke of Marlborough, an English soldier and Statesman.
715 Robert Harley (1661-1724), 1st Earl of Oxford and Earl Mortimer, a British politician and Statesman and Defoe's employer and protector.
716 I have not been able to identify this vessel. It is possible that Desmond has misheard and that the reference is to a German U-boat commander called Von Hippel.
717 A city in the Finistère department of Brittany, France.
718 Military abbreviation: Royal Indian Army Service Corps.
719 A lecture presented with slides.
720 Alsace has long been fought over by France and Germany but reverted to France following WW1.
721 A wooded mountain range in Baden-Württemberg, Germany.

Saturday February 22nd

Snowy again and the showers were not very hot. My foot is much better now, though I still keep it powdered. The showers in our building function no more and I had to scrum in with the mob and try and get under 4 rather spasmodic streams of lukewarm water. I spent the morning on shorthand; we are now doing the x and l hook which shortens words very much though it is rather difficult. The day was very ordinary and I worked on at Russian and my German book. For supper we had tinned Christmas pudding, a 1/3 of a tin each and it was lovely, only wanting brandy sauce. We also had a delicious bread pudding and got up feeling really pleasantly full "Je suis plein!"[722] The evening was taken up with "Capt Brassbound's Conversion". The scenery was really wonderful and showed John Mansel to be a supreme artist. The costumes were, as usual, very effective and the production up to Langham's usual standard, especially the way in which he managed to get 20 people on to the minute stage. Barrie, as Lady Cicely, gave a well studied and entirely feminine portrayal. The small parts were all good especially Gowan's as Sir Howard Hallam. He looked a very prosperous Jew, though he himself is an "anti Juif par excellence".[723] McHall, as Drinkwater, a cockney ruffian, was almost unintelligible and Brassbound (Clough Taylor) was wooden and not word perfect. The final scene fell very flat as the worthy Capt made love by numbers and hobbled through his lines. The play left no exhilarating taste in my mouth; rather an empty dissatisfaction. I was sorry for L after all the work he had put into it; I almost feel that if he had left me in the part, I could have done it satisfactorily. <u>News</u>. Eden and Dill in Egypt.[724] Far East still tense.

Sunday February 23rd

I am writing this a fortnight later and, as it is taken from very rough notes, it is difficult to remember everything but I wish to keep the continuity so I shall do my best. The weather was rather dismal and after church I wrote up the diary and then read Disraeli. I am reading it in French. The style is very clear and most readable. This is not the first impression that I got. I felt it to be rather split up and not flowing; but after a few pages I began to appreciate the well chosen adjectives and vividly balanced short sentences. The early life of 'Dizzy' is very well described and his exotic nature and artificiality would be revolting if they were not a means to an end. The end being to get himself into a position where his influence would be great enough for him to put over his ideals of "Young England", the ideals of his country as a second Israel. He used his personality and appearance as bribery, always taking risks: "The adventures are for the adventurers". He knew that when he was young he must make full use of his youth and as he was young and strange, these were his means to take public fancy, especially the fancy of the influential. The ways of politics were intricate: to be a success he must be intricate: and he was a success. "To succeed late is not to succeed: it is to achieve immortality and death". The feature of the book that appealed to me most was the way in which the contrasts between Gladstone, the grand old man who lived with his ideals and used them at the opportune moment, and Disraeli, the practical man whose ideals were worldly and who watched public opinion and also the relationship between ideal and fact. His motto was Imperium et Libertas.[725] "I prefer the rights of the Englishman to the rights of man". His character, so socially perfect and artificial on the surface, belies a real spirit for his adopted country and for his Queen. "A little frivolity to acquire the right to be grave".

---

722   French: literal translation is 'I am full' although if a French person were to use the word 'plein, they would be referring to pregnancy in an animal! Desmond is perhaps unaware of this.
723   French: a supreme anti-Semite.
724   Antony Eden , Foreign Secretary and the Chief of the Imperial General Staff, General Sir John Dill, met in Cairo on 22nd February 1941.
725   Latin: Empire and Liberty.

Lace ruffled and coloured waistcoats to acquire the right to make an Empress of India and rule the Suez Canal. I also read an article called "England's Position". This showed a very different front; England could not be broken by air raids, we were 'tough' and the way was economic starvation. <u>News</u>. Indo China has still gone on bombing Siam with British planes and there are many troops in Singapore, Chiappe's death attributed to the Secret Service. An English ship "Canadian Cruiser"[726] flying US flag sunk in Indian Ocean.

Monday February 24th

The snow was with us again though it was not very cold; the weather is most perverse and unexpected. Lovel dealt with the 18th Century, the age of corruption and bribery. The inactivity of the first George[727] gave Parliament a very strong prerogative and the cabinet system of unity grew up in "the best club in Europe". The interesting feature of this age is the fact that there was not class hatred between the highly educated and broad minded aristocracy, the well to do bourgeois and the labouring peasants who knew their position and were content with it and their beer. The French influence on prose and poetry was strong and the unities of time and place became more well known. The day was exciting for we had definite orders to move on Wednesday. The suitcases had to be measured to ensure that their size was not too great for the train accommodation. Rumour has it that officers in Canada are badly treated and that we are going to a 'tough' camp. Another rumour that we are going with the overflow from Salzburg to Johannesbrunn. Rumour is one of the livelier pastimes of prison life; no one knows where they start and everyone who passes them on disclaims all responsibility. A list of the officers for repatriation was read out and these had been examined by two Swiss Doctors who had been quite encouraging. We are unfortunately losing MacLean who is a wonderful man and always means every word he says; many people have this blessing but not all have Padre's manner in which it is evident that he is sincere. A sing song Scottish accent and a sense of the dramatic make his sermons absolutely gripping. "A nation is a work of art and time". Time is the real factor and it is our Time that will save us. The time will always be there; the art must be made to follow the time and, when all this is over, we must examine and remodel the art on the basis of time. I wrote to Zabette though I don't think I shall hear from her because she can only write back on cards which I supply her with.

Tuesday February 25th

The snow was much deeper though I did not have much chance to go outside as I spent the day packing. I read my diary through for any indiscretions and felt very pleased that I had kept it. My case was nearly filled up with books and cigarettes. I must have amassed about 500: still, they will probably have their uses. There was a general air of expectation and panic and so much hilarity that one might have thought that we were going home. 6 great drawing books came. I sold three and may carry on my diary in the other three, though the paper is not very good. I wrote to Aunty and Mummy. Writing letters takes me a very long time for I copy them out into a book; also with so few letter cards, every sentence must be thought out. The idea of keeping a record is so that I will not put the same thing twice; I mentioned the move. At tea time the move was cancelled; no reason was given and no date was given. An ideal chance for the rumour mongers. Our acting Camp Officer left us and thanked us all for our discipline and good behaviour; rather charming, he was a Lieutenant with a rather high pitched voice and receding chin who saluted a great deal and looked at the feet of the front rank: Appell was over very quickly. I don't know what his name was, something like Glucose. He was very new to his job and very polite. We had three new officers

---

726   Canadian Cruiser, an armed merchant ship, was sunk by German naval forces in the Indian Ocean on 23 February 1941.

727   George I (1660-1727), King of Great Britain and Ireland from 1714 until his death.

in who had done 5 months solitary for escaping. The two elder ones, Wright and Lowden, gave us the news; it was given definitely and in a very amusing way. They both had beards and one wore a monocle: their voices had the calm boredom of announcers and everything they gave was well weighed before it was given and they did not throw out fantastic rumours. They again mentioned the invasion attempt. The position in France is very severe but the morale is good. I spent the evening chatting about Norway with Tony Strachan, the ethereal young man who writes novels. I must say that I like him now: his words are well chosen and have a twang of cynicism. His pose is the post war recklessness of drugs and dance music. He works very conscientiously and reads a great deal with a dictionary at his side. He is quite an authority on the modern novel. He was in the unfortunate position of satisfying nature's wants when a German tank shelled the house in which he was situated. An even better story was of one man who went to a Norwegian house and asked them to inform the Gs of his presence. They were not willing to, so he rang them up and after a good night's sleep and a good breakfast he was collected. Another of an officer and 80 men trying to stop cars and give themselves up but no one would have them. News. Mussolini gave a speech in favour of the Axis[728] and Italy's enthusiasm. There was a denial of heavy East Coast air fighting.

Wednesday February 26th

Today it was freezing hard and the children were tobogganing down the hill outside the gate, about 5 toboggans tied together. They were having great fun. I was amazed to see one little boy give us a thumbs up and grin hugely. He, like a very pretty little girl with a sweet smile, had been putting out his tongue and in reply FF had put his thumbs up: hence the innocent salute. The little girl, however, still smiled angelically and put out her tongue; she was tiny with lovely blonde hair and a chubby red face which matched her woolly cap. In History Lovel told us about R Walpole,[729] his bribery to put himself in power and his cynical "Every man has his price". RF gave a lecture called "George and Margaret on buying a house" in which he stressed the importance of employing an architect to check a house over; the Major is an architect. His lecture was about drains and damp and smoke rockets and a lot of very practical but rather dull information. I'm afraid that I continued reading Lord Bacon by Ld Macaulay which I had begun the previous evening. Macaulay is very clear and very Victorian, meaning that life for him is achievement and progress, as his notes about the greater importance of a cobbler over Seneca's[730] words on anger show. Bacon was too mean when seeking after the seals and when seeking after truth. In the former, he was corrupt, insincere, malicious and egotistical: in the latter, he was practical, useful and progressive. His wit was the power of perceiving analogues between things which appear to have nothing in common. He took all Knowledge to be his province and he conquered with chalk, not steel. His philosophy was to mitigate human suffering and multiply human enjoyment. Philosophy of a spiritual nature was interesting but wasteful of energy and time. A man must have "Industrious observations, grounded conclusions and profitable discoveries and inventions". I wonder if Grandpa studied Bacon, or Bacon as portrayed by the Whig, Macaulay. Facts to join to honesty and truth: a philosophy of usefulness. The News was dominated by Hitler's speech in which the increase of the submarine war was threatened.

---

728   The Axis Powers was the alignment of nations who fought in WW2 against the Allied forces.
729   Robert Walpole (1676-1745), British Statesman and first Prime Minister of Great Britain.
730   Lucius Annaeus Seneca the Younger (4BC to 65AD), a Roman Stoic philosopher, Statesman and dramatist.

Thursday February 27th

This morning we had a glorious walk. The snow was still on the ground but it was beautifully crisp and clean. We went up behind the camp and up the hill from where we got a lovely view of the castle. We did not come down the hill as usual but went through the woods, the sun filtering through and making golden patterns on the snow. We climbed down the hillside and it was like a romp, as we tumbled over uneven, snow covered ground. We joined the road just before we got into the village and I felt quite weary. I found a parcel for me from a Mme Herbulet[731], a friend of L J Cook; the parcel had a pair of socks, a piece of nut and fruit cake and 2 packets of cigarettes, 1 Egyptian and 1 English; it is very kind of her, especially as they are so short of food in that country. There were also two letters for me, one from Lola sent off 28.1.41 and the other from Wendy who seemed very full of life and fun. Lola and family all seem to lie in London and she has sent me books from Selfridges. The order for the move came and it was for Saturday, so the afternoon was once again taken up with packing. In the evening I went on with Lord Bacon while FF held an auction sale and vests went for 20 Marks and other fabulous prices were reached. <u>News</u>. Balkan activity military attaché left Sofia, 50 English arrested. Eden – Dill in Ankara.[732]

Friday February 28th

The yard was full of slush, about an inch deep and my shoes leaked like a sieve. The morning was fully occupied with having our suitcases searched. Mine was turned inside out but nothing was taken. Then our cases were stored in the parcel room, ready for the move. The NCO denied the rumour that there was rioting in Norway: first we'd heard of it. During the afternoon, I read various essays of Macaulay from a Collins Edition "Miscellaneous Essays".[733] "The Succession in Spain"[734] which was most interesting for the passage about the Spanish character, also the Earl of Peterborough seems an interesting character. He performed some wonderful military feats but Lovel told me that he was unreliable and a Whig; hence Macaulay's great love for him. Civil disabilities of Js which attached anti J measures and supported Js as privileges are power; foreign attachments are fount of domestic misrule (to be read again). A severe criticism of Croker's "Boswell's Life of Johnson",[735] Croker's book was like a leg of mutton, "ill fed, ill killed, ill kept, ill dressed". Boswell was a terrible old bore and inquisitive scoundrel, so we get such a good biography. Johnson, an eccentric full of spicy statements "A man who cannot get to heaven in a green coat will not find his way in a gray one". The Friends realise this. Machiavelli who is much maligned: his book is "History of Florence"[736] and "The Prince."[737] The afternoon soon passed and at tea time the move was cancelled: what a country. Here we are with no kit and no prospects. <u>News</u>. Very heavy raid on Malta. Explanation of new types of our aircraft.

---

731   I am not sure if this name is transcribed correctly.
732   Capital of Turkey.
733   "Critical and Miscellaneous Essay" by Thomas Babington Macaulay.
734   "War of the Succession in Spain" by Thomas Babington Macaulay.
735   "Boswell's Life of Johnson", by John Wilson Croker, published in 1831.
736   "History of Florence" by Niccolo Machiavelli, 8 volumes published between 1520 and 1525.
737   "The Prince" by Niccolo Michiavelli, published in 1532.

Saturday March 1st

The morning was wet, rain streaming down, the river rushing as a torrent. I was awakened by the squealing of a pig being killed; sinister screams and blood curdling yells which went on for about ten minutes. This had a very depressing effect and I had a feeling that Stube 17 was a Dante's Inferno.[738] Pig killing here is a very rare event but when it is done, we hear and see it: after the screams we see the carcass hanging outside the farm door and pools of blood stain the road; this was most curious when the roads were frozen and the surface was like a sheet of red glass. I spent the day reading some Macaulay and then a book on the English Constitution by E Freeman[739] which developed the Teutonic theory of Comitatus[740] which developed into a society of three grades, Monarchic, aristocratic and democratic. In the evening there was a race meeting and I had the rather dull occupation of working at the tote. I'm afraid I don't like gambling: if I started, I expect I would like it and I know that I should lose at the beginning and I don't like losing. Baccarat[741] is the big craze now and this evening one chap won 1400 Marks. Money here means nothing. We get 72 Marks a month and there is practically nothing to buy if you do not go in for books, which I do. I am sure that I have mislaid a great deal of this money and I never think to count it, I just throw the money on the Canteen counter and buy as much as is there; any odd book I buy or any new kind of brilliantine or mirror, without thinking of value. It will be difficult for some of these fellows who gamble all day to settle down to play with real money. Two new doctors arrived and another Indian. We have now 6 Indians, because four Indian Viceroy Commissions from the RIASC[742] came a few days ago. Only two of them speak English and their room is fixed up with prayer mats and all the paraphernalia of Mohammedenism. Jumbo Muzundar, RAMC,[743] who is a Brahmin[744] will have very little to do with them. I begin to realise the religious troubles of India and the difficulties of Home Rule. Jumbo, who speaks perfect English, is a strong nationalist and was not very favourable to us. Since his visit to hospital, he has changed his ideas a bit. The doctor gave us some good news, mostly about N Africa and one or two very amusing stories. He was very reassuring and we felt quite cheerful. Frank-[745] told us that Bulgaria had entered the Axis Powers. I wonder what Turkey will do. The news has been leading to such a step.

Sunday March 2nd

It was beautifully fine and very warm. I lost my temper for the first time for many a long day. The moving rumours had been making life very uneasy and the Bulgarian rumour was rather disturbing. I sat on my bed and looked rather dreary so Kennedy, who is the fount of knowledge on every known subject and who washes every day with his overcoat on, began to try and drag me into some argument. I remained silent for some time and his clever words fell stupidly on my ears. At last I could bear it no longer: I stood up and told him, in no uncertain manner, to mind his own business and if I wanted to be miserable, I would be miserable and I didn't want him to go on talking tripe. No sooner had I said that than I saw how ridiculous I had been and I began to laugh and apologise. So it

---

738 Italian: Hell. A reference to a 14th century epic poem by Dante Alighieri.
739 "The growth of the English Constitution from the earliest times", by Edward Augustus Freeman, published in 1872.
740 A Germanic friendship structure that compelled kings to rule in consultation with their warriors.
741 A card game.
742 Military abbreviation: Royal Indian Army Service Corps.
743 Military abbreviation: Royal Army Medical Corps.
744 A scholar class in the traditional Hindu societies of India and Nepal.
745 Desmond's abbreviation for Frankfurter, the newspaper.

is with all my tempers. I always see the funny side and I hate to be thought unpopular. I am getting the better of this attitude slowly. It is better to do what you think is right and be unpopular than to do what others expect you to do. MacLean's sermon was as good as ever. He dealt with the temptations and showed that they were mental afflictions that every man must go through, hunger, sin and power. Every great man takes himself into solitude to prepare himself for the struggle of life. Padre compared this life of ours to that period of contemplation. I do not agree. A period of penance is spent alone and in contemplation: life here is much too personal to contemplate deeply. Every attempt at thinking is disturbed by someone talking. The only thing to do here is to work; in work you can forget yourself and prepare for the time after the war; this is active thought and not contemplative. I have not examined myself here: rather have I tried to improve myself by reading and listening and I have learnt a great deal. I somehow felt that this would be the last time I should hear Padre and his sermon was all the more enjoyable; the enjoyment of a final tasting, sentimental enjoyment. During the afternoon, I began "Rebecca"[746] by Daphne du Maurier which I enjoyed very much: there was a sense of mystery which pervades the whole story. I think I enjoyed the book because it was a novel and I had not read one for a very long time. I also learnt a few German words which is a very dull but important part of learning a language: going to a country does away with this boredom because words learnt in conversation seem to stick.

Monday March 3rd

Today was the day of Connors' prophecy on which he predicted a very vital event but he could give no nearer definition. Time will show whether he was right. Lovel lectured on George III[747] and his desire to be a benevolent despot. From the Treaty of Paris,[748] in which we did not consult Germany, we got the Perfide Albion[749] reputation. The colonial system, which was to draw as much as possible from these colonies, came to an end with the revolt of the American colonies. With all my books packed, the only thing to do was to read so I finished "Rebecca" and spent the evening writing up an appreciation of the book. Writing comes more easily to me but I must do more practise. Still I do want to do German and these languages can only be mastered by real hard work. The evenings now are very light and it is lovely walking about in the balmy evening air. No papers came up so we got no news: this Bulgarian question is very worrying because the Greeks can be taken in the rear and the Germans may be able to use a Mediterranean port, which would hinder our transport which must now be almost normal for I am sure the Italians are nearly finished.

Tuesday March 4th

The day was beautifully fine and the village looked lovely in the bright sunlight. These timbered houses are very attractive and the red painted beams stand out and form a pattern on the white background, which adds an air of artificiality to the real scene of little children playing and geese prancing up and down. Every morning the geese fly up the stream, with their long heads pointing forward they look like some vicious aeroplane and their wings beat the air like great propellers. The air here is always rent with the cacklings of the ducks and the roar of the stream as it pours down the weir. The houses are high, with a loft in the attic, and the people are always working. Even

746 "Rebecca" by Daphne du Maurier, published in 1938.
747 George III (1738-1820), King of Great Britain and Ireland from 1760 until his death.
748 The Treaty of Paris, signed on September 3rd 1783 ended the American Revolutionary War between Great Britain and the United States of America.
749 French: Perfidious Albion, a pejorative phrase used within the context of international relations and diplomacy to refer to acts of duplicity, treachery and infidelity by monarch or governments of Britain (or England).

the old women work in the farms and it is no strange sight to see a horse and a woman attached to a cart. The soil calls, the people answer. During the morning, we had to pay in our lagergeld and then at 11 we heard that we were to move in the evening and to leave the camp at 5.30. Lunch was earlier and the afternoon was spent packing hand luggage and saying our farewells. My old sack came into its own again and I tumbled all my things into it. A sack is much easier to pack than most cases and I shall adopt a kit bag after the war when I go travelling. It is not very good for suits but for shirts and things it is ideal. Tea was at 3.30 when we each had a 1/3 of a steak and kidney pudding and 6 slices of bread. At 4.30 we were searched and then lined up to move off. I was very sorry to leave Col Gibbs with whom I had had many talks: his courage was wonderful and never did he complain, though he must have felt very sad. His old age ruined, his wife and child in prison and his other relations cut off by the barrier of war. He had become much thinner but he holds himself erect and keeps his military bearing; a fine gentleman. The Padre stayed behind, for which I was very sorry. He was a sincere Christian who spent his life trying to help and instruct and he redeemed many parsons for me. The MDs[750] and Grand Blessés[751] also stayed. A great guard, about 50, attended us and they had two Schnuffel hounds[752] who were very fierce; I whistled very agreeably to one and he leapt at me, his black face wreathed in snarls (they are trained to attack Khaki) and I was very glad that he was on the leash. We were issued with ¾ of a loaf of brown bread and then we set off. The whole village turned out to see us off; they exhibited neither pleasure, nor sorrow: we were just a flock of unfortunate sheep. We trod the well known path, past the Elbersdorf church, under the Schloss hill, past the dentist and so up to the railway station, along the road I had come down about 18 weeks before. At the station orders were read out. We were told that we had been leading a complacent life and now we were under strict discipline: many words about orders to shoot and the usual shouting. We then drew a piece of sausage. By this time the Schloss prisoners had come down and we were called out to go into the train which was waiting. The RAF looked very picturesque, most of them had long beards and even longer hair; this may have been to frighten our hosts. I was sent to a carriage with Mortimer, the librarian of our camp who was in the Coldstreams, Frank Murphy, Husson, and two fliegers,[753] Murphy, who knew Peter Browne very well, and Murdoch. The train was a corridor train and the compartments had wooden seats and held six comfortably, if comfort can be had on a wooden seat, and seven with a decided squash. The guards stood in the corridor and only one man from each compartment was allowed to stand up at a time. The window was wired and the light was at only one end of the compartment. As the train was not due to leave till nine, I ate my slices of bread and a bit of sausage, a new type on me but quite edible. At 9 we moved off and so left Die Schöne Spangenberg[754] behind. I had been quite happy there and I had done a lot of work: if I had heard from home, I would have been very happy. Incidentally Col Ford had heard from the US embassy and they were going to help us: this was marvellous news and pleased us no end. Still, we shall have to wait and try not to be impatient. The discomforts had been mastered and the food ration had been sufficient, or rather we had learnt not to be hungry. It had been a little community that ran easily and instructively. Leaving it was rather like leaving a home. I had lived in the same small area and had so disciplined myself that I very rarely thought about outside pleasures. I thought of home and quiet and Mums, but social activities never entered my head. I wonder if I shall ever return. At 9 the train moved off and we settled ourselves down for the night: one of the chaps climbed into the luggage rack and the rest of us shifted and twisted until we dozed off. A wooden seat acted as a type of inoculation though not a very effective one. We talked with one of the NCOs, an aspirant who had given us a Lantern Lecture, and I tried out my German. At present it is very halting but I feel that with some conversation, it would soon come. During the night we went through Nordhausen and Göttingen.[755] (Letter from Lola 6.2.41, card from Mme Herbulet).

750	Abbreviation: From the Latin Medicinae Doctor, Doctor of Medicine.
751	French: Severely wounded, very sick (the intention being to repatriate because of their ill health).
752	POW slang for guard dogs.
753	German: airmen.
754	German: beautiful Spangenberg.
755	A university town in Lower Saxony.

Wednesday March 5th

I spent a very restless night and woke about 7 to find that we were on a siding of the station Lutherstadt Eisleben.[756] As the sun rose I could see factory chimneys springing out of the mist from the distant valley and slowly the world came to life; engines puffed up and down the line and men unloaded wagons. We stayed on the siding till about 8 and then moved off very slowly, only to stop again at 9 for a 3 ½ hours wait. The train was in an uproar, the officers and guards running up and down for all they were worth. 3 fellows had escaped during the night and no one knew where they had jumped off: John Surtees, RB[757], was from our camp and 2 Fliegers.[758] I do hope they make it. Their big difficulty will be the cold at night, but I imagine they went well prepared. At 12.30 we moved off again after Capt B had inspected all the compartments; he must be very worried and I don't think sympathy will fall to him. We were passing through cultivated, undulating country which was not very interesting. At Halle, a huge junction, we stopped for quite a considerable time and we had a little soup that the guards could not eat, we were lucky to be next to their carriage. At 3 we moved off again and now the view was of flat, swampy fields and a few towns, Eilenburg,[759] Torgau,[760] where we crossed of the Elbe. There was a very fine old castle standing right upon the river and the appearance of a modern bombing plane made a very curious contrast, war of two ages, stone and metal. At Beilrode[761] we saw a lot of fierce children who shouted and yelled but I don't know whether it was in joy at seeing the guards or in hate at seeing us. Falkenberg[762] platform was covered with a lot of very dull and apathetic people who struggled to get into a train. Women are treated as men when courtesy is in question. During the night I slept on the floor and passed a very good night only being woken up about 1 o'clock by a nurse bringing some disagreeable Ersatz.[763] The whole night long the train stopped and started but we did manage to get across the Polish frontier. To pass the time, I had been reading "The 1890s"[764] by Holbrook which was quite instructive but rather lost its interest when I could not refer to the works mentioned e.g. Aubrey Beardsley's,[765] Street's "Autobiography of a boy",[766] "The Green Carnation".[767] The book was very good during its biographical passages e.g. Oscar Wilde,[768] John Davidson,[769] etc. I noted it as I always do now and I can refer to the books when I get home. I am rather interested in this period of purple patches[770] and decadence. My own writing is rather purple. I began "Vicar of Wakefield",[771] quite fun but very dated.

756   A town in Saxony-Anhalt.
757   Military abbreviation: possibly Rifle Brigade (?).
758   German: airmen.
759   A town in the district of Nordsachsen.
760   A town on the banks of the Elbe in north western Saxony.
761   A municipality in the district of Nordsachsen.
762   A town in the Elbe-Elster district in south western Brandenburg.
763   i.e. substitute (coffee).
764   "The Eighteen Nineties: A Review of Art and Ideas at the close of the Nineteenth Century" by George Holbrook Jackson, published in 1914.
765   Aubrey Vincent Beardsley (1872-1898), an English illustrator and author.
766   "The Autobiography of a boy" by G S Street, published in 1867.
767   "The Green Carnation" written by Robert Hichens and published anonymously in 1894.
768   Oscar Wilde (1854-1900), an Irish writer and poet.
769   John Davidson (1857-1909), a Scottish poet, playwright and novelist.
770   A purple patch is a section of writing characterised by rich, fanciful or ornate language.
771   This was by Oliver Goldsmith and published in 1766.

Thursday March 6th

I got up from my hard and dirty couch about 7.30 and looked out on flat plough land dotted with odd woods of silver birch and fir, all made more miserable in the dull morning light. The whole landscape was very like Silesia[772] and I began to wonder who wanted Poland anyway. We went through Eichentlast[773] and Opelantza[774] and the land became even more depressing with its swampy flatness until we came to Posen.[775] We stopped in the station for a long time and had the pleasure of seeing a Speisewagen[776] with a plate of cream cakes and quite a reasonable blonde, a rare sight for a POW. The suburbs of Posen must have inspired Dostoyevsky to write "Crime and Punishment".[777] Building plots with an odd, ugly, square building here and there amidst the swampy dirt. The crowning feature was an old fort surrounded by barbed wire, a lager;[778] a few miserable khaki clad figures were walking up and down and gazing at the uninspiring view of water and weariness. Our hearts did not leap for joy. Everyone looked poor and dreary and poor old women were digging amidst broken down red brick buildings. I was very pleased when we left this depressing civilisation and got out into the flat fields, an occasional hayrick breaking the monotony. No hills anywhere. Kostchin,[779] Gultawy,[780] Tischdorf,[781] Wreschen[782] where I saw special carriages for the Poles: they are treated rather like animals and are not allowed to mix with their rulers. The country here was extensively flooded and communication was carried on in little punts: the miserable little hovels which went for houses were almost lost in the waters. The sun was shining now and the land looked a little less mournful; never have I seen such flatness, not a mill, not even an undulation. The winter winds must sweep across and be as uncomfortable as the summer heat pouring down on to this almost desert. We stopped for a long time at Kutno[783] and then turned North, in the direction of Thorn,[784] our destination, having made a detour of 2 sides of a triangle. When darkness fell, there was no attempt to black out the windows and it was a strange sight to pass through stations that were blazing with light and to see cars flashing along the roads, their lights playing on the road. Our astonishment at this sight was not so great as the joy of the guard NCO who leapt and sang with joy. He was a very smart little man who smoked huge cigars and sang snatches from his repertoire, he being an opera singer by trade. Our guards had been quite pleasant and only obeyed orders when they took our shoes away from us at night. We had a great deal of hanging about and false alarms about arrival; at last, after much shunting and jolting, we drew into Thorn. The platform was lit up by arc lights and car headlights and a great many troops were there, their rifles at the ready. We were ordered out and lined up in fives. Then we moved off, led by the senior officers with whom was Brig General Somerset who had been at the Schloss. After about a quarter of an hour's trudging through thick mud, we saw lights, barbed wire and soldiers ahead, the view of a prison camp at night. Within a few minutes we were

---

772   A region of Central Europe located mostly in Poland, with smaller parts in the Czech Republic and Germany.

773   I have not been able to identify this town/location. It may be incorrectly transcribed.

774   I have not been able to identify this town/location. It may be incorrectly transcribed.

775   Posen (German spelling), a province of Prussia from 1848 and part of the German Empire from 1871 to 1918. In 1919, according to the Treaty of Versailles, Germany had to cede the bulk of the province to the newly established Second Polish Republic.

776   German: Dining car (of train).

777   "Crime and Punishment" by Fyodor Dostoyevsky, published in 1866.

778   German: Camp

779   Kostchin (probably German spelling), a town in Poland.

780   I have not been able to identify this town/location. It is possible that it is incorrectly transcribed.

781   Tischdorf (probably German spelling), a town in Poland.

782   Wreschen (German spelling), a town in central Poland.

783   A town in central Poland.

784   Thorn (English spelling), a city in northern Poland and the location of Stalag XX-A. The main camp was located in a complex of 15 forts that surrounded the whole of the city.

inside a great red brick wall with vast iron gates. A blaze of light met our eyes and, by the beams, we could see a draw bridge over a deep empty moat, and this bridge led to a dark passage, the doors of which had been flung open. We were marched into this Château d'If[785] and were halted in a damp tunnel harshly lit with electric light which reflected on the whitewashed walls. All along this tunnel were little doors covered with iron railings. No sooner had we halted than a German officer, his hand on his holster, began shouting, his fierce voice echoing in a sinister way down the dungeon tunnel. He spoke in German and I did not catch all he had to say though I had an inkling, which was confirmed by an English speaking officer, small and with glasses, who informed us that we were here by orders of the High Command. Prisoners in Canada had been put into the Kingston penitentiary, Fort Henry, and were being treated as criminals, not officers.[786] We should be kept here until their treatment had been alleviated. Rumour had been correct and it was not long before we saw what our treatment was to be. In groups of 16 were marched off, with much shouting and noise occasioned by one officer who was smoking, to our sleeping quarters. We were led down one of the side passages, down some steps, through an iron grill and along damp passages until we were shown into a room. It contained a stove, a table, 16 stools, 8 double beds with two blankets and a wood wool palliasse, which were all very damp. A potato stew was ready for us and we certainly enjoyed it; it was washed down with Ersatz coffee. I did not take long to climb into a top bunk and prepare myself for the night. The guards came round and locked us in and the lights were switched off. My night was not very comfortable because my wood wool palliasse had a great lump in the middle. I had sat next to a red haired fleet air army man at supper and he told me that the Guernsey show had been written off as a bit of bad luck. Our dungeon is bad enough but what must the cooler be like? 6 of our officers are due for 5 days for playing cards after Lights Out, Bibbings being the ring leader. They were surprised and left a pack and some money on the table: bad luck. Also Lovel and a few others, for refusing to remove their boots in the train.

Friday March 7th

A bugle blew reveille at 6 for the men and our door was unlocked at 7.30. I got up quickly and went out for a wash. The wash place consisted of a trough with a pipe running along the top which was perforated in several places to allow water to trickle through. This primitive arrangement worked from 7.30 to 8, 1.30 to 2 and 5.30 to 6. Breakfast was some Ersatz coffee. The Appell bugle went at 9 and we trooped up the long tunnel and out onto an earth covered yard with high banks all round, on which earth had been thrown up to the limit of the wire; two sentries surveyed us, one with a machine gun. The Commandant inspected us from a bank and the Camp Officer, elderly and quite genial, examined us very closely, asking each one his age and saying "Young man", "Small man", "High man", as the case might be. After Appell we were sent to choose our roommates. I was very slow off the mark, hesitating to push myself into a good room, or rather a congenial company. At last I found myself in room 12 with rather a dull crowd; Kennedy and his bunch, L J Cook and Husband, who I like, and some others. I was sorry to be separated from Colin who was in a Flieger room. Prison life is a question of acting and asking questions afterwards, or, as GBs say 'Do what you want to do and then prove you are right'. Lunch was brought in after the 12 o'clock Appell, it was a potato stew. I spent the afternoon walking round and met some of our orderlies who had gone to the Schloss. We had some tea made; it was a wonder that our orderly, Brookes, managed to do this. He is a scruffy little ex regular who is bone from the neck up; as a postman in civil life he must have been like the child who did not know the difference between an elephant and a pillar box. We had an extra Appell at 5 at which a letter was read to us, giving the alleged conditions at Kingston. Very little light, guards with truncheons, locked in at night,

---

785   The Château d'If is a fortress (later a prison), located on the island of If in the Bay of Marseille, France.

786   The inference here is that the POWs were to be treated harshly as a reprisal for the treatment of German Officer prisoners in Canada.

Lights Out at 9.45 and 10 in a room, bad sanitary arrangements. As reprisal, our windows are half boarded up and we always have the lights, the guards carry truncheons, we are locked in and our physical wants are supplied by a pail, our Lights Out are at 9 and we sleep 16 in a room. The sanitary arrangements are extraordinary. The WCs are formed round a central shelf and look rather like pews. There is no flush and chlorine is the disinfectant. The urinals are very ornate and look rather like a Dutch salamander stove, a wrought iron hood comes from the wall and the effect is quite majestic. We shall be here until all is well in Canada. A sweet little tabby cat with perfect markings found his way into our room, he was most affectionate and it was the first cat I had seen, except for a black and white one that had run across the courtyard one evening. Our tea was of a ¼ of a loaf each, some butter and Ersatz. At 8 o'clock there was a room Appell and lights went out at 9. I soon fell asleep. Others did not fare so well, for many of the beds are very unstable and it is no rare occurrence to hear a splitting crash, followed by many swear words as the occupants of a bed meet in the darkness.

Saturday March 8th

The same procedure as yesterday took place except that I had a shave in hot water and I did not feel it a great luxury: I would just as soon have cold. Appell was very long as we had our hand luggage searched and it was nearly time for the next Appell when we were finished. Lunch today was of fried Klippfisch (Ling[787]) and potatoes and it was really quite good. I investigated the library which was full of quite good books and I took out "Tess of the d'Urbervilles"[788], which I began, finding it rather heavy going but quite enjoying the descriptions of the countryside and intrigued by the word fetishistic. We were allowed to take some things from our suitcases; the big snag is that we have no cupboards at all and I put all my things on the floor, kept in Red Cross boxes. The showers are very well installed but as we were the last to have one, the water was cold. After the bath, we played a game of dominoes which brought back common room memories. I was playing with a set of double 8 and the 5 and 3 combinations and I was fairly beaten by a fellow from Sheffield called Salt, a quiet but pleasant lad who had had 5 months solitary with the Gestapo[789] for trying to escape. We have a great many Völkischer Beobachter[790] deposited in the library and the Reading room, two pleasant rooms on the ground floor. The news was trivial though the Italians claim to have dispersed 50 of our planes over Albania with 5 of their own. There were a few pictures of Channel Island Free Mason emblems which were on show in Berlin. They speak of the Jewish sign on Guernsey's flag. The paper is the party one. I have not yet made out a programme but I intend to do some Russian, shorthand and read a bit of German, read and write. From now on I will write on both sides of the paper as it is rather scarce and it would be very annoying to be held up for lack of paper.

Sunday March 9th

This morning after Appell I paid a visit to the sick bay, a large airy room next to the RIAMC, a very pleasant old gentleman who is very painstaking and sympathetic, rather a change from the slap dash George Gorrie; there are also 2 Belgian doctors who are a little fed up with life because they had expected to go home but had been held

---

787   A cod like fish.
788   "Tess of the d'Urbervilles" by Thomas Hardy, published in 1891.
789   German: abbreviation of Geheime Staatspolizei (Secret State Police).
790   Völkischer Beobachter – German: People's Observer, a daily newspaper published by the Nazi party in Germany from the 1920s until the fall of the Reich in 1945.

back to look after us. One is very pro German and he told me that I was about the first officer he had seen, because in Belgium he saw no English. I do not argue with him, it is very difficult. The actual sick bay has a staff of 3 very superior orderlies who are very polite and conscientious and a complement of about 8 beds which are always occupied as there is a great deal of flu, accompanied with high temperatures, probably due to the damp. I made my visit because the blister on my heel had made very little progress and had some poison in it. The doctor had an anti flogistin[791] dressing put on it and told me that the trouble here was lack of vitamins and wounds took a very long time to heal up. At 4 o'clock I went to the church: this was a brick lined tunnel, set into the main tunnel: it was very chilly but had some resemblance to a church, for an altar had been made and we were each given a hymn book and a prayer book supplied by the Society for Propagation of Christian Knowledge.[792] The hymns were accompanied by a cornet and a violin. This cornet player is a very good musician and, as well as playing hymn tunes, he also plays the bugle calls: it is quite inspiring to hear "Lights Out" in a prison camp, rather more romantic than "put that b---- light out". The service was taken by an Irish Padre and it was the C of E service, the lessons being read by the Brigadier Gen Somerset. The Padre has a strong brogue and a loud voice; the prayers had to be read so the quicker they could be got through the better; he knew them by heart and it was rather annoying to have to say them: still, I suppose work must be done. That was the impression he gave me. His sermon was on the temptations and had some quite good advice, telling us to prepare ourselves for the time of trial that was to come. It was presented in a muscular manner and I had a feeling that much of it was directed at the interpreter, especially bits about the strength of the Israelites. When I left I did not have the feeling of peace that MacLean's quiet, earnest voice used to give me. M's prayers were always new and seemed sincere. Today's were gabbled and stereotyped, the responses given with the precision of a printer's press. I used to enjoy the moments of silent prayer, today there were none; keep their feet from falling, their hearts from weeping and their soul from death. Why do I go to church? For unity of purpose. By this, I mean that I can concentrate on one definite thing, hoping, and with my hopes I mingle prayers to a rather vague deity who I feel must be there to hear me. In church I am not disturbed. It is perhaps the only place where peace from conversation is possible. Conversation breaks into thoughts as a knife goes through butter. I go to church for peace and quiet, to concentrate all my thoughts in one direction, the safety of those at home. M's services were quiet, this man's are noisy: but I shall continue to go, for as the prayers become more familiar I can shut them out from my mind and they will be like a soaring surf, always present in the background but never disturbing. What I should really like is a meeting where no outside influence would distract me. More of disturbing influences later. The lunch was the usual stew of potatoes and turnips all mixed up and boiled. There is no meat in these stews and the rations are much less than at IX A. I spent the afternoon writing up my diary. With my foot I was not able to go out to the Sports Platz[793] but I hope to visit it at some future time. Those who did go brought back some branches of fir and some catkins, which made our room look less dreary. My pictures had been put up on the wall and, though they are only sketches from the Frankfurter, they make the badly plastered walls look more civilised. The plaster is that kind that rubs off on your clothes and it is very marked with nail holes and other eyesores. In the evening I sent a card home to Mums and just mentioned the change but did not fill the card with gruesome details. The day was made quite exciting by various foraging expeditions, the result of which was to provide us with a washing up table and, more interesting, some vegetables from which we made a stew, the kitchen cooking but asking no questions.

791 Desmond makes a mistake with the spelling. Antiphlogistine, a topical analgesic introduced in 1919.
792 Society for the Promoting (not Propagation as Desmond says) of Christian Knowledge, commonly known as SPCK, the oldest Anglican mission organisation, founded in 1698.
793 German: square.

Monday March 10th

The weather was cold and raw but our room had fortunately dried up and was quite habitable. We had managed to raise quite a stock of coal and the fire, a high glazed tile affair, gave quite a good heat and could be used to cook food on. The morning Appell supplied a change. The Camp Officer stepped onto the Platz and we heard his voice say "Britische Offiziere, Guten Morgen".[794] There was a silence of embarrassment and then Murray's voice, "Say Good Morning to the Captain," and then a rather weak "Good morning." The German officers are much more polite here and evening Appell is always taken by a captain who salutes very politely before he sees us locked in. The actual locking used to be done by an English Corporal but it is now done by the German senior NCO, a very hearty fellow who, for obvious reasons, is called Scarface. He was a prisoner in Scotland during the last war and he seems to have been well treated judging by his kindness to our boys who swear by him. His knowledge of English is very rudimentary but very expressive, being composed of the floweriest of English swearwords. I spent most of the day writing my diary, for I was a fortnight behind. Lunch is at 12 o'clock and is always the same stew, at least it is really hot. After lunch I read till 2.30 when we make a cup of tea which is always most welcome and helps to break up the afternoon. My reading today, "Tess of the D'Urbervilles", which I was quite enjoying. The story was rather common place with the blushing young maid, the good looking dangerous squire and the charming young gentleman who Tess always loves. The story is made more intricate by the forcible characters of Tess and her husband who will suffer all mental hardships during separation for the sake of their pride. The final scenes are very tragic; Tess, living with Alec, not for love but for the sake of peace of mind and the well being of her family, is found by her husband. Exasperated by Alec's coarse humour at her expense, she murders him and the last scenes depict Tess and Angel, her husband, reunited, fleeing from justice; both happy in the other's love and doing their best to shut out the terrible future which pursuing them relentlessly, overtakes them as they shelter among the haunted shadows of Stonehenge. The finest passages are those of farm life and the dawn gradually breaking over the fertile pastures of Wessex. The scene of Tess's seduction is quietly shown, the great sadness shrouded in the darkness of a wood. It was a book that pleased me for a change but I was not over enamoured with the length and similarity of the fine descriptions. I must read one or two others, for an author cannot be judged solely on one work. During the afternoon the orderlies that we had brought with us left for one of the other Forts of which there is a circle around this Fort, Fort 15. When men are here they sleep 40 to a room and the animal life, it would seem abounds. From talking to the MDs,[795] it would seem that many of our boys had lost all sense of self respect. They will not even look after themselves and will not bother to take a bath, even when the opportunity presents itself. In the evening we fried some sausages which we eat with some 'scrounged' potatoes. The kitchen stores of IX A had been divided up and we had quite a good assortment of tinned stuff. I went to pay a visit to Colin who is in a room full of airmen. It is not often that I see him now, for living in separate rooms makes life more cell like and there are some men I have not seen since I've been here. Colin's room contains a number of amateur musicians and the air is rent with saxophone wails and accordion jingles: a gramophone just completes the musical picture. A number of copies of the Völkischer Beobachter are put in the library and I try and get a look at them every day: the paper is a popular press one and the writing is journalistic and extravagant and, as the party direct this organ, the news is very biased. The Frankfurter always had a great deal of English news and it was better reading. The German papers consist of news and stock prices. There is nothing like the 4th Times leader or the light Columnist such as Castlerosse;[796] the

---

794   German: British Officers, good morning.
795   Abbreviation: From the Latin Medicinae Doctor, Doctor of Medicine.
796   Valentine Edward Charles Brown (1891-1943), styled Viscount Castlerosse, was a journalist for the Sunday Express, and a director of the Evening Standard, The Daily Express and The Sunday Express.

whole layout stresses the political ideal of the party: rather dull to read and for me, rather depressing, especially the reported ship losses which must be exaggerated. Another journal in the library is a weekly "Das Reich"[797] which has political, sporting and literary supplements. The tone of the papers is that of a whip trying to use public feeling against England and also USA by reports of speeches and articles of obscure men which give extravagant war aims, e.g. the complete prohibition of aeroplanes in Germany should that country be defeated. The general style is an intensification of propaganda. <u>News</u>. Reports that USA has guaranteed Yugoslavia.

Tuesday March 11th

The weather was rather wet, unusual for this area I am led to believe, and I was not able to take much air. I began to make my programme. I spent my morning at shorthand. I have decided to work by myself using the instructor, as the classes are very slow. The greatest difficulty of shorthand is the practice. The rules themselves are very reasonable and I find the building up of words most interesting and the time till 12 o'clock Appell simply flies by. After lunch I read till 2.30 and then do some Russian till the coffee is served up. This Russian is not too difficult if it is taken slowly and I never do more than an exercise a day. I intend to complete the small grammar and get knowledge of all the words: I think that will be sufficient for my purposes and should be enough for ordinary reading and the beginnings of conversation. We had a lovely hot shower during the afternoon and it was very pleasant to come back to a warm room instead of having to dash across a bitterly cold passage and stand about in an ice cold changing room with a very dirty floor. The news was full of a very heavy raid in London and a Swedish report that the "saison"[798] had begun. I do hope that precautions are now fully organised. I often feel very guilty sitting in the port of Poland, with no danger and no real worries, in spite of the rumours that troops are massing on the Russian frontier and refugee trains are moving westwards. After Lights Out at 9 o'clock (they are switched off from outside with no warning) conversation continues till about 10.30, usually finishing up on the usual topic of women: the conversation of the three fs. My bed is very hard and I am never quite sure when the boards will fall out of the bed of the man above me, for the beds are very rickety. I thought about a short story. It was to be written in the 1st person dealing with Hobson's tragic accident. His attractive wife offers great possibilities to portray hardness and ruthlessness. The scene in the restaurant could be one of life suddenly turned cold. The years of blindness at the Haras,[799] at last made habitable by the arrival of Blanche, would give much scope for pastoral Hardy-like writing. I think I should put it into the first person to make it more real and make the relations more personal; still, that would be a subsidiary matter to arrange; first person for a short story, third person for a novel.

Wednesday March 12th

My foot did not seem to be healing very much and it was still quite infected. I am sure that such a blister would never cause me so much trouble in normal times. It must be the lack of vitamins in the skin. The morning was interrupted by the inspection of a visiting General. He arrived in the middle of the morning and came to our room, accompanied by a large staff of officers. He was a little man, with a prominent chin and a monocle. His uniform was covered with red braid which seemed to match his face which was crimson with rage. This rage was brought

---

797   German: Das Reich, a national socialist newspaper.
798   French: season.
799   I am not sure if this word is transcribed correctly. There is a commune, Le Pin-au-Haras in the Orne department in north western France.

about by his reception in one of the RAF rooms, where his appearance had made no impression except an arousing of mild interest. He swept into our room, almost running down G Woods who had leapt in front of him to say "sechzen officiere".[800] The General glanced at a bed and began to shout. His shouts, being interpreted, were to the effect that a blanket was untidy. After a little more critical noise, he swept out. A few minutes later Murray appeared and told us that our room was not tidy enough and we must stay in until it was put straight. We brushed and cleaned until the Camp Officer appeared; he made no observations as to the tidiness of the room but he told Woods that he was to be the father and mother of his young flock. He spoke in this vein for about five minutes and was very charming when he could have been very unpleasant. The General had quite obviously been out to find trouble. Still, all inspecting Generals seem to have the same mentality. I finished Tess and did some Russian. So the day came to an end, with some 'scrounge' stew to make it more bearable. The great trouble here is that the water is absolutely undrinkable and we must always wait for tea or Ersatz to quench our thirst. The news was full of the forthcoming visit of Matsuoka[801] to Hitler. Also Portsmouth has been heavily bombed. I am gradually getting used to the people in the room, though I get very tired of the early morning noise and I could brain a very Yorkshire gentleman called Gowlands who croons to himself and sings some dreadful song which seems to consist entirely of the line "And they don't wear the pants", which is repeated over and over again. Kennedy is usually talking rubbish about how the war is to end and how we must set about bringing peace. L J Cook is an authority on every known subject. Crawford is very public school and never finishes a statement except by the words "you see." Kelso and Hill manage to pass the time talking to each other in diaconal language, interspersed with vulgarity. So the happy days go by. You will agree that prison life is not one in which contemplation is easy.

Thursday March 13th

My foot did not seem to be making much headway so I had hot poultices which, painful as they were, had the consolatory effect of excusing me from Appell. I sat in the room and waited for an NCO to come and check me off the list. It is very annoying not being able to take any fresh air and walk about; still, I suppose I shall have plenty of time to take air before this war is over. I did my usual work. After lunch I read an essay of Wilde's "De Profundis"[802] written when he was in gaol. It is very attractively written but there is something rather unpleasant in the man's abject apology for his having "drunk the cup of life". He realises that his life was one that never counted sorrow and suffering; now he sees that suffering is real and true and not a veneer and from it he draws the conclusion that depth in life is essential, for he feels that his depth has come with sorrow.

> *"Who never ate bread in sorrow*
> *Who never spent the midnight hours*
> *Weeping and waiting for the morrow*
> *He knows you not ye heavenly hours."*

The most delightful passages are those in which he deals with the life of Christ, of his love for the sinner, his love for the individual. The word painting is very fine and this 'purple patch' writer seems to put all the simplicity of Christ into the lines. He feels that he must ask for less of the world than ever he asked and in the elemental forces of nature, the sea, the sky, the woods, the flower, he will seek to purify himself. It is a shock to read such a book but it should be read and it gives a sense of pity to see such a man through his soul, open to the world. Is it just another show or is it true? I am inclined to belief in its truth; two years of reality could change such a man's

---

800   German: sixteen officers.
801   Yōsuke Matsuoka (1880-1946), a Japanese Diplomat and Minister of Foreign Affairs of the Empire of Japan during the early stages of WW2.
802   "De Profundis" by Oscar Wilde, published in 1905.

nature. The book is full of useful thoughts, "Whatever happens to oneself happens to another". How true in my own case, what words to combat selfishness. "Nothing is more rare in a man than an act of his own" (Emerson).[803] What a truth for Wilde's early life; are my acts my own or are they dictated entirely by social circumstances; I must examine myself carefully after a month of liberation, "I have got to make everything that has happened to me good fortune." I certainly have to and I am trying to do it. Prison life makes me see people and things as they really are. How do I see myself? Working to prevent myself thinking; living in a world of imagination which pays little attention to physical troubles. A book that I must study again. I intend to read all Wilde's work and then write some appreciation or criticism! A great many new books came from the top camp and it was great fun walking around. There is so much to read and it is such a temptation to devote my whole time to reading and writing. My theory is to learn new languages here because I have the time but, if we are here next year, I shall set about real writing. I must try a novel. I ordered a fountain pen at the Canteen but I have small hopes of ever receiving it. As yet we have had no money.

Friday March 14th

We were greeted this morning by the rumour that the US was in the war. I think this rather unlikely as yet. The usual monotony of the day was relieved by the arrival of some "pain d'épice"[804] and some sweet biscuits which was greatly appreciated. The first lot of beer turned up as well, so life looked quite normal; I'm used to the iron bars now and with my work and reading "iron bars do not make a cage". During the afternoon I read some Keats.[805] "Isabella",[806] a very sad tale, and also some sonnets. I found them very readable and I liked the use of alliteration: it was not forced and seemed to come quite naturally. Once again we were allowed to get to our cases but were not allowed to take them to our rooms: at present we have no cupboards and it is all very awkward. The evening was made gay by some fishcakes of tinned fish and some potatoes which came to our hands: the coming was, of course, assisted by our own efforts. They were very tasty. We were all inoculated against diphtheria; I was jabbed with a very sharp needle and did not feel anything and my arm became only very slightly stiff. I had a new book out "Great Englishmen of the 16th Century" by Sir Sydney Lee.[807] It was most readable and I read Sir Thomas More[808], that advanced thinker yet conservative believer; some of his remarks on marriage rather intrigued me "a man taking a wife is like a man who puts his hand into a bag of snakes in which there is one eel". But, once married, he says "Enjoyment of his family is a necessary part of a business of a man who does not wish to be a stranger in his own house". Sir Philip Sydney[809] had the poetic desire to emulate the classics. All the essays were good. Raleigh, Bacon of whom I intend to make a great study when I return home. Here I can merely read and digest his essays and endeavour to put out an essay about him. The news spoke of more bombing of Portsmouth and London. There was a fantastic story of a bomb exploding in Ambassador Rendel's[810] luggage after he had left Bulgaria.

803	Ralph Waldo Emerson (1803-1882), an American essayist, lecturer and poet who led the Transcendentalist Movement of the mid 19th century.
804	French: spiced bread (more like a cake).
805	John Keats (1795-1821), an English Romantic poet.
806	"Lamia, Isabella, The Eve of St Agnes and Other Poems" by John Keats, published in 1820.
807	"Great Englishmen of the 16th Century" by Sir Sydney Lee, published in 1904.
808	Sir Thomas More (1478-1535), an English lawyer, social philosopher, author, Statesman and noted Renaissance humanist.
809	Sir Philip Sydney (1554-1586), an English poet, courtier and soldier.
810	George William Rendel (1889-1979) was a British diplomat caught up in a huge bomb explosion at the Pera Palace Hotel in Istanbul. It was claimed that the Germans had planted the bomb in luggage as the party left Sofia.

Saturday March 15th

I had to waste a long time in the sick bay and when I had finished I went and did some shorthand, concentrating on revision: at present my work might be called an extra long hand. Still, one day I might become proficient. Lunch was of fried Klippfisch and at least it was a change, if nothing else. I had rather a headache in the afternoon so I decided not to do any work and spent the time playing dominoes with Salt. This time we used a set of double sixes and got on much better. At 6 o'clock FF organised a concert and conducted community singing in his usual indomitable fashion. The "theatre" is a tunnel next to the chapel and it was a great credit to the performers that they were able to banish the rather dismal surroundings. A jazz band of drums, saxophone, and accordion very well played by P O Smalley, Hash sang his good Irish songs. There was a very vulgar "Albert in London", the cornet solo and community singing. It was very cheering and it showed that the surroundings cannot quench all spirit. After Lights Out I told the story of Maugham's "The Rain"[811] which I had read on the way here. All beards are off by order, except Naval men. My shaving is now done in hot water, though it matters not much to me.

Sunday March 16th

The day was very fine. I could see this through the windows for at present I do not go on Appell and waste about one hour in the sick room. The blister is still very raw and does not seem to heal up at all. The old doctor tries all sorts of things: caustic, zinc ointment and then in solution and still the skin does not seem to get any energy. It is very annoying not being able to walk about and take exercise. Life here is much more cellular. By that I mean that there is very little communal life and it is amazing how seldom I meet old friends. The only general room is the library, which holds about a dozen, and a reading room for lectures. Most people stay in their rooms and the camp is not so homogenous as Spangenberg. There is also a dividing factor in having the RAF here, for the rooms are usually made up entirely of army or airforce. The RAF are very good chaps but very rowdy and, except for a great aptitude for playing jazz music and conversational bridge, they are not very useful to the life of POWs. I went up to the church clad in all my pullovers and coats, for it was very cold. The Padre rattled through the service at a merry pace, though as I explained last week, my thoughts were quite my own and were not stereotyped to Mr MacIntyre's words. He is an Irishman who was offered some good terms, but would not play in the end. His sermon was based on the words "He who would be great should be the slave". He begged us to be humble and work for good, not for power, as some had done. The singing was rather ragged as the cornet player was not quite sure of the length of the verses. That, however, did not worry me: I would not mind if there was no singing. After lunch I read an essay on Shakespeare which showed very well how greatly Shakespeare had been revered by his contemporary dramatists. The age was one in which merit was recognised by pleasure, failure recognised by real criticism which spared no words. Ben Johnson describes him as "The applause delight and wonder of our stage". During the afternoon I wrote my diary which is usually a good day's work. The day's news was all rumours; Yugoslavia was supposed to have joined the Axis and Greece was reputed to have asked for peace because she had not enough aid from her allies. The Belgian doctor was the source of these. He is a great believer of all G news and he is a Flamand. He is not interested in the result, he just wishes to see the end and would as soon see the other side victorious. He is very dangerous here and I shall be quite glad to see his back. He is of the Perouse type and he can cause us a lot of trouble when it is all over.

---

811 "Rain" by Somerset Maugham, published in 1921.

Monday March 17th

The morning was very cold and, to make it even more unpleasant, our chimney became blocked. One of the orderlies, a sweep by trade, came down and attended to it but not before the room had become like an ice box. When he had fixed the chimney, the fire burned like an express train and, in order to save coal, we had to let it go out in the evening, a practice which will be continued. The morning was enlivened by a first class rumour. Hitler, Mussolini, Molotov and Halifax, who was to represent England and USA, were to meet in Rome to discuss peace terms. The speculation was intense until it was realised that the originator was Scarface. It was later divulged that Scarface starts a rumour every day for the benefit of the gullible officers. This camp is much more prone to Bobards[812] (the English term for these news flashes is not very polite), the reason for this surfeit of news is the great number of sources. The orderlies who come in to work have seen train loads of wounded coming from Russia, and troops going up to the frontier. The Poles who come in and work tell us about the terrible treatment inflicted on Lithuanian Germans. The Belgian doctor gets some tit bits and the guards know all sorts of things. The men here are fighting men of a "panzer"[813] group and they are much more polite and considerate: perhaps they feel that they might one day be in the same boat. After lunch (still the same stew; potatoes, turnips, carrots and water) I copied out my "Rebecca" article for Beckwith's magazine which should be produced shortly. A shower bath changed the day a little. The showers here are much better than at IX A. There are 11 good sprays, instead of 6 bad ones. The water is always hot and, instead of 30 bathers, we go in 16 at a time. During the afternoon I was all excitement for the evening's entertainment, The St Patrick's Day Dinner. I had put myself down as Irish, having Mulholland and Murphy on the male side. The dinner had been organised by Glazebrook, a very handsome Major (he had jumped from Lt to Major with a very speedy movement) who had very piercing brown eyes and with his beard, which he has now lost, he looked a typical Italian of the Renaissance; by Hash, who in sea boots, well polished, and Polish breeches looked like the foreman of a racing stable; and by Charles Bonham, a regular who spoke with the smattering of a very attractive brogue who did all the collecting of food. G Woods and I gave one of the tins of steak and kidney from our room stores. Dinner was to be at 5.30, all diners had to arrive equipped with tin plate, knife, fork, spoon, mug and ration of blut wurst[814] and butter and a slice of bread. It was rather like a fashionable fork supper; I enjoyed it quite as much. The dinner was held up for the distribution of letters in which I had a particular interest, for there was a letter from Nanny. The envelope was decorated with a 20 pfg[815] stamp which did not please me very much and the letter was written in the usual spindly scrawl which now pleased me as it had never done before, though I couldn't help asking myself why Nanny did not buy a decent fountain pen. The letter was charming: I had feared a cold letter which would tell me facts and then close. This letter was usual in its tenderness except for one thing, which worried me more than anything else: there was no mention at all of Mums. What can have happened to her! Am I to take the non mention to mean that all is as it should be and that she has written herself or is it that she is not in a position to either write or give any news? I was terribly glad to receive the letter but it did not disperse my horrible fears. I strive to think that no news is good news. N seems to believe that we are treated here as university students and that our intellectual needs are attended to by a competent staff. Fortunately, we have some talented companions and some of us wish to learn; otherwise we should not get very far. The excitement of receiving the letter put me into a mood of restlessness which would be satisfied by the variety of a new type of entertainment. At the door of the reading room we were met by Glazebrook who gave us each a tot

---

812   French: rumours
813   German: tank, armour.
814   German: blood sausage (similar to black pudding).
815   German: pfennig.

of Schnaps.[816] Schnaps is the German word for liqueur and this 'tot' was brandy of a sort; at least it was warm and biting. The room was laid out in a fashion like this:-

****[817]

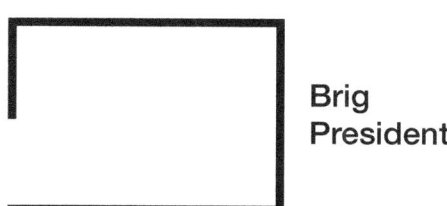

The Padre said grace and we sat down to dinner at a table which was covered with a table cloth (red sheets). The meal consisted of Hors d'oeuvres (sardine, vegetable salad and wurst), Meat pie (a gamel[818] between 5), Steak and Kidney pudding (one to three) and peas. Then a mixed fruit pudding, which was very tasty, followed by biscuits and coffee and more Schnaps to follow. Hash had been responsible for the preparation of the meal and it was a triumph almost equal, in substance not spirit, to the feeding of the 5,000. "The King" was proposed by the President, the MD Col Morris, Ireland by Capt Brush and St Patrick by Bonham. He gave us a poem of Jimmy O'Deas[819] which was to show his own position, half orange, half green. He then told us that St Patrick had travelled all over Europe and had even been to Poland, so it was very fitting to drink his health here. The toast of Irishmen in the services was by F O Murphy who, to prove that our services had always been the home of Irishmen, gave us the anecdote that when Julius Caesar came to England he saw a mass of men on the shore, recognised them and cried to his men "Row back to Rome my lads, here's the Dublin Fusiliers".[820] Brigadier Somerset spoke for the guests. He had been told that an Irish stew was not a product of Ireland; if this was a sample of an Irish dinner, he would garrison any man who said that cooking did not originate in Ireland. It was the best meal he had had since he had been a prisoner and in that I definitely agreed with him. We had to disperse at 8 o'clock and the Appell bugle came all too soon. This same bugle had heralded in the toasts. As the doors were locked, I felt that I had passed a very peasant evening. My hunger was satisfied and I felt pleasantly hazy; three bottles of beer (Englische Pilsner[821] it was called) and some Schnaps are a lot for a Gefangener.[822] My eyes wanted to shut and my tongue to wag. A comfortable arm chair and the wireless playing some slow dance music, the fire glowing in the darkened room. That was what this ugly room should have become!! News. Glasgow and Liverpool were heavily bombed.

Tuesday March 18th

I was still off Appell and usually spent the morning doing shorthand; I am getting along quite well but it needs endless practice. I find it very dull reading through the exercise I have done, I fear I have a horror of reading through any sort of work. I love to get on and do something new. I must get out of this aversion, if I wish to become a successful writer, for it is impossible to get the right phrase at once. However, I feel that the inspiration

---

816 German: any kind of strong alcoholic drink.
817 Here Desmond draws a sketch showing the layout of the tables.
818 I am not sure if this word is transcribed correctly and cannot identify its meaning.
819 Jimmy O'Dea (1899-1965), an Irish actor and comedian.
820 A reference to the Irish folk song "The Dublin Fusiliers".
821 German: English Pilsner (a type of pale lager).
822 German: prisoner.

of a moment is very much better than the struggle of coining phrases. What I must strive to get is a style which is spontaneous in its theme and can easily be perfected into polished work without the appearance of hard work. During the morning our friend, the General, returned but he was a very different man, for he was accompanied by Jefferson Patterson,[823] who is first councillor of the US embassy. JP took a great many notes, especially on the conditions of the men who are not very happy: they sleep 45 in one of these rooms and the places are swarming with livestock. They have a great many complaints against our own NCOs who often behave very harshly. Most of the men realise that they need discipline but they do not like to see their own privileges taken from them to placate their captors. JP asked a great many questions and kept the authorities on the hop, especially the senior man who was most ingratiating. He did not come to our room; I should have like to have seen him, if only because he was a friendly civilian who spoke English. I often wonder what these visiting Americans think of conditions in the camps and if they feel sympathetic towards us. Our lot is not too bad when we get used to it but I think that it must be rather depressing for freemen to see us. I wonder what their feeling about war can be, do they wish to join in when they can see it at such close quarters? I don't know whether it was coincidence that caused a consignment of Bulk stores from Geneva to arrive or whether it was to impress our visitors. Whatever the cause, the stores arrived about 4.30, a tin of condensed milk, a slab of chocolate, a box of Knäckerbrot[824] and a box of Biscottes.[825] It did not take me long to make a hole in this food. The chocolate went first and then I started to crunch the Knäckerbrot; this is a very crisp type of biscuit, "pain croustillant".[826] I rashly made two holes in my tin of milk and it did not take much to persuade me to start sucking. The sweet, sticky, delicious whiteness oozed down my throat. It is a wonderful sensation soon over. I received a letter from Aunty which acknowledged my November letters. My clothing parcel should soon be along. Aunty had still no news from home. I spent some time reading Hitler's speech in which he made many strong assertions that the war would be over this year. Italian indignation is high over the sinking of a hospital ship[827] by TA[828] aircraft. It was leaving Albania. It may have been the extra food that made sleep so difficult but it was long after 4.30 before I at last dropped off. Once asleep, I did not wake up till the door was unlocked. Conversation at night runs usually along the well grooved channel of smut; that at least is fairly free from complete tripe and it may be nature's outlet. It is over 8 months since I spoke to a woman. Strangely enough, I am not very worried by this and it is only occasionally that desire takes hold of me. There is no doubt that I wasted much too much time on this subject before the war; still, I don't really regret it. This "drinking of the cup of life" leads me to O Wilde's "Picture of Dorian Gray"[829] which I had been reading for some time. The story is good and the supernatural charm of the painting is well reproduced. The style is very artificial and it is very clear that the writer is putting forward his shocking tactics by coining exotic phrases and new pleasures that are entirely sensuous. Dorian's collection of stones is to give him sensual pleasure; their cost and their associations are his desire, not their geological value. I felt that the book was written to print as many startling epigrams as possible. All life is self examination and all experience, however criminal, must be co-opted into the philosophy of life, of self. The love of words and of sensations is rather Elizabethan. The difference is that in the earlier age the writers were experimenting in new fields whereas in the "Fin de siècle"[830], the writers were resurrecting the life that had been subjected by rules and conventions. They were as children who have been made to keep quiet during church on Christmas day. They have been thinking of their presents and longing to speak. When their mouths are loosed, their words flow over with expression and pent up emotion. So it was with

---

823	Jefferson Patterson (1891-1977), a US career diplomat.
824	German: a flat and dry type of bread or cracker made from rye flour.
825	French: light, soft bread, toasted or crisped in an oven.
826	French: crusty bread.
827	An Italian hospital ship, HS Po, was sunk by a British torpedo bomber inside the Bay of Valona, Albania on 14th March 1941.
828	Military abbreviation: Territorial Army.
829	"The Picture of Dorian Gray" by Oscar Wilde, published in 1890.
830	French: end/turn of the century.

the Decadents.[831] Their fathers had had their desires but had façaded them with sobre covering. At last the mouths were loosed and the sensations were given a voice to their body. The pent up desire to talk and to describe these sensations led to a style that put these desires into the very words. The world became a place to vent the desires and not a place in which to live: the world was a dinner table, where conversation and epigrammatical cynicism were the most vital factors. Wilde says that "a man who can dominate a London dinner table can dominate the world". For Wilde the world was a dinner table and to enjoy this book you must be one of the diners who enjoys the delicate flavour of the hot house peach and not the diner who likes to smother his taste with Worcester sauce.

Wednesday March 19th

The weather was now very fine but the East Wind was biting. The day was rather like one of the IX A days for I went to a lecture by Lovel who dealt with the position in France that led up to the Revolution, only one class paid taxes, the poor. John Surtees was brought back as well as the 2 airmen. JS had got 40kms when he went into a barn and fell asleep. He was found next morning by a farmer who took him to be an escaped lunatic and handed him to the authorities. One of the airmen was knocked unconscious when he jumped from the train and when he came to he was very shaken and, in a doze, walked into some railwaymen. The other got 300kms: his feet were in a terrible state and, as his progress was very slow, he moved off too early one evening, was seen by a small boy and reported. They were all of them very well treated and are in very good spirits. I would be heartbroken to come back. Barrie gave a lecture on musical theory and showed us how music was composed and the aids to composition. He gave us some opening bars and we had to write 8 bars. He was very pleased with mine. I hope he will continue this series because it is great fun. Without a piano at hand, all the work has to be done in the head and this is the ideal way to learn. I began Emerson's Essays "Representative Men".[832] His style is very complex and involved, full of semi colons and theatrical questions. His theory is that great men must be admired and studied so that there may be greater men. His essay on Swedenborg[833] intrigued me. This man was a mystic who believed that knowledge raised the soul of man, "The wiser a man is, the more will he be a worshipper of God". Nature, assisted by man, would become more and more perfect in every plain. As the animal kingdom became perfected, so man through knowledge would grow, "Till man in his perfection was Heaven". He thought without the retrogression of War! (This to be studied later). Montaigne[834] was a Sceptic, the man who takes a middle course between sensation and morals. This view is constructive, if it is used to choose the best of both sides, and to realise that a change is not the end but the beginning of a new phase in which the course must be steered, "If my boat sinks, 'tis to another sea". The paper was full of the criticism against the bungles of the War Ministry. It is rumoured from London that Matsuoka will go there. This is denied here.

---

831   The Decadent Movement was a late 19th century artistic and literary movement of Western Europe. Oscar Wilde was a leading figure in the movement.
832   "Representative Men" by Ralph Waldo Emerson, published in 1850.
833   Emanuel Swedenborg (1688-1782), a Swedish scientist, philosopher, theologian, revelator and Christian mystic.
834   Michel de Montaigne (1533-1592), writer and essayist, commonly thought of as the father of modern scepticism.

Thursday March 20th

The History lecture dealt with the French Revolution,[835] M Antoinette's[836] meddling with the idea of foreign help raised the national violence of Henrietta Maria's intrigues and the influence of the Czarina[837] and Rasputin?[838] An interesting study on Queen Consorts could arise. I spent the afternoon doing my washing. I had to do it all in a wooden bucket and it was all rather primitive and would not have been a good advertisement for Persil. Washing clothes is a tedious necessity which needs a great deal of practice; I must try it with Lux[839] one day. I had a long chat with Gaffrey, a very cheerful little orderly who was with us at VIII E. He is a barman at the Ecu de France[840] and he would be ideal as a valet-chauffeur, which is the job he would like. I am getting his address and will think of him if ever I become affluent enough to indulge in such a luxury. He is cheerful and keen and he seems to like me for he forced me to take a Sam Browne[841] which he had found. His address is:-   ****[842]   In the evening I had my first TAB[843] inoculation; these do not worry me now and I hardly feel the needle. For tea we had some porridge from Red Cross stores: it was good but much too watery, not burnt as it was at Lowood:[844] I am reading "Jane Eyre"[845] which I am enjoying very much. It is so clear and unaffected and gives a very vivid picture of the times. The poor little orphans were much worse off than POWs. Like the Rev Mr Collins in "Pride and Prejudice", Mr Brocklehurst[846] raises all my wrath and I should love to kick his shins. I shall write more about the book when I have read it completely. I sat out in the sun after lunch and saw a nasty sight. The beds in the sick bay are riddled with bugs and they were fumigating some of the beds. Not an invitation to go sick. I ordered a suitcase. The Canteen here is quite good and it is now useful to us, for we have been paid. I bought some very good bachelor buttons[847] because I do hate having to sew. The big rumour is that the entire Luftwaffe went over England last night. It sounds like Scarface again.

Friday March 21st

Today I received two letters. One from Mrs Rankin who told me that she had forwarded a letter for me and that they all went in the Embassy bag. Wendy wrote her usual type. Full of dancing and fun. She said that she and her friends nearly went crazy if they could not go out every night. I make no comment. She gave a description of some needle work she was doing. This is the second time that she has gone into these intimate details; I must remind her of them when I get home. I also received a parcel from WH Smith containing 2 packs of cards, a set of Dominoes

---

835   French Revolution (1789-1799), a period of radical social and political upheaval in France in which the absolute monarchy that had ruled France for centuries collapsed.

836   Marie Antoinette (1755-1793), Queen of France and Navarre from 1774 to 1792, executed by guillotine for treason to the principles of the Revolution.

837   Alexandra Feodorovna (1872-1918), Empress Consort of Russia as the wife of Nicholas II, the last Emperor of the Russian Empire.

838   Grigori Yefimovich Rasputin (1869-1916), a Russian mystic and advisor to the Romanovs, the Russian Imperial Family.

839   Lux brand laundry soap.

840   A well known restaurant in Paris.

841   A wide leather belt supported by a strap passing diagonally over the right shoulder.

842   Here Desmond leaves a blank, obviously intending to write in the orderly's address but he never does.

843   An inoculation to give protection against typhoid.

844   A reference to the burnt porridge in the school for orphans in "Jane Eyre".

845   "Jane Eyre" by Charlotte Bronte, published in 1847.

846   A character in "Jane Eyre".

847   A type of snap on button.

and a game called Gambo[848] which I may try one day when I have become a sufferer of Gefangener Blues. A great many clothing parcels came so mine should soon be here. I am going to write for a battle dress and my coloured cap. Everyone looks so smart now that I feel very dowdy. After lunch I sat up in the Platz and smoked a little pipe that I had just bought, a Bruyère Garantie.[849] I smoked tobacco extracted from Gauloises[850] and Turkish "Hellas". I would like to smoke a pipe and eschew cigarettes. It is very comforting and not too expensive. The German tobacco "Brinkmann" is mild and quite good. During the afternoon I had a haircut. There is a Barber's shop here which is quite well fitted. The barber would insist in cutting my hair in line with my ears, a habit which I have now discontinued and I now have short sideboards which Uncle M always advised me to have. In the evening we had a chat with a Pole who came to mend a window or rather he came to superintend his little boy mend the window. He told us that the USA and Russia would help us, also that letters from Bulgaria intimated that all was not going too well and that there was quite a lot of trouble. We gave him some cigarettes which he said he would keep as a treat until he went to bed. The curfew is 10 o'clock here. He spoke in German and I understood most of his conversation. I wish I could get more practice in conversation as I am sure that I should soon speak the language. The news was full of the strengthening of Yugoslavia's attitude towards the Axis.

Saturday March 22nd

The weather seems as contrary as Spangenberg for today was snowy and cold. My foot does not seem to have healed at all; it is very annoying. We had a lovely shower. In the afternoon I went to a lecture by Major Gee, a Master at Clifton. He spoke of the History of plays. They came from church anthems; developed so much that they had to be held first in the church yard and then in the village square. All plays seem to originate with a religious ideal and in England all plays have had a comic character. We cannot sit through an entirely emotional play without a light moment. At 5 I went to the "Theatre". The old curtain was up and the spot light and the little tunnel was very intimate; it was rather like a little theatre club for the production of banned plays. Jim Lubbock, the compère, gave us some good jokes which would be banned anywhere, (POW and cobwebs): wobble it about a bit; green paint, etc. The show was the IX A nonentities and we had "The Cads of the Air Force", followed by a new one "Table Stooges". The same old Max Miller act by Dross and Flanagan and Allen "Green fields and cow pastures", "Where – I never saw her". The whole show was bright and cheerful and was a great credit to the producers. The music was by Slim Smalley and his band. As we trooped out, we were met by the second house coming in. Quite like home. This evening our doors were not locked and we had the lights till 10 which was a great improvement. I wrote a card to Lola who had written to me twice; I asked her for Hugo's Spanish and Pitman's Shorthand English and French. After lights out, jokes and limericks were the order. I made up a few and found them very easy. The new rumour is that we leave on Thursday. Great story about Churchill and Another Fox who is a network commissioner and an ex white slaver![851] Heavy raid on London on Thursday.

---

848   A card game.
849   French: a type of pipe known for its good quality.
850   A brand of French cigarettes.
851   I am not sure if this sentence is transcribed correctly (in particular, Another ....network..)

Sunday March 23rd

(As I have been in hospital during this week I am a bit behind with writing this up: I was foolish enough to lose my notes and my informatory sources of daily events are rather slender). My foot did not seem to be healing up and I had to waste about an hour and a half in the sick bay. I went to church but was not very interested in the service. The Padre's strong Irish accent, especially when he says 'here and there', is very trying and I shudder involuntarily when I realise the words are coming: this rather spoils my powers of concentration. I spent most of the time hoping for a letter from home. The service I attended was at 6 o'clock and I think it was the first evening service I had ever attended. Col Ford read the lesson in a very dull manner; he read it as I expected he would. The Padre is very aggressive and used the word G- in his sermon. It seemed rather shocking though it was an ideal word for the Pharisees. In this case, it was the leading spirit who was under subjection, the peace maker gave way. Now the leading spirit has been violent and for the moment violence has won. The Padre is not a preacher of the meek and mild type, as an argument between him and Clout showed. I cannot go into the Ethics of Christian Love here, for obvious reasons. Still, the time will come. After church we sat down to a very fine meal of bacon, scrambled egg (a postage stamp of dried egg) and some Danish sausage which was presented to us by Robert Smailes, a quiet Solicitor Student, who was celebrating his birthday.

Monday March 24th

Today was full of escape stories. The first intimation that anything was amiss came at lunch time for everyone was on Appell till 1.30. It transpired that 3 airmen had been caught. It was soon discovered that their places on parade had been taken by 3 orderlies. After about an hour's investigation, it was found that there was another orderly on parade. The officer missing was John Hyde Thompson who used to sleep next to me in IX A. If the airmen had not been found out, JHT would have been well away, for the Germans had no idea that he had left. The sporting orderlies, who had been so useful, received 28 days "in the Bunker" but the authorities were not too severe on them and they did not waste away. When the airmen were brought in, we got their story. They had had their heads clipped and they had gone out on a working party. The three of them then attached themselves to a party who were going to the aerodrome. Once arrived there, they took off their khaki and underneath they were wearing blue dyed canvas and false side caps. They walked on to the field and, to their dismay, the 'plane that they hoped to get was not there. But they were not going to let this fact daunt them. They went into the hangar, saluting officers and getting their salutes returned very punctiliously. Inside they found a large bomber and climbed inside. For half an hour they tried to find the starter. Then they began to get desperate. Seeing a 'plane coming down, they thought of a desperate scheme in which they hoped to signal the 'plane to stop, put the pilot out and fly off before the engines were stopped. They ran on to the field and began signalling the pilot to stop. He, misinterpreting their signal, turned the 'plane round and taxied away from them. Full of disappointment they moved back to the hangar but not before they had been seen by the airport controller. He sent for them and they were marched into his office. He proceeded to shout at them for breaking the rule about walking on the tarmac. They did not answer and all went well until he asked them a question. They could not answer. He was even more enraged. Suddenly he detected something. He looked more closely at the caps and nearly jumped out of his skin. They told him who they were and he saw the humorous side. He ordered that they should be given a meal. They were well treated by the Fliegers[852] and then handed over to the army who took a more serious view. The result of their escapade was 4 days in the cooler. I think that their experience would be worth a month. John HT was not retaken and no news was to be had as to his whereabouts.

---

852   German: airmen.

Tuesday March 25th

This day was a real red letter day. We sat down to a very fine tea of 1/3 of a steak and kidney pudding and some minced meat. It was a grand meal and I hardly raised my eyes when letters were brought. Two were thrown at me. No stamp and very puerile writing. I slipped the letter out and my heart literally leapt for joy. I let out a cry of delight. It was the thick fountain pen scrawl on thin white paper and at the head of each letter was printed Le Paradou[853]. Never have I felt so happy. For months I had prayed, in my own way, for news that would relieve my awful fears. The first letter was dated Feb 11th. It was just like one of the old ones that used to arrive weekly. Full of gardening news and fresh air. The other letter of March 8th was more serious. Mums knew that I had heard of her trouble; she had never said a word about it in her first letter and I can never thank her enough for her strength and sympathetic understanding. Her second letter assured me that she had been very well treated and was now home and leading her normal happy life. The expense, however great, will be repaid. It will always be a spur to me. I shall think of the joy that her letters brought me and it will bear me up. By hard work, I have lived through these days of worry: by hard work, I will live through all worry. Mums can put all her trust in me, and I shall make up for her troubles. In the evening I wrote to Nanny and put a great deal into the letter. During the day I had read some essays of Froude[854] which I found very readable. Clear precise wording and clear cut conclusions. In his "Representative Men"[855] he asked for a model man that we could copy, "There is always one man who is the best in every walk of life. Find this type". His essay on Spinoza[856] was rather complicated but I got an inkling I must read it again when I have read my book on Logic. The latest rumour is that 150 new officers were coming. I went to sleep in peace.

Wednesday March 26th

My foot had made no progress at all and I was advised to move up into the sick bay. I seized the opportunity willingly for the two letters had given me quite a mental shock: I had worried for so long that the alleviation of my troubles was almost too good to be true. I moved in at 3 o'clock and was given a top bunk over little Smith from Jersey. The bed was much more comfortable, for it had a straw mattress. My bag sheet was filthy but I could not face several days in blankets. The food in the Revier[857] is just the same as usual but we usually get some Ovaltine in the evening. I had been driven nearly crazy by the noise and stupidity that went on in the room. But peace did not come for Major Clout, a very vigorous business man who knows all, sees all and hears all. He reverts all arguments to the last war and lives in a state of complete optimism as to the speedy end of this one. A liver attack that ruffles the face of one of our hosts will lead him to say that the war is very nearly over. He is certainly very well informed but he cannot argue quietly: he flares up and holds any contrary opinion as a personal insult. After a long argument with F O Thompson (shot down through engine failure in Sept 1939) in which Clout used "my boy", "my young fellah" and other similar convincing phrases, he challenged Thompson to answer the question as to whether Wilson[858] was culpable not seeing that he had the confidence of the USA. Thompson's reply clinched the argument. In an attractive American drawl, he replied "Well, Major, I shan't reply because whatever I say will be

---

853   "Uncle Mickie's house in Guernsey (see Introduction).
854   James Anthony Froude (1818-1894), an English historian, biographer, novelist and editor of Fraser's Magazine.
855   Desmond appears to be confusing Emerson and Froude here. "Representative Men" is by Emerson, not Froude.
856   Baruch Spinoza (1632-1677), a Jewish-Dutch philosopher.
857   German: sick bay.
858   Presumably Woodrow Wilson (1856-1924), President of the United States from 1913 to 1921.

wrong." The talk for the night was over. "Oh – er don't think I'm trying to force you into my views." These were his last words on the subject. When my foot was looked at in the evening, it was decided to try a new method. The wound was cleaned up and then sealed up in elastoplasts, a system that was adopted with wounds in the Spanish War. I'll try anything if it will cure this depressing affliction.

Thursday March 27th

The air was full of rumours. Molotov had been shot and six generals with him and Litvinov[859] had taken his place. More serious for us was the one that John HT had been recaptured and had been wounded, receiving 3 shots in the leg and one in the lung. He was reported to be lying at Fort 17. The day here begins at 7. From 9 o'clock onwards, there is a concentration of new-comers who have to pass by us to visit the doctor. The staff consists of 2 sergeants, one of whom, Roberts, is very superior and works in an interior decorators near Harrods, and two corporals who squabble most of the time. It is rather trying having to listen to them but, on the other hand, they work quite well. I began writing a short story with the Hobson plot and found it very fascinating. My big problem is trying to concentrate description and put only vital things in. I had finished "Jane Eyre." I enjoyed it very much though I found it rather long. I thought that the conversations with St John Rivers[860] might have been curtailed. I was not impressed with this fanatical unsympathetic Christian who knew that he would kill the young girl if he made her his wife; his character was brilliantly contrasted with the characters of his amiable sisters. The exposé of the orphanage was cruel to read and the little girls lived lives that compared very badly with the lives of POWs. I was amazed to read the fiery descriptions of the madwoman and the passionate love of Rochester.[861] The final scene of blindness made happy is not ruined by over sentimentality. Though I was amazed by the forceful characters, I always had the feeling of restraint and naiveté. I think that Daphne du Maurier will be called the Bronte of our era. Her book "Rebecca" held the mystery which always lives through Jane Eyre. In "Rebecca" the mystery is the power of a dead spirit. Charlotte Bronte fills her story with the rugged, strong spirit of Rochester and all through the book his voice seems to call. The English is clear and well chosen and the country scenes are as good as Hardy's, but they are more artificial, country as one would see it through a drawing room window and not the pure air of the farm yard before dawn. If "Jane Eyre" was written to promote the cause of woman's emancipation, its sympathetic feeling must endear its cause to the most ardent misogynist. The most attractive part of the day in the Revier is the fact that the lights do not go off till about 11. When I went to sleep, I slept with no difficulty the whole night through.

Friday March 28th

Today I read G B Sterne's "Sentimental Journey"[862] which I found rather difficult to read. The style was very clipped and I get tired of hyphens between sentences. There were several bons mots.[863] A French woman is coquette, then Deist and then dévote (is the English woman not the other way round?). The journey, being sentimental, did not occupy itself with a great many towns. I should very much like to do a journey in France after the war but spend

---

859 Maxim Litvinov (1876-1951), a Russian Revolutionary and prominent diplomat.
860 A character in "Jane Eyre".
861 A character in "Jane Eyre".
862 Desmond has made a mistake here. His description of the novel and the quotations he gives confirm that this is "A Sentimental Journey" written by Laurence Sterne (not G B Sterne) and published in 1765.
863 French: witticisms.

my time writing on political ideas and hopes for the future. Cycling from St Malo[864] to Montpellier[865] should give me plenty of scope for, as Sterne says, "An Englishman does not travel to see Englishmen." That may have applied then but Edward VII soon changed that. One friend of mine found that the only thing to say about Rome was that you can get a lovely cup of tea. Stube[866] 12 has tea at 10.30 but far be it from me to make a voyage to Thorn to drink that tea. A good subject for an essay. English travellers should read this little book if they can get used to the rather old style. "Travelling teaches us men and manners; mutual toleration is mutual love". We had a chat with Scarface about flyers. His answer was "Alles s-----."[867] As a POW last war, he said that 26 parcels were sent to him and he received three. I doubt this. A new doctor arrived, Lt Col MacKay of the 5th Division, to replace Col Morris. I had a chat with the Padre who told me all about Parker who had fallen into a post. He also told me about Martel[868] and that he was well. I was very glad to hear this and I hope to hear confirmation of this. Parker also had some fun in Paris. Lilliput,[869] which I read this evening, amused me very much and I could understand the stir that he had created with his book, especially the great conflict between the big enders and the little enders. Also, the choosing of councillors by seeing who could jump the highest. I had a long chat with Roberts and he was very pleased to have people to look after who took an interest in themselves. In some of the Forts, the men have got very slack and take little care of themselves. Sleeping 45 in a room is not conducive to hygiene.

Saturday March 29th

The day was very snowy and unpleasant so I was quite glad to be in the Revier. The rumours about trains of wounded were very cheering, also a speech reputed to have been made by a very violent Russian. I went on with Gulliver and read of his trip to Brobdingnag.[870] I was very fascinated by the imaginative powers of Swift and it was a fine effort in criticism for the benefit of the masses. These early books e.g. Gulliver, Robinson Crusoe, appeal to all sections and ages, adventures for the young, construction and destruction for the grownups and amusing anecdotes for the old. I went on with the story and found it much easier and words seemed to come to me. I am very wicked in that I want to get on and I hate having to correct what I have written. I must break myself of this habit. (Bryant's "Macaulay"[871] tells of what pains the old History took to make every sentence flow and to make it seem fresh and spontaneous. I feel that this diary must be full of mistakes, yet I haven't the courage to go back and delve into them. I will have to revise it one of these days). As it was Saturday we had Klippfisch. I have got accustomed to the very salty flavour but this does not alleviate the pangs of thirst. I had been feeding very well up to now for we had a parcel each last Thursday. Mine was a Scots Red Cross and, after the room stores had been removed, I was left with a fruitcake, 1lb of chocolate, some shortbread, a tin of condensed milk and a box of sweets. I was forever dipping into the box and it soon went. I am incapable of saving chocolate. I know that a whole bar will taste no better than a small piece and that I shall not have it for so long, yet I cannot refrain from going right through the bar. Oh for the day when I can go into a shop and buy a big slab of Cadbury's milk! The food here consists of a stew, potatoes, turnips and carrots. Occasionally there is a shred of meat. In the evening we get 1/5 of a loaf, some butter and some sausage twice a week. Ersatz honey, made from rose leaves and very palatable, turns

---

864   A walled port city in Brittany in north western France.
865   A city in southern France, capital of the Languedoc-Roussillon region.
866   German: room
867   German: All s-------.
868   Philip Martel who accompanied Desmond on Operation Anger, the scouting mission to Guernsey (see Introduction).
869   A reference to Jonathon Swift's novel, "Gulliver's Travels" previously referenced.
870   From Vol II of "Gulliver's Travels".
871   "Macaulay" by Sir Arthur Bryant, published in 1932.

up every now and then and we get little caraway dog biscuits instead of bread on Saturdays and Tuesdays. Still, I get used to it slowly. Tea drinking can stave off hunger, as can a pipe. I smoke about 4 a day and have made myself a mixture which I call continental: German, English cigarettes, Bulgarian, Greek, French and Belgian. It is rather hot but I find it quite palatable. It will put me in the way of smoking cheap brands. I began "Kenilworth"[872] and found it rather difficult to get into. I do wish these classics would be printed in decent sized print. I read "Jane Eyre" with great pleasure for I was not frightened away by the minute writing. The edition was that which Uncle Mickey has got; green cloth, uncut pages and a great many photographs. An ideally presented book.

Sunday March 30th

On Sunday I was told that I could leave the sick bay. My foot had healed a little but I had still to stay on my bed. It was not very pleasant having to come back to my hard wood wool mattress and my bed is a bottom one, with the light in front of me, which makes it rather awkward to read. Fortunately, I can lie on my right side, my favourite one for reading. When I got down to the room I found that Jones, our orderly, was sick and that old Choppin of Johannesbrunn fame had taken his place. He is bald with no teeth and he has a sing song North Country accent pitching his voice on the most mournful key possible. He is a great talker and loves to tell of his ailments. I can't help feeling sorry for him though I must admit that he is not the most rapid of workers. He seems to like me, for he is always coming round and asking "Is everything alright Mr Moololland?" and his conversations always end with "Very good, Sir." I think he found that being a room orderly was a bit too strenuous and it was not long before he went back to pumping water, a quiet and peaceful occupation in which he would not be harried from pillar to post with cries of "Hot water," "Where's my knife" and less printable phrases. I finished the story during the afternoon and felt quite pleased with it. The Revision may alter my opinion. Tea was a gala meal for we had half a Christmas pudding each and they were very fine puddings. "Quill" arrived. This is a collection of work by various officers and it was quite amusing. Beckwith, the compiler, did some quite amusing little poems. Tony Strachan, our budding novelist, had a feminine conversation, giving the sabre toothed side of women's conversation. My "Appreciation of Rebecca" was quite well received though I am not quite sure what it is supposed to be. That is, whether it is a criticism or merely just words to make a picture. It is written to make other people read the book, and endeavour to recreate the air of mystery and excitement that I felt on reading that masterpiece of Miss du Maurier. The rumour that caused great consternation was that we were to be put in rooms alphabetically. This did not worry me very much though I have got used to the idiosyncrasies and annoying habits of my roommates. I can retire into my shell and be quite peaceful. Or at least peaceful for a POW.

Monday March 31st

My rear quarters were getting very tender for this bed is not a Vi-spring[873] and is far removed from those sensual double beds that adorn the American Flatlets. I seem to miss women very little and it is only with an effort that I can make myself think of those enjoyable hours that I spent in their company. What I ask for is the peace and quiet of home; my own room and someone to make a fuss of me. I must have a few days at home before I throw myself into the hardships of life. I shall not avoid them and I'll go through anything. But I do long for a lie in on Sundays and Mums bringing my breakfast. Still, it's no good thinking of these things. I spent most of the day cutting and slashing at my story and I brought it down from about 5000 words to 3000. I cut out the long conversation between

---

872   "Kenilworth" by Sir Walter Scott, published in 1821.
873   A popular brand of bed.

Dan Symons and myself and put his story into condensed Oratio Obliqua[874] which I think was an improvement. I got down to my Italian and learnt words. I am giving Russian a break for it was beginning to get me down. I shall take it up later and crack into getting the vocabulary. Life here is made more agreeable by having friends. Racket would be another name for Stalag. I finished "Kenilworth". I must confess that it was an effort and I was guilty of some skipping. The descriptions of Elizabeth's court were very virile and the words ideally chosen but they drew me away from the story and it was often very difficult to get back the thread. I prefer to have descriptive writing dove-tailed into the plot so that all is thrown into the mind at once. Scott gave the idea that he was writing a book and not a story. References to chapter and telling the reader that he will learn certain things if he reads further annoyed me. Varney[875] was the best character; all the Elizabethan virility and unprincipled adventure were in him. The little boy, Flibbertigibbet,[876] amused me and there was something ghoulish about him; it seemed that he was created for Cruickshank[877] to draw. I cannot judge Scott on one book but I did think it heavy going. He is one of those writers who must be picked up and read carefully, little extracts over and over again. I shall try" The Lady of the Lake"[878] and another novel on Scotland before I make my judgement.

Tuesday April 1st

I went right back to my childhood this morning. I called Choppin over and told him that there was a mouse under my bed. Never will I forget the sight of his poor face as he looked under my bed and said "Wait till I get my goon." I had a good laugh and scotched the April fool racket. Choppin laughed dismally and said "Ee you had me there." What a child I am becoming. I began reading Crichton's book on Logic.[879] I shall study this carefully as it is bound to be of use to me. I also began "Wuthering Heights" by Emily Bronte.[880] Some cigarettes and chocolates came in from Mrs Marshall; she has been most painstaking in helping us and I hope that she will be well looked after when it is all over. I was very lucky to draw for a pair of Red Cross pyjamas. They are light grey flannel and are a real luxury. It is grand to get into bed like a civilised being and not like a pie bald Elizabethan for I used to wear a brown pair of Hungarian pants and a red French shirt. We heard all about the fun and games that goes on in the Forts and it is certain that the English soldier is no fool when his comfort is at stake. I read one of Bacon's essays on Dispatch[881] "Long and curious speeches are as fit for dispatch as a robe or mantle with a train is for a race". "To choose time is to save time".

Wednesday April 2nd

I decided to get dressed today but I had to spend most of my time on my bed. It gets very hard and sleep does not come very easily. Our room was destined to have four more occupants and the new beds were squeezed in. I took the opportunity to get a new mattress which does at least hide the gaps in the boards. Arthur Watts, who had been to the dentist, came to tell me that he had met my old friend, Joe Eames. The latter had seen a list of officers and had asked after me. He was looking very fit and seemed as cheerful as ever, not dead as I had been told. I wrote

874	Latin: indirect speech.
875	A character in "Kenilworth".
876	A character in "Kenilworth".
877	George Cruickshank (1792-1878), an English caricaturist and book illustrator renowned for his social caricatures of English Life.
878	"The Lady of the Lake", a narrative poem by Sir Walter Scott, published in 1810.
879	Possibly James Crichton (1560-1582), a Scottish polymath. I have not been able to identify this book.
880	"Wuthering Heights" by Emily Bronte, published in 1847.
881	"On Dispatch" by Francis Bacon, published in 1612.

him a note and gave him all the news. I expect big things of him as he is in the magazine. I got myself put on to the dentist's lists and should go in about a month's time; I am 60th. We were inoculated again for Diphtheria and I had no ill effects though I still do not enjoy the sensation of the needle; the thought of bacteria entering my blood is most distasteful. Some fellows have had very swollen arms which have had to be lanced. I had an interesting talk with a young man who was very fed up with life, perhaps even more than some of us. The new arrivals came about 4.30 after an 8 hour journey from Posen. They had been sent to Posen from Salzburg (Laufen)[882] and had not had a very pleasant time. They were charmed with 20 in a room, being used to 40, and the idea of a bath was a great surprise. They were quite a pleasant quartet; Hooth, a tall, long haired springy young man who sings songs all day and uses a young captain, Lindsay Renton, as his stooge. Clever who is at Clare[883] and a member of Lincoln's[884] is very quiet and pleasant. Walker, a gunner, is good looking and attractively cheerful. I hesitate to think of what they will think of Bedlam. Whenever I come back to the room I say "Back in Bedlam". Turner, giggling like an insane girl and trying to smoke cigarettes with little puffs. Crawford fighting his way through life crying "Stab me, what". Kelso and Hill bickering like two old hens and Gowland crooning American lyrics in an almost Foreign Yorkshire accent. Kennedy holding forth on all subjects with his air of aged wisdom and old Imperial (L J Cook) the Russian Error[885] giving us the answer to all our problems. Oh, we do have fun. The big moment of the evening was when the new arrivals left some of their stew. They did not leave that stew to be wasted. It was quite a thrill to have the lights out at 12.30.

Thursday April 3rd

I heard that Tony Twysden was fit and full of life down at VII C and his accordion was in great demand. I'll always remember the "Waves of Tory"[886] in Damsies[887] Barn. I went on with the Logic book and it gets harder every day; still I'll stick to it and plod along. Lance Pope is at Laufen and he had an amazing experience and rather a strange reception. I bought a pipe for 5 RM at the Canteen and it is a much cooler smoke; it has a Dunhill mark on it and must have been made for our market. At last we were allowed to take out our suitcases, which makes storing clothes much more easy, though I myself have only one vest and one shirt, I can always travel light. The taking out of cases had an amusing result. One officer tried to get his out after hours and Scarface took out his pistol and fired amiably into the ceiling. The officer had the nerve to lodge a complaint. Two officers made an attempted escape which failed rather dismally and the two gentlemen are now in the cooler. I began copying out my story which is slow but quite amusing work. The German papers are full of the Yugoslav atrocities against Germans; this must be the beginning of an attack.

---

882   Oflag VII-C was located at Laufen castle in South Eastern Bavaria, close to Saltzburg.
883   Clare College, Cambridge University.
884   The Honourable Society of Lincoln's Inn, one of four Inns of Court in London to which the barristers of England and Wales belong.
885   I am not sure if this word is transcribed correctly.
886   A Scottish country dance.
887   I am not sure if this word is transcribed correctly.

Friday April 4th

My foot had made very little progress and it is getting very worrying. Still, I suppose I must wait in patience. I am lucky to have nothing worse. Some of the flea bites of the Posen boys are terrible and they are causing terrible sores. One poor man had dermatitis on his head and he has been bandaged for over five months. It was a beautiful afternoon and I sat out in the sun and it was quite summer like. I was able to finish "Wuthering Heights" which I enjoyed very much. It is stark tragedy and the characters are all vital, almost to a kind of insanity. Heathcliff is a fiend and his only feeling that can be called human is his rather brutal affection for the uncared for Hareton. Heathcliff hopes that Hareton will live to be his own replica. The book is sophisticated and rude, filled with the wildness of the moors. Only Ellen, the maid, is really human and even she had difficulty to stand out against the impulses of little Catherine. Edgar Linton lives quietly but his eyes are blinded by Catherine Earnshaw and his hate for Heathcliff ruins his tender mind. Young Linton is an abject pampered creature who seems to have no right to live in this hard world of conflicting characters. I was even more amazed that this book could be written by a young girl who was brought up in a strict family. What was it that brought these fantastically evil people into her mind? I shall study these sisters with the aid of Mrs Gaskell. I wrote a card to Geneva (asking Lloyds bank to wire good news to Aunty).

Saturday April 5th

I read "Macaulay" by Arthur Bryant. It was a very readable book and confirmed my opinion of Macaulay's intense working power and his great love of reading, "I would be a poor man in a garret with plenty of books than a King who did not love reading".[888] His motto was "My task, did my task, my task and something over". I learnt that he took endless pains with his writing and turned every sentence over in his mind before he put it down. He marked all his books with marginal comments and his powers of perception were astonishing. His ambition had been to become a man of letters and it was with this end in view that he took a position out in India. His parliamentary views were liberal in home politics and their form was to support the growing industrial middle class against the landed Tories. His international politics were as national as Palmerston's[889] and in his own words, "England is so great that an English man cares little of what others think of her or how they talk of her". There is no doubt that he was biased in his historical decisions but they are well worth reading, if only for the wealth of description that has been devoted to each incident. Here is a fine writer and I was most impressed with this fair account of the materialist Victorians. Some battle dresses were given out but I did not get one this time but I will get one next time. My tunic has been made to fit and it looks quite smart now. I fear that I shall have to settle down and clean my buttons. In the evening we had some very good pancakes made from Yorkshire pudding mixture. I was very glad to have a shower and get my hair washed; it is almost back to normal length now and it sticks down quite well. I am training it back so that when, if ever, I play tennis again it will not fall into my eyes. What a pansy I shall be? Lovely exotic bath salts, eau de cologne to rub on my face, shaving lotions and brilliantine. Silk shirts and bow ties, suede shoes and a pin stripe suit. This life of dirt and noise makes me long for comforts. Always noise, always people getting in the way. Fighting to toast bread at the fire and balance a little tin of shaving water on the corner of a table. Struggling to get at the little drips of water that trickle from the horizontal pipe. But most of all I want to walk down the valley and look up at the red roof and catch a glimpse of Mums as she hangs up the washing. Home and quiet, these are really more important than luxury.

888   Desmond is not quite correct here. The quote actually is "I would rather be poor in a cottage full of books than a King without the desire to read.

889   Henry John Temple (1784-1865), commonly known as Lord Palmerston, was a British Statesman who served twice as Prime Minister in the mid 19th century.

Sunday April 6th

Just another day of lying on my hard bed, only electric light to cheer me. Struggling through Crichton, learning Italian words, reading German and Macaulay. His essays on Burleigh and Hampden[890] were not startling though the first gives a new light on the great Queen; she was neither ardent Catholic nor ardent Protestant. Supremacy of the throne was her aim. He went to great lengths to show her admirable tact which reached its culminating point in the manner in which she dealt with the Monopolies.[891] HT[892] was brought in. He had got nearly to Warsaw and went as a G arbeiter.[893] Going to a Polish house he asked the way. They mistook him for a G and told him to go down the road to another house. This he did and found that he had fallen into an Arbeit[894] camp. His next stop was Thorn where he was very well received. He certainly had bad luck.

Monday April 7th

Today was a great day for letters. Nic and Jim received their first and all was well. The whole island turned out to meet them. Nanny has been poorly but is better now and has been for a drive. In a buggy or with Victor I cannot tell? Our names were sent over Bremen and picked. They are out of tea. I do wish I could send them some from here. It is tea that really makes life worth living. It turns up at 10.30 and 1.15 and I stew it up about 3.30. It tastes like wood spirit but it is tea and I have made my reputation as champion tea drinker. Harold's first letter was full of depression and he was longing to join up. He did admit that he would rather be in his position than mine. Old Ernest was on leave and looking very smart and all "outpost of the Empire". I must get H to send me some photos of his fiancée. He must make me Godfather to his first son! The German paper was very bitter about two POWs who were returned from USA but they enjoy talking about the capture of Benghazi. We are a little nervous here but we finish up by saying "It's bound to be alright in the end". I heard an amusing story of Lowden who was with Bob Salt in Lille. When he was discovered he asked if he might take a book with him to read before he was shot. These fellows had 5 months in solitary confinement, no light and no exercise but they are as right as rain. Bob is very sane and lets very little worry him. I like him for his quiet humour. His stories of his flash Uncle are most amusing.

Tuesday April 8th

Days here are very dull. With my foot in its present state I have to spend most of my time lying on my bed so I do not come into contact with many people. The great cry now is "thank God I'm normal". This has rather lost its significance by its constant use. Often I wonder if the words are a prayer. Turner seems to be nearing a state of insanity. He giggles at nothing and occasionally lies on his back and just screams. He has always been very spoilt and though he has a very quick brain, as his quickness at learning Russian shows, he adopts the pose of being very young and stupid. I have gone into my shell very much here and I'm afraid that my tongue is getting rather bitter.

---

890 "Burleigh and his times, John Hampdon and Horace Walpole" by Thomas Babington Macaulay, published in 1832.
891 During the last years of her reign, Queen Elizabeth I came to rely on granting monopolies as a cost free system of patronage rather than ask Parliament for more subsidies in a time of war.
892 Lieutenant John Hyde-Thomson for whom this was the first of many escape attempts including from Oflag IVC (Colditz).
893 German: worker.
894 German: Labour (camp).

I have always been moody and this life of sameness often brings the same moods. That is, one day I am very high spirited and talk of silly things, another day I never speak a word. Fortunately, I realise these moods and it rather amuses me to play a part. I often feel the lack of sympathy and this life of everyone for himself is very sickening. The way to be happy is to exercise the mind, learning a language not only gives mental exercise but ambition to become successful is a great spur. Shorthand is very interesting as it is so reasonable; every lesson is ideally graded so that new work is assimilated with very little effort. The practicing is the dreary part. I was very glad to get a letter from Uncle Alfred; he was leading his usual life and the letter breathed a spirit of peaceful routine and his rather archaic language is most attractive; the summer was coming on, war or no war, and I know that his thoughts are centred on his work and he is convinced that all will be well. He has dispatched 3 books on Quakers for me; I shall study them carefully, for I feel in need of a belief that can be permanent. Now I just waver and I can't bring myself to think; it is so much easier to work at black and white. I daren't get myself thinking too hard here on indefinite matters. Life is so different, no worries and no peace. I must get something definite that will not be knocked down by the first trial of a normal existence. The Von Bs wrote from Jersey all about their little cat "Darby"; it makes me hungry to think of the fat pampered little beast. Victor's card was very reassuring and life was going on as ever. I went on with writing up my story. The next one I do I shall revise each page thoroughly, work with a dictionary and copy it out before I go on. I must conquer this desire to get on. It is hard to believe that Flaubert[895] sometimes spent a day in finding a word. It is better to write a sentence that will live than pages of rubbish. I find it a struggle to write imaginatively. I am much better at straight descriptive stuff. I was very surprised to receive a parcel of 1000 Gold Flake[896] from Daddy. I gave about 20 packets away and am wading through the rest. I like a cigarette after a meal because it cuts the gnawing desire to eat more. The paper is full of hate at America's hand in the Balkan game and Col Donovan[897] is mentioned; I remember speaking about him earlier on.

Wednesday April 9th

I received a letter from the Red Cross telling me that Daddy had subscribed for a parcel. I don't know what they are doing with the 5 million that they received before the war. The quality of their goods is not very high and we get a parcel about once a month. I will not deny that I enjoy them very much but I somehow feel that a lot of money is being wasted. The Government battle dress is being held down at Stalag and it is very hard to get any. Grey trousers have been given to repatriated Ukrainians. There are rackets which it is best not to go into. The Brigadier gave a long talk on Appell. The Camp Officer is not interested in our discipline. The Brigadier has formed companies and platoons and has tightened up the discipline all round. He has been criticised and he has offered to hear any complaints or reasons as to why we should not conduct ourselves as soldiers. No one has found a reason. The main objection is that it makes life too easy for the counters. His argument is that he wishes to give as many people an occupation as possible. Also we must behave before our hosts. I grumble at having to stand to attention but I realise that it is essential to keep self respect. Since I have been confined to my bed I have found a languor coming over me. It is almost too much trouble to go along the corridor to get a wash. There is no discipline in the room. I agree that it must come from the top. "Obey your inclinations with an eye on the policeman". The Brigadier is the policeman and he has said that he does not wish to report us after the War. The anti complex is still there but it has been subdued with this threat. We had a very fine, light pudding made from crushed biscuits, fat and sugar. It was delicious and with a treacle sauce. I imagined myself eating one of Peggy's. I read an essay of

---

895   Gustave Flaubert (1821-1880), a French novelist.
896   Gold Flake cigarettes.
897   Colonel William J Donovan (1883-1959), a US soldier, lawyer, intelligence officer and diplomat best remembered as the wartime head of the Office of Strategic Services during WW2.

Trevelyan's "Englishmen and Italians".[898] It dealt with England's part in the political movement in Italy which led up to the Risorgimento.[899] Italian culture was studied by all the leading politicians so that they became imbued with the right of the Italian cause. Would things have been different if our politicians had gone into the cultural life of other nations and those nations had sent their representatives, not to threaten war, but to teach the beauties of their art and language? It is a subject to reflect upon. Should war ever come with France, I shall find it very difficult to raise my passions. Macaulay's Essay on Hallam[900] was a diatribe against the friends and followers of Charles II. It is in these moments that I rather despise Macaulay. If his attacks were not so studied, I should read him no more. But they are thought out attacks and every cutting word is the work of deliberation. I compare him with Emerson, the short clear sentences with the involved phrases of the American. One reading of Macaulay is sufficient. Emerson wants to be read and read again. <u>News</u>. The waited attack against Yugoslavia has begun. I wonder when we shall be in action. An American reporter states that we have from 150,000 to 300,000 troops.

Thursday April 10th

The weather was very bright and I sat out in the sun during the afternoon. There were several handball games in progress which made it rather dangerous to sit next to the goals; we have been promised the freedom of the roof which should be very nice. I'm finding my sun glasses useful now. I received my first letter from Russell who has at last passed his second exam. He is contacting John Gabb for me; I wonder when Russell will be finished with medicine. He must have been at it for nearly four years now. In the evening I wrote to Valéry at his home address; I do hope he gets home soon. I began reading S Maugham's "Of Human Bondage"[901] and I think I am going to enjoy it very much. He seems to get into the very soul of his characters and no detail escapes him. His characters are described and summed up in a very few well chosen words. I did not get to sleep for a long time and I thought out ideas for a novel. It will be rather autobiographical and will be mostly dealing with French provincial life leading up to the climax of the War. I cannot get on with it yet as I want to finish my shorthand and Italian. The paper was full of an article of Liddell Hart's[902] who was advising us to stay out of Greece.

Friday April 11th

A cold wind but warm enough to sit out before lunch. Our lunch was a variation but not for the better. A plate of barley and sugar. I do not feel so very hungry now that I smoke a pipe, though it is a hard task with just a 1/5 of a loaf. In the evening I went to see Masefield's "Good Friday".[903] Beckwith produced it. The play is centred round Pilate's decision, his desire to save Jesus is overcome by his fear of dangerous rebellion to Rome. Glazebrook acted very well in the role of the Jew from the Sanhedrin who comes to raise Pilate's fears of revolt. Chancellor, a blind beggar, gave a convincing portrayal of a tragic character. Gee as Pilate was too much the school master. The costumes were very good and the stage was simply draped, the lighting very effectively dimmed during the centurion's speech. The poetry was sonorous and some of the lines were most effective, especially the blind man's speech about the wild duck. The occasional rhyme was rather jarring and gave a feeling of bathos.

898	"English Men and Italians" by George Macaulay Trevelyan, published in 1919.
899	The Italian Reunification of the different states of the Italian peninsula to form the single state of Italy in the 19th century.
900	"Hallam", essay by Thomas Babington Macaulay, published in 1828.
901	"Of Human Bondage" by W Somerset Maugham, published in 1915.
902	Sir Basil Henry Liddell Hart (1895-1970), an English soldier, military historian and leading interwar theorist.
903	"Good Friday", a play in verse by John Edward Masefield, poet laureate, published in 1916.

Saturday April 12th

I was very thrilled for I had finished my story and gave it to my friend Bob Salt, who is an Arts student at Sheffield. He is very well read and has a critical mind. He said the story was excellent but the style was lousy. That was pretty shattering. I asked him what he meant. He said that it was rather florid and that I did not pay enough attention to punctuation and spelling. I am convinced that I must not be so anxious to get forward. I must think over my work and make it perfect. I sat out for some time in the sun again and my foot is much better. I received two letters, one from Mums was all about the garden but told me that she had no coupons to send me new underclothes. But it doesn't worry me that I can get no parcels; as long as I know that all is well, that is all that I want to know. Wendy's letter was as cheerful as ever. It is grand of her to keep writing to me. I should love to see her. Her pretty little face and her blonde hair. Such a flirt but very sincere.

Sunday April 13th

Easter Sunday. It was very wet though this did not worry me very much as I was confined to my dungeon. I wasted a great part of the morning queuing up to get my laundry. The four Polish washerwomen had made a very good job and my sheet had regained its virginal whiteness. It was grand to have clothes that were really clean. I wrote to Mummy and will save my other letter till the end of the month. In the evening I went to church and quite enjoyed the sermon. The Padre has an aggressive and dramatic manner. He is original but his heavy Ulster accent is not too easy to follow. The Easter appearances show that Jesus will reveal himself to all men and will forgive the unfaithful and teach the doubting. The music at the service was that of the cornet and an accordion which sounded rather effective. The day ended with a gramophone recital, the instrument provided by the Germans. Unfortunately the airman who presented the programme was ignorant and nervous. He did not seem to know what the records were, by whom they were played or by whom the music was composed. It was lovely to hear a full orchestra and I was thrilled with "The Overture to the Barber of Seville."[904] "Lohengrin"[905] was powerful and mighty and "Musetta's Waltz"[906] song beautifully sentimental. It was strange and exciting to hear a woman's voice again, romance and sentiment throbbed in the smoky tunnel which we call our theatre. Every face was smiling, eyes were bright and the pleasure that pervaded every mind was visible on the faces. A woman's voice singing in German and being reproduced on a rather rickety machine. But memories thrive in sordid surroundings. Men are very sentimental. The weakest link in this chain of music was a jazz rendering of "The Count of Luxembourg";[907] it sounded like a child playing on a tin ukulele in a railway carriage. And they played this with Wagner. One of the first things I do when I get home will be to go to a Wagner concert to hear the woodwinds rising in crescendo. It was a very enjoyable evening. I hear that the troops had a dance among themselves.

---

904   "The Barber of Seveille", Opera buffa in 2 acts by Gioachino Rossini, first performed in 1816.
905   "Lohengrin", a Romantic opera in 3 acts by Richard Wagner, first performed in 1850.
906   "Quando m'en vo" also know as "Musetta's Waltz" from "La Bohème" by Giacomo Puccini, first performed in 1896.
907   "The Count of Luxembourg", an operetta in 2 acts with English lyrics and libretto by Basil Hood and Adrian Ross and music by Franz Lehár.

Monday April 14th

Bank Holiday. The working party did not come up from Stalag and we received no letters. In the evening there was a very bright concert. Forester was in his usual hearty form and gave us one or two good jokes especially those ....

The Final Curtain

I do not know why Desmond stops in mid sentence or whether he finished the diary or, if he did finish it, where the rest of it went.

Eventually Desmond was liberated and he returned to England where he applied for a job as a lawyer on the Control Commission. This was not to be unfortunately, as after being accepted for a post on the Control Commission, he went down to stay in Brighton with the parents of a girl who was, he hoped, to become his fiancée. He arrived at her home late on the night of 2nd September 1945 and the following morning got up late. After breakfast he decided to have a bath. After what seemed a long time, his intended fiancée thought he might have gone to sleep and decided to wake him up. After knocking on the door for a minute or two and receiving no reply, realised something was wrong. She asked a friend from next door to get into the bathroom by the window. So, climbing a ladder, he did just that and found Desmond lying apparently asleep. He did, however, smell a strong smell of gas and realised that the geyser was still on or faulty. Having turned off the gas they sent for an ambulance which took him to the Royal Sussex County Hospital where, unfortunately, he was found to be dead. The cause was of course due to Carbon Monoxide poisoning.

So ended what could have been a brilliant career. I believe Desmond did manage to get home to see his mother and grandmother for a brief time after his repatriation as the Channel Islands had been liberated on 9th May 1945. He is buried at the Saint Martin's Cemetery on Guernsey, alongside his Grandfather and Grandmother. Nanny Moorhouse died in August 1955 aged 85, after a long illness probably brought on by the years of deprivation during the occupation.

Winston Churchill had expected great things from Operation Ambassador and had not been amused when he heard the outcome. "Let there be no more silly fiascos like those perpetrated at Guernsey".

Desmond's father died in April 1956 aged 73, his mother, Dorothy, in May of 1959 aged 65, also after a long illness and Uncle Mickie in June 1965 aged 85.

"Since well I've done my past, then gentles pray
Applaud and send me with your thanks away"

Entry in the Register at Elizabeth College, Guernsey

MICHAELMAS TERM, 1932

4037. **Mulholland, John Desmond**—born in London on the 17th July, 1919; son of the late John Mulholland and Dorothy Moorhouse; Elizabeth College 1932-1936.
✠

Shooting VIII., 1935-36; 2nd XI. Hockey, 1935-36. Passed Final Exam. for English Bar, 1938. Caen University, 1939. War Service: Lieut., R. Guernsey Militia, 1939-1940. D.C.L.I., 1940. Prisoner-of-War, 1940-45. Passed 2nd Class, R. Society of Arts Exam. in Russian, Advanced Grade, while at Oflag VIIb. M.C. Barrister, Grays Inn, London. Died as the result of an accident, September 3rd, 1945. *Note*—In July, 1940, in company with Lieut. Philip Martel (No. 3673) he volunteered for reconnaissance service prior to a raid by British Forces on Guernsey. The plans for their rescue failing, they finally fell into German hands after spending some three weeks in hiding in the island. They remained prisoners-of-war in Germany until the end of the war. For their services each was awarded the M.C.

Excerpts from the Elizabeth College School magazine.

100   THE ELIZABETHAN.

The majority of the members of the Bisley Team won prizes in the Guernsey Rifle Meeting, Blampied, Le Cheminant, Avenell and Higgs being the most successful.

Shooting colours were awarded to L/Cpl. A. Le P. Avenell early in the season, and to L/Cpl. B. F. Higgs, C.Q.M.S. E. G. Le Tocq, L/Sergt. P. H. Hocquard, and A/Cpl. J. D. Mulholland after the Bisley Meeting.

THE ELIZABETHAN.   107

During the Easter Holidays the Groundsman, Mr. W. Allen, was married. The School subscribed the cost of a clock and a pair of bronze ornaments, which were presented in the Hall on May 9th by the Head Prefect. The clock bore the inscription, "Presented to Mr. W. Allen on the occasion of his marriage by the boys of Elizabeth College." Presentations were also made by the Principal and Mrs. Hardy, and by the Staff.

J. M. Symes has been made Assistant Editor of "The Elizabethan."

J. D. Mulholland has been made Assistant Librarian.

O.T.C. Notes.

MEMORIAL SERVICE FOR HIS LATE MAJESTY KING GEORGE V.

The Contingent was represented by two officers and thirty other ranks at the Memorial Service for His late Majesty, held in the Town Church on Tuesday, January 28th.

PROCLAMATION OF HIS MAJESTY KING EDWARD VIII.

The Contingent at full strength, less recruits, paraded as a Guard of Honour with the Royal Guernsey Militia and the British Legion at the Proclamation Ceremony. The Company was drawn up in line facing the Royal Court steps.

PROMOTIONS.

The following promotions have been made with effect from January 14th, 1936:—

To be C.S.M., Sergt. Blampied.
To be L/Sergt., Corpls. Borne, Guille.
To be Corporal, L/Cpl. Wolley.
To be A/Corpls., L/Cpls. Harwood, McLeod.
To be A/L/Cpls., Cadets Atkins, Avenell, Bichard, Bruce, Constantine, Creasey, de Longueuil, Douglas, Groves, Higgs, Hocquard, Mulholland, Pearson, Quevatre, Randell, Renier, Sarchet, Symes.

The following promotion has also been made with effect from February 29th, 1936:—

A/L/Cpl. Hocquard to be confirmed in rank and to be A/Cporl. while N.C.O. i/c. Band.

STRENGTH.

The following having left the Contingent were struck off strength with effect from January 14th, 1936:—

C.S.M. Carey; Sergts. Raleigh, Le Feuvre; Corpls. Brouard, Collas; Cadet Carey ii.

The following have been taken on strength as cadets and posted to No. 4 Platoon:—Gill i, Gill ii, Keyho, White, Luff, Wiscombe i, Dorey, Honey ii, Green, Rabey, Brooks.

CERTIFICATE "A" EXAMINATION.

The Contingent presented twenty candidates for the Certificate "A" Examination held in November, 1935. Of these, nineteen passed; the remaining candidate failed in one paper only.

This is a record for the Contingent both in number of entries and in successes, and we offer them our hearty congratulations,

The following were the marks:—

	1st Paper. Max. 200.	2nd Paper. Max. 200.	Total. 400.
Cadets Atkins	89	99	188
Avenell	108	96	204
Bichard	80	107	187
Bruce	80	89	169
Constantine	114	114	228
Creasey	112	99	211
De Longueuil	104	80	184
Douglas	94	92	186
Groves	109	80	189
Higgs	86	142	228
Hocquard	126	115	241
Mulholland	82	119	201
Pearson	120	88	208
Quevatre	88	131	219
Randell	99	93	192
Renier	100	116	216
Sarchet	123	100	223
Symes	111	126	237
Wolley	115	131	246

LONDON GAZETTE 21st February 1946:

"The King has been graciously pleased to approve the following award in recognition of gallant and distinguished service in the field:

MILITARY CROSS
*Second-Lieutenant Desmond Mulholland 107259,
The Duke of Cornwall's Light Infantry."*

The Military Cross awarded to Desmond in 1946

The Diary Of Lieutenant Desmond Mulholland MC

ROYAL GUERNSEY

Front Row: Drum/Major H. F. Le Page; L./Sergt J. A. Renouf; L./Sergt. J. Le Gallez; L./Sergt. N. Torode; C.S.M. F. Moore
Major N. R. Blockley (Staff Captain); Major E. A. Wheadon (Officer Commanding); H.E. the Lieut.-Governor, Major-Gene
Lieut. J. D. Mulholland; 2nd Lieut. H. Nicolle; Capt. E. W. Bartie; R.S.M. H. Hopkin (Sherw

Second Row: Pte. A. J. Edmonds; Pte. F. Smith; Pte. D. Le Pelley; Pte. L. W. Batiste; E./Sergt. W. Earnshaw; L./Sergt. R.
H. Champion; Sergt. S. G. Tew; E./Sergt. D. Vaudin; L./Sergt. A. R. Elliott; Sergt. D. B. Edwards; Sergt. E. A. Guilbert; E./
Girard

Third Row: L./Cpl. L. Dodd; Pte. C. J. Jehan; Pte. D. Stonebridge; L./Cpl. R. P. Carré; L./Cpl. R. E. Prigent; Cpl. E. P. Lanoe
Robinson; Pte. E. C. Falla; Cpl. T. Le Sauvage; Pte. A. G. Marquis; Pte. T. Bougourd; Pte. L. C. Smale; Pte. T. Heaume; Pte

Fourth Row: Drummer C. H. Bichard; Drummer E. C. Le Flocq; Pte. J. W. Salmon; L./Cpl. H. W. Falla; Pte. S. Brache; Pte
D. G. M. McKane; Pte. D. G. Richings; Pte. R. V. Valpied; Pte. J. H. Renouf; Pte. J. Trebert; Pte. A. Eker; Pte. L. J. Sarch

Fifth Row: L./Cpl. E. A. Ryan; Drummer N. Laurent; Pte. W. J. Le Sauvage; Pte. T. J. Ozanne; Pte. C. W. Queripel; Pte. R.
A. Ayres; Drummer A. J. Priaulx; Pte. R. J. Gavey; Pte. W. H. Garland; Pte. C. J. Brehaut; Pte. T. J. Martel; Pt

Sixth Row: L./Cpl. R. F. O. Lowe; Drummer C. Tourtel; Pte. P. Le Sauvage; Pte. H. H. Bretel; Pte. F. Norman; Pte. H. R
Drummer F. Chandler; Pte. E. Simon; Pte. A. Young; Pte. L. Damarell; Pte. A. Breban; Pte. A. H. Do

Back Row: L./Cpl. A. Le Flocq; Drummer H. Burch; L./Cpl. A. Le Page; L./Cpl. L. Le Ber; L./Cpl. L. Burgess; L./Cpl. H
Vaudin; Pte. J. H. Renouf; Pte. W. Broome; L./Cpl. D. T. Sarre; L./Cpl. F. H. Loaring; Pte. R. J. Dorey; Pte. F. W.

ITIA: December, 1939.

J. Ferbrache; P.S.M. A. R. Dingle; 2nd Lieut. P. Martel; 2nd Lieut. P. de Putron; 2nd Lieut. H. W. Poat; Lieut. H. A. M. Drake;
Telfer-Smollett, C.B., D.S.O., M.C.; Capt. H. Cantan, D.C.L.I. (Adjutant); Capt. O. Priaulx, Capt. V. M. G. de Vic Carey;
rs); R.Q.M.S. B. G. Jones; Sergt. P. Le Page; L./Sergt. A. J. Bridle; L./Sergt. A. W. Falla.

Sergt. A. Barrasin; Sergt. R. Blondel; Sergt. L. Vining; Sergt. H. Vaudin; E./Sergt. W. Holladay; Sergt. O. Jones; E./Sergt.
Carteret; Sergt. D. Brouard; E./Sergt. W. Tapp; E./Sergt. A. Patterson; L./Cpl. E. E. Carter; L./Cpl. F. Napper; Pte. C. N. Giles.

Gallez; Pte. R. F. Thoume; Pte. H. N. Roberts; Pte. H. N. Fallaize; L./Cpl. P. M. F. Babbé; Pte. A. Wakeham; L./Cpl. S. C.
; Pte. J. S. Falla; Cpl. J. D. Loaring; Pte. W. A. Elliston; Pte. A. J. Allen; Drummer W. T. Ellis; Pte. C. J. Brehaut.

uvage; Pte. P. J. Pinchemain; Cpl. G. C. Sheppard; Pte. H. Guilbert; Cpl. R. J. Bray; Pte. E. P. Langlois; Pte. F. J. Smith; Pte.
lwen; Pte. D. Girard; Pte. W. Martel; Pte. C. Hamon; Drummer H. Barnes; L./Cpl. T. J. Young; Pte. G. McInerney.

/Cpl. A. J. Le Page; Pte. B. L. Le Page; L./Cpl. T. H. Robert; Pte. A. T. Le Page; Pte. H. Gauvain; Drummer A. G. Mills; Pte.
y; Pte. R. Chapman; Pte. A. Hocquet; Pte. H. G. Pike; Pte. S. G. Le Sauvage; Drummer L. Harvey; Drummer G. Lowe.

. de Bertrand; Pte. S. C. Torode; Pte. W. N. Gavet; Pte. L. N. Damarell; Pte. F. Baker; Pte. E. Julou; Drummer C. J. Mahy;
Dunning; Pte C. J. Henry; Pte. G. Queripel; Pte. R. Nicolle; Drummer R. Quertier; Drummer H. Martin.

te. L. Bourgaize; Pte. F. H. Rowland; Pte. C. E. Robin; Pte. E. Ogier; Pte. W. H. Lainé; Pte A. Le Prevost; Drummer W.
Pte. R. Le Morellec; Pte. W. J. Luce; Pte. F. McCormick; Pte. A. Mourant; Drummer P. R. Hewlett; Cpl. R. Carpenter.

Courtesy of Guernsey Museums & Galleries, States of Guernsey, 2013

DESMOND MULHOLLAND'S POW CAMPS

1. After his arrest on 28th July 1940 on Guernsey he was held in a room in the **Channel Islands Hotel**, which at that time was the German HQ.

2. From there he was flown to France on 30th July 1940 where he was eventually detained and interrogated at the **Hotel de Ville** in Rennes and then on 31st July 1940 to the **Hotel Bellevue** in Dinard.

3. **Camp des Pionieers** – Rennes. A transit camp in France from 2nd August 1940 until 10th August 1940. Known to the Germans as Frontstalag 133.

4. On the 10th August 1940 he was transferred to the **Colombier Barracks** in Rennes where he remained until 29th August 1940.

5. From 29th August 1940 until 7th September 1940 he was in an **unnamed barracks** in the Rennes area.

6. **Oflag VIIIG** at Weidenau (Now Vidnava, Czech Republic). From 12th September 1940 until 14th September 1940.

7. **Oflag VIIIH** at Oberlangendorf (Now Dlouhá Loučka, Czech Republic). From 15th September 1940 until 12th October 1940.

8. **Oflag VIIIE** – Johannisbrun, Sudetenland (Now Jánské Koupele, Czech Republic) from 12th October 1940 until 28th October 1940.

9. **Oflag IXA/H** at Elbersdorf (Spangenberg lower camp), Germany. From 30th October 1940 until 4th March 1941,

10. **Oflag XXA (Fort 15)** at Toruň (Thorn), Poland. From 6th March 1941. This was a very harsh camp where POW's were sent to in reprisal to German POW's treatment at Fort Kingston in Canada. It was a series of old forts surrounding the town and was known collectively as **Stalag XXA**. This camp was emptied around 10th June 1941.

11. On 11th June 1941 Desmond and many of his fellow prisoners were returned to **Oflag IXA/H** at Elbersdorf (Spangenberg Lower Camp). He remained there until 6th October 1941

12. From 6th October 1941 until 12th September 1942 he was trnsferred to a camp near Warburg, Germany. This was **Oflag VIB** near the village of Dössell, which is now part of Warburg.

13. **Oflag VIIB** at Eichstätt, Germany from 13th September 1942 until 14th April 1945. On 14 April 1945, as the American Army approached, the officers were marched out of the camp. Unfortunately, only a short distance from the camp the column was attacked by American aircraft, who mistook it for a formation of German troops. Sixteen British officers were killed and 46 were wounded. The camp was liberated by the Americans on 16 April 1945.

14. After a long march the final camp was probably **Stalag VIIA** at Moosburg from where he was flown home.

15. He eventually arrived back in the UK some time in May of 1945.

DESMOND'S PRISONER OF WAR CAMPS ACROSS EUROPE

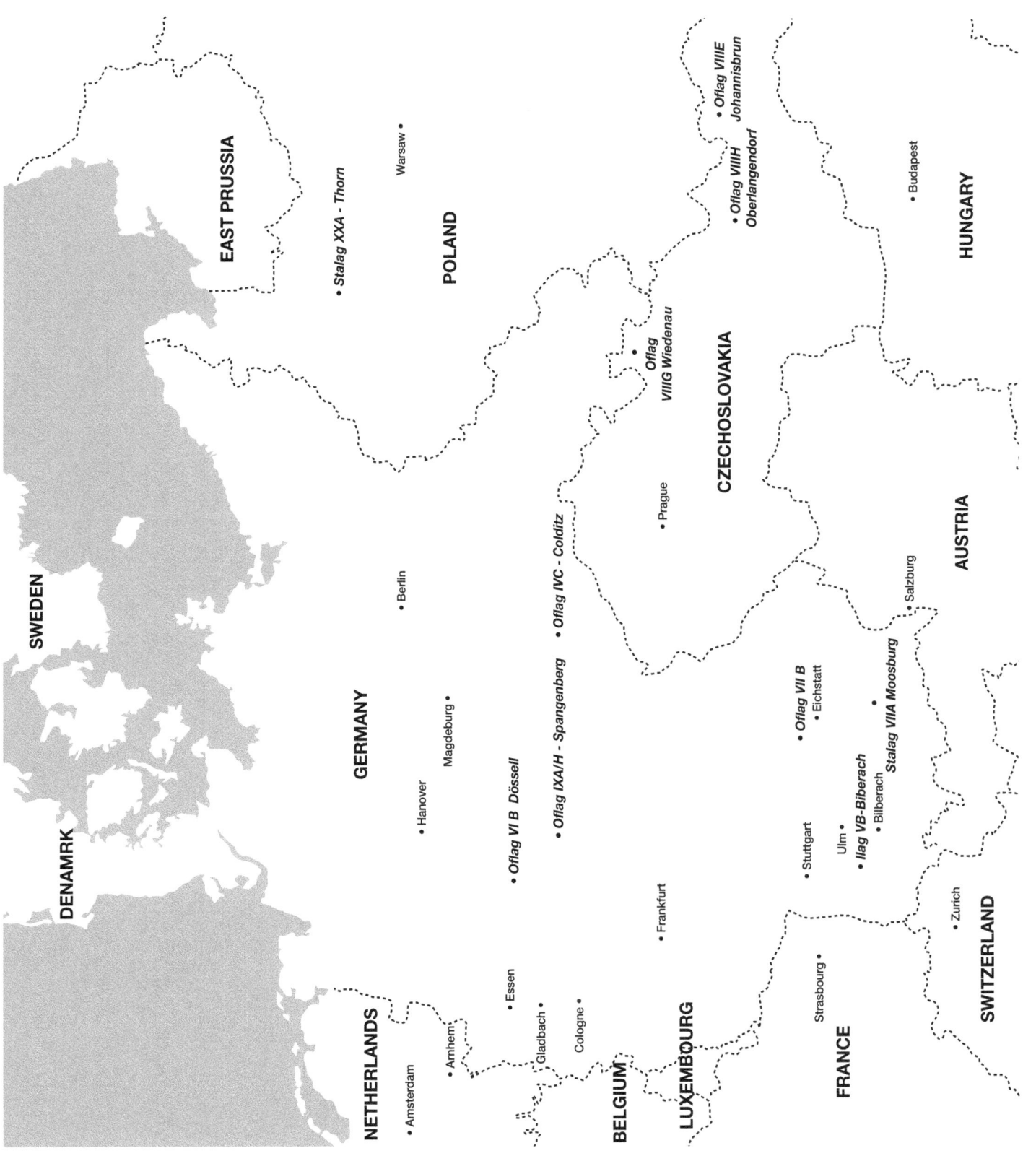

INFORMATION SOURCES

The German occupation of the Channel Islands by Charles Cruickshank.

The Daily Telegraph Obituary of Philip Martel M.C.

The family of Philip Martel.

The Commando who came home to spy by William M. Bell.

The States of Guernsey Archives.

La Société Guernesaise.

The German Occupation Museum, Guernsey.

The States of Guernsey Museums and Galleries.

Le Priaux Library, Guernsey.

Keith Ronald Pike, Douzeniere of St. Peter, Port Guernsey.

The Commonwealth War Graves Commission.

The Imperial War Museum.

Elizabeth College, Guernsey.

Guernsey Ancestry.

Ancestry.co.uk

INDEX OF NAMES

Amath 14
Anthonie 54
Arnoulde, Helen (Spence's wife) 17
Aunt Wendy 54
Aunty (Gladys Jesson nee Moorhouse) Intro. 34, 54, 58, 67, 73, 89, 94, 110, 128, 139.
Bachelerie, Captain 7, 8
Barbottin, Commandant 11
Barbu 12
Beckwith, E.G.C. (Ted) 44, 61, 90, 126, 136, 142
Benedict, Monsieur 6
Bernard 12
Bibbings 47, 48, 49, 52, 54, 65, 107, 118
Bishop, A.H. (Bish) 58
Boislambert, de 29
Bonham 126, 127
Bonnefaut, Le Marquis de 12
Booth, Captain 57
Boyer, Marcel 9, 31
Brady, Alma 68
Brookes 118
Brosses, Charles de 9, 12, 31
Browne, Peter 115
Brush, Captain 127
Buisson, Captain de 14
Casankuve, Commandant 28
Cantan, Colonel Harry Introduction, 90
Carey, Victor 103
Chancellor, Francis 142
Choppin 35, 136, 137
Cirod, Captain Le 14
Claude 68
Clever, Francis 138
Clout, Major 39, 102, 132, 133
Cocheri, Vivi 29
Connors, Captain (Hash) or ("H") 16, 18, 24, 26, 30, 34, 39, 47, 49, 55, 65, 66, 67, 80, 84, 91, 114, 125, 126, 127
Consley 103
Cook, George Littlejohn (LJ) 42, 73, 95, 112, 118, 123, 138
Cooper, Captain (Doctor) 43
Cornish 1
Coudere 12

Curtis, Lady 9
Daddy (John Edward Mulholland) Intro, 3, 43, 68, 141
Davidson 105
Delbarre, Lieutenant 9
Dobson 59
Dross 91, 131
Eames, Joe 137
Edgar (Driver) 13
Edie, Charles 42, 69
Edwards, Captain 61
England, Private Thomas, Hampshire Regiment 8, 9, 11, 12
Falry 29
Ferbrache, Sergeant Stanley Intro, 79
Fevrier 11
Fielding, Captain Alan Forester 38, 44, 49, 66, 85
Fielding, David 51, 61, 85
Fontenay, J. de 54
Ford, Colonel (Sherwood Foresters) 39, 115, 132
Fox, Captain (Medico) 66, 67, 74, 91, 92, 105, 131
Frémont, Captain 5, 7, 11
Gabb, John 142
Gaffrey 130
Gaguerand, Captain de 19, 27
Garrett, Major Lovel (LG) 41, 42, 44, 45, 49, 51, 53, 54, 57, 66, 74
Gee, Major C.H.R. 43, 95, 131, 142
Geneviève 7, 8, 13, 67, 68, 89
Gibbs, Colonel 17, 18, 19, 27, 34, 68, 80, 115
Gilder, Doctor 94, 105
Glazebrook, Major 126, 142
Gooch, Sub Lieutenant (Fleet Air Arm) 108
Gorrie, Doctor George 57, 92, 101, 119
Gowan 109
Gowland 123, 138
Grandpa (Edward Moorhouse) Intro, 1, 15, 31, 57, 75, 84, 96, 97, 111
Gray, Sergeant 64
Grayson, Barrie or Barry (Mus. Bac. LRAM.) 40, 45, 47, 62,
64, 66, 70, 71, 75, 77
Gros, le 14, 15
Gross J. 34
Harris, "Bing" 5

153

Harris, Captain Duggie (RASC) 56, 89
Herbulet, Madame 112, 115
Hervier 31
Hill 123, 138
Hobson 12, 29, 122, 134
Holland, David 47, 55, 66, 70, 74, 104
Hooth 138
Hunter "Bing" 92, 105
Husband 118
Husson 115
Hyde-Thomson, John 132, 140
Jackson, Captain 51, 64,
Jacobson 47, 54
Jessup, John 79
Jones, Private 38, 85, 136
Kampman 12
Kate, American friend. 20, 53
Kate, Monsieur 13
Kelso, Lieutenant J.A. 64, 123, 138
Kennedy, J.A. 113, 118, 123, 138
Kents, R.W. 56
Keppel. Sergeant (Gloucesters) 13
Knowles, Miss Christine 85
Krabb ("K") 4
Langham, Eric 41, 46, 50, 59, 109
Laing, Kenneth 42, 45, 67, 68
Lola 112, 115, 131
Lowden 111, 140
Lubbock, Jim 131
MacIntyre, Padre 120, 125, 127, 132, 135, 143
MacKay, Lt. Colonel (Doctor) 58, 135
Maclean, Padre Norman 40, 44, 47, 50, 53, 57, 60, 62, 70, 75, 81, 86, 92, 98, 105, 110, 114, 115, 120
Maclean, Sergeant Victor or "V" 6, 7,
Magee, Private (Cook) 98
Manon, Toto 25
Mansel, Captain John 47, 59, 69, 109
Martel, Lieutenant Philip ("M") Intro, 3, 4, 7, 8, 16, 17, 79, 135, 149, 152
Martin, Raymond 5
Maxwell, Lieutenant P. 73
McHall 109
McLeod, Douglas (Mac) 16, 18, 26, 28, 54, 65, 101
Meyer, Michel 17
Moidrey, de 14

Morris, Colonel 127, 135
Mortimer, Roger (Librarian) 115
Mummy or Mums (Dorothy Michael) 1, 9, 30, 34, 43, 44, 58, 63, 79, 87, 92, 105, 110, 115, 120, 126, 133, 136, 139, 143
Murdoch 115
Murphy, Flying Officer Frank 115, 127
Murray, Sq. Leader 121, 123
Muzundar, Jumbo 113
Nanny (MaryMoorhouse née Cotton) Intro, 61, 108, 126, 133, 140, 144
Neave, Airey Intro, 52, 66, 68, 70, 72, 79, 83, 96, 102, 108
Nicholls, Captain (Doctor) 44, 48
Nicolle, Lieutenant Hubert Intro, 79, 97, 105
Oldman, Brooke 90
Pat 43
Paverner 57
Perouse 29, 30, 125
Picot, Lieutenant 11
Pinel 13
Pirot, Captain 11
Ponsonby, Major Wilfred (Royal Corps of Signals) 40
Pope, Lance 45, 72, 73, 138
Racky, Mr. 32, 33
Raux, de 29
Renaud 14
Renton, Lindsay 138
Rivière, La 12
Roberts, Major 39, 49, 60, 63,
Roberts, Sergeant 134, 135
Roth, Oberleutnant 40
Roubaix 7
Russell (Dr. Russell Jesson) Intro. 94, 142
St. Sauveur 12
Sally 90
Salt, Bob 119, 125, 140, 143
Sanglier, Captain 11, 13
Schiller, Eric 13
Shortman, QM 47, 54
Smailes, Robert 132
Smalley, P.O. "Slim" 125, 131
Smith, M ("Little Smith from Jersey") 50, 54, 56, 57, 62, 64, 65, 67, 84, 85, 102, 133
Somerset, Brigadier General 117, 120, 127
Soulignac 14

Spence 17
Spinks, Lieutenant 107
Spriet, Monsieur 12
Stephenson, Herbert 18, 87
Strachan, Tony 66, 70, 111, 136
Surtees, John 116, 129
Symes, Lieutenant James Intro, 79, 97, 105
Symons, Dan 137
Tangye 34
Taylor, Clough 109
Tether, Sergeant 7,
Thompson, Flying Officer 133
Thorp 35
Triplet 14, 15
Twysden, Tony 138
Uncle Alfred (Moorhouse) 42, 141
Uncle Mickie or Mickey (Arthur Cadogan Michael)
  Intro. 1, 44, 63, 79, 88, 89, 133, 136, 144
Valéry, Jean 10, 12, 13, 15, 27, 55, 142
Vallée, Captain 11, 14
Veryard, Corporal 7
Verstraeten 67
Victor (Nanny's gardener/driver) 140, 141
Vissier, Lieutenant 59, 85
Walker 138
Watson, Colin (Gordon Highlanders) 17, 19, 26, 28,
  33, 38, 47, 52, 65, 71, 89, 101, 118, 121
Watson, Jean 21
Watts, Arthur 56, 89, 137
Wendy 87, 112, 130, 143
Weysom, (RMA) 18, 28,
Woods, G. 123, 126
Wright 111
Zabette. 11, 16, 34, 43, 56, 71, 79, 94, 110